VIETNAM, JEWS AND THE MIDDLE EAST

Also by Judith A. Klinghoffer

ISRAEL AND THE SOVIET UNION: Alienation or Reconciliation (*co-author*)

THE CITIZEN PLANNER

THE FEDERAL COLLECTION OF CRIMINAL JUSTICE STATISTICS

Vietnam, Jews and the Middle East

Unintended Consequences

Judith A. Klinghoffer

St. Martin's Press
New York

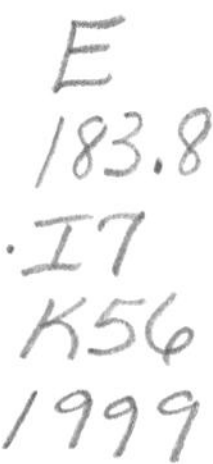

VIETNAM, JEWS AND THE MIDDLE EAST

For information, address:

St. Martin's Press, Scholarly and Reference Division,
175 Fifth Avenue, New York, N.Y. 10010

First published in the United States of America in 1999

This book is printed on paper suitable for recycling and made from fully managed and sustained forest sources.

Printed in Great Britain

ISBN 0–312–21841–9

Library of Congress Cataloging-in-Publication Data
Klinghoffer, Judith Apter.
Vietnam, Jews and the Middle East : unintended consequences / Judith A. Klinghoffer.
p. cm.
Includes bibliographical references (p.) and index.
ISBN 0–312–21841–9 (cloth)
1. United States—Foreign relations—Israel. 2. Israel—Foreign relations—United States. 3. Israel-Arab War, 1967—Causes. 4. Vietnamese Conflict, 1961–1975—Influence. 5. Vietnamese Conflict, 1961–1975—Israel. 6. United States—Foreign relations—1963–1969. I. Title.
E183.8.I7K56 1999
327.7305694'09'046—dc21 98–38446
CIP

To Joella and Arthur

Contents

Acknowledgments

I owe many thanks: Yaakov Talmon taught me to look for global connections, Bela Vago to read diplomatic cables, and Lloyd C. Gardner to follow my instincts and to "hang in there" whenever the going got tough. He, along with Warren Kimball, Michael Shafer and Ziva Gallili, were kind enough to read and comment on an earlier lengthier version. Miriam Eshkol gave me access to her husband's archive as well as to her own invaluable insights. Richard Parker provided me with his working translation of pertinent sections of Mohammed Heikal's book *Al Infijar*, as well as with useful advice and comment.

Paul Nitze let me read his classified oral history; Denis Healey and Robert Komer replied to specific queries; and Meir Amit, Lucius Battle, Zbigniew Brzezinski, Myer Feldman, Nicholas Katzenbach, Robert McNamara, Benjamin Read, Eugene Rostow, Walter Rostow and Joseph Sisco spent varying amounts of time graciously and patiently answering my often impertinent questions. Max Kampelman also provided me access both to his papers and to his memories. Alas, he along with Dean Rusk, John Roche, Aharon Yariv and Avraham Harman are no longer with us. It was an honor to have known them.

No place could have been more supportive than the Lyndon B. Johnson Library staff in Austin. Not only did the library help underwrite my research with a Moody grant but it also did yeoman job assisting me with the declassification of an enormous amount of documents, and even invited me to present some of my findings at a conference on international perspectives of the Vietnam War. I owe special thanks to David Humphrey, John Wilson and Ted Gittinger.

This study has also benefited from the help of numerous archivists and librarians working at Rutgers University, the Minnesota State Archives, YIVO (the Institute of Jewish Research), the Jacob Blaustein Memorial Library, Haifa University, the Dayan Center for Strategic Studies, Israel State Archives, and Yad Eshkol.

I am most grateful for the insights of friends and colleagues from Rutgers University, the Foreign Affairs College in Beijing, the Norwegian Nobel Institute, and Aarhus University, as well as for the unwavering support of my American and Israeli friends and family. Finally, no one could have done as well the endless job of listening as my daughter Joella or the tedious job of editing and reediting as my husband Arthur. I am forever in their debt.

List of Abbreviations

AID	Agency for International Development
ACJ	American Council for Judaism
AJC	American Jewish Committee
AIPAC	American Israel Public Affairs Committee
AJCL	The Blaustein Library of the American Jewish Committee
ARAMCO	Arabian American Oil Company
CCAR	Central Conference of American Rabbis
DCSS	Dayan Center for Strategic Studies
GAHAL	Gush Herut Liberalim (Israeli National Liberal Party)
ISA	Israel State Archives
JCS	Joint Chiefs of Staff
JTA	Jewish Telegraphic Agency
JWV	Jewish War Veterans of America
LBJL	Lyndon Baines Johnson Library
LBJ–OH	LBJL's Collection of Oral Histories
MAPAM	Mifleget Poalim Meuchedet (Israeli Marxist Labor Party)
MOSSAD	Israeli Intelligence Service
MSA	Minnesota State Archives
NCNA	New China News Agency
NCNP	National Conference of New Politics
NCRAC	National Community Relations Advisory Council
NEA	Near East Agency
NLF	National Liberation Front
NSC	National Security Council
NSF	National Security File
NYT	*New York Times*
PLA	Palestine Liberation Army
PLO	Palestinian Liberation Organization
RAFI	Reshimat Poalei Yisrael (Israeli Labor Party)
SCA	Synagogue Council of America
UAHC	Union of American Hebrew Congregations
UAR	United Arab Republic
UNEF	United Nations Emergency Force
UNRWA	United Nations Relief and Works Agency

WHCF	White House Central Files
WJC	World Jewish Congress
YIVO	Institute for Jewish Research
ZOA	Zionist Organization of America

The Buried Story

The June 3, 1967 issue of the *New Republic* reprinted a *Chicago Sun Times* Bill Mauldin cartoon showing President Lyndon Johnson drinking coffee at a restaurant. A sign above his head reads "WATCH YOUR HAT . . . AND COAT." Johnson, holding two pistols, dutifully watches the hat called "S.E. ASIA" totally unaware that behind his back Leonid Brezhnev is busy stealing a coat entitled "MIDDLE EAST."

There was nothing iconoclastic about the Mauldin cartoon. His understanding of the origins of the 1967 Middle East crisis was widely shared by the world media and public. A Harris poll published during the war revealed that, by better than two to one, Americans believed that Moscow encouraged the outbreak of the Six Day War in order to divert and weaken US efforts in Vietnam. Experts, especially those versed in Middle Eastern affairs, also freely acknowledged at the time, and continue *privately* to admit, that the only rational explanation for the sudden spring 1967 crisis was a Soviet decision to create a "Second Vietnam." That was the reason Georgiy Kornienko, the 1967 chief of the American Department in the Soviet Foreign Ministry, not only spent the international conference held on the twenty-fifth anniversary of the Six Day War trying to refute a "Second Vietnam" thesis no one had *officially* espoused but, afterwards, devoted numerous hours to delving into the Soviet archives only to be forced to admit that "Soviet representatives committed 'blunders,' which, if one wished, could be wrongly interpreted . . ."[1]

Curiously, though there is no dearth of studies of either the Vietnam or Six Day wars, the close connections between the two got effectively buried. Buried with it were the far reaching effects of their unintended consequences. Those consequences include the 1967 realization that the chief American Cold War rival continued to be the USSR, not China; that the American concentration on the Southeast Asian "hat" (i.e. Asia) endangered the more important Middle Eastern "coat" (i.e. Europe); that the Soviet Union was just as willing to sacrifice small countries in pursuit of Cold War advantage (Israel) as the United States (Vietnam); that far from being an unwelcome burden, Israel was a significant strategic asset; and, last but certainly not least, that the Communist USSR had replaced Nazi Germany as the number one enemy of the Jewish people.

Ultimately, Brezhnev's failed attempt to steal the Middle Eastern "coat" proved disastrous to the Soviet Union. It rejuvenated the American and European Atlanticists, split the left, militarized Israel, united Jews everywhere, and gave birth to "Neoconservatism" in the West and to the dissident movement in the East. In short, it not only dramatically altered the fate of both the Middle East and Southeast Asia, but played a significant role in the eventual collapse of the USSR.

If so, how could the Vietnamese–Middle Eastern connection have been so effectively buried? The answer seems to rest not only in the tendency of analysts to specialize in a single region but also in the interests of the major players. American policy makers were widely criticized for permitting their preoccupation with Vietnam to lead to the neglect of the Middle East, and later they were constantly accused of being willing to sacrifice Israeli interests on the altar of an advantageous exit from Vietnam. The Soviets were accused of inciting the Arabs to war, and then "selling them out." Both superpowers defended themselves by vociferously rejecting any relationship between the two conflicts. Israel, which was stigmatized by the Soviet–Arab camp as a colonialist American stooge, certainly had no interest in connecting her case with the unpopular Southeast Asian War. Nor did it help the Arab cause to acknowledge that its statesmen tried to exploit the American embroilment in Vietnam to eliminate Israel. Similarly, Atlanticist opponents of the Vietnam War, often ridiculed as "Dawks," and Pacificist supporters of the war, often derided as "Hoves," understandably emphasized the differences between the two conflicts.

I have to admit that historical research, not memory, was the cause of my own discovery of the Middle Eastern fallout from the Vietnam War. During the early eighties I was involved in a study of the history of Soviet–Israeli relations, and I came across numerous references to Vietnam. At the time, I did not have the opportunity to explore the connections fully, but they remained on my mind. At first, I was sure they had been explored by others. When a bibliographical search failed to produce any systematic examination of the subject, I attributed it to a lack of evidence. However, to my joy and chagrin, too much rather than too little raw material emerged as the real problem. The point is that this work is the result of historical curiosity, not a political agenda.

In fact, the structure of this study is specifically designed to overcome its highly political nature. Objectivity is a difficult quest. However, as a wandering (and wondering) Jew, born in Romania, raised and educated in Israel, and working in the United States, I believe myself well situated to do the protagonists justice. Moreover, to avoid the pitfalls of vilifying some, and canonizing others, events are recounted from three central points of view, though the voices of their opponents can also be easily discerned.

Thus, regardless of the obvious differences in power, each of the protagonists is portrayed as both a subject and an object rather than as a victimizer or a victim. The alternating triangular focus helps to legitimize inevitably different goals, explore efforts at influence and delineate the way distant events in places about which the actors knew little transformed each of them.

Ultimately, this being a crisis history, it lends itself to the dramatic structure of a four act play. The first section examines the protagonists' initial response to the Vietnam imbroglio; the second follows the way in which America's growing difficulties in Vietnam affected its relationship and events in the Middle East; the third, the climax, zeroes in on the direct role the Vietnam War played in the May 1967 Middle East crisis and the Six Day War; and the fourth examines the short and long term consequences of that swift, but paradigm-shifting war. Each section is divided into three chapters, each examining one of the actor's perceptions and responses to the aforementioned developments.

The theme stressed throughout this work is that a dual system of causality operated between events on the two great Cold War fronts. Developments in the Middle East were influenced by those in Vietnam, and they, in turn, affected the course of events in Southeast Asia. Thus, the American decision to concentrate on the Vietnamese front, without a significant mobilization of additional economic, military, political or ideological resources, could not but alter US force distribution in other regional theaters. The American success or failure in thwarting a war of national liberation could not but influence the thinking of other revolutionary groups searching for ways to counter superior Western technology. American friends and allies along the rest of the containment line could not but became reluctant to support an American policy which increased their vulnerability, and the lack of allied support could not but help undermine the American homefront support for the war.

Similarly, American rivals could not but seek ways to exploit the obvious weaknesses of her one front war strategy. The longer the war lasted, the more manifest American weaknesses became. Consequently, when the Soviet Union opened a second front in the Middle East, an increasingly isolated US could only delay but not avoid reevaluating the wisdom of her Vietnamese focus.

The emergence of the Middle East as a major Cold War front at a time when the US was mired in Vietnam left Israel visibly exposed. The Jewish state's very survival became dependent on her ability to secure the ideological, diplomatic and strategic resources necessary to withstand an increasingly effective Palestinian liberation war and deter a potential Soviet backed Arab onslaught. In this context, the Six Day War represents the failure of conventional deterrence.

Israel's special relationship with the Jewish diaspora aided her pursuit of national survival, but eroded her already limited ability to avoid the Cold War crossfire. Nowhere was this conundrum more apparent than in the enormous pressure the US and the USSR brought to bear on the Israeli government to take sides in the Vietnam conflict. In the end, Israel's stance towards the Southeast Asian War emerged as a measure of her declining post-1967 independence.

Size, location and group achievement made American Jews the most significant component of the Jewish diaspora. In addition, the preponderance of Jews within the intellectual community made them into assertive and influential players in the formation and articulation of sixties' liberalism. Shaken by the Holocaust, fearful of a nuclear war, worried about the war's effect on the country's domestic liberal agenda, and determined to demonstrate the practical value of their faith, American Jewish religious and secular intellectuals emerged as early, vocal and effective opponents of the Vietnam War. The President singled out Jews, and publicly warned them that their Israeli and Soviet brethren would pay the price for their anti-war agitation. The Middle East crisis (which Jews viewed as a potential second Holocaust) erupted before they had a chance to evaluate this unsettling warning. It convinced an increasing number of Jews, especially in America, not only to put ethnic concerns first, but that they could only be secured by remounting the anti-Soviet Cold War barricades. Thus, if the Vietnam War united the liberal-left and raised doubts concerning the strategic validity of applying the principle of containment to China, the Six Day War split the left and reaffirmed the validity of containment against the Soviet Union.

As always, the unequal availability of sources presents the most formidable obstacle to the recovery of the past. The post Cold War American archives are overflowing with liberally declassified materials, and with archivists and librarians eager to help. Similarly, former policy makers eager to shape the manner in which history judges them, write detailed biographies and spend hours answering questions. Newly declassified Soviet materials are especially pertinent. The same is far less true about Israeli policy makers and American Jewish leaders. They consider themselves far too vulnerable for extensive self exposure. Still, many Israeli documents have been declassified, a major Jewish organization has made its archives available to historians, and some Israeli and American Jewish leaders have been willing to be interviewed even on a subject they still consider much too sensitive.

Thus, if evaluated with great care, the available materials do reveal most of the picture. The Johnson Presidential Library is an ever growing treasure trove. Its documents have been supplemented by those found in the Congressional Record, Divrei Haknesset (minutes of the Israeli parliament), the Hubert Humphrey and Max Kampelman Papers, the American Jewish Committee archives, the Israeli State archives and Yad Eshkol. Especially useful published contemporary materials include the huge collection of Arab newspapers and broadcast transcripts translated into Hebrew by Israeli intelligence and housed in Tel Aviv University's Dayan Center along with the Israeli foreign ministry's published sources. Interviews with many of the major players, including Dean Rusk, Robert McNamara and the Rostow brothers helped fill in the details of this long lost story which has so radically, if unexpectedly, altered the course of so many lives in so many places.

NOTES

1. Georgiy Kornienko, "The Cold War: Testimony of a Participant," as translated in *The Six-Day War; A Retrospective*, edited by Richard B. Parker (Gainesville: 1996), 71–2.

Part I
The Stage is Set

1 American Foreign Policy Realigned

VIETNAM AND THE TRANSFORMATION OF AMERICAN FOREIGN POLICY

Lyndon B. Johnson assumed office surrounded by longtime Jewish friends and advisors, men like Abe Fortas, Ed Weisl and Abe Feinberg whose liberal agenda he shared. As Senator and Vice President, he enjoyed a stellar reputation as a staunch supporter of Israel going back to January 1957 when he led the Congressional opposition to President Eisenhower's attempt to force an unconditional withdrawal of Israeli forces from the Sinai through economic sanctions. In June 1963, the Second Lady disregarded Arab protests and served as the honorary chairperson of Israel's independence ball.[1]

Johnson, like Kennedy, assumed that the road to the Jewish electorate ran through Israel. Unlike his predecessor, he found a willing partner in Israel's new prime minister, Levi Eshkol. When Kennedy told David Ben Gurion that he knew he owed his election to American Jews, and asked if there was "something" he could "do for the Jewish people?," Ben Gurion had suggested that he do his "best for the free world." Consummate "wheeler dealer" Eshkol had no such qualms.[2]

Johnson's first offer was extravagant: he was prepared to fulfill all Kennedy's promises, and even consider replacing Dean Rusk (who had opposed Israeli statehood) with Averell Harriman as Secretary of State. But the real bargaining occurred during Eshkol's May 1964 official visit to Washington when, as Johnson wrote Associate Justice Felix Frankfurter, the two leaders "had some serious business to transact" and managed to reach "a good understanding."[3]

Indeed, Johnson not only wanted Israel to forgo the nuclear option and base its ultimate security on the Sixth Fleet but to permit Washington to tell Nasser that she did so. In return he promised to initiate feasibility studies of a joint desalting plant and to set up a joint commission to evaluate periodically Israel's defense needs.

In essence, he undertook to maintain the military status quo in the region. Johnson also called Myer Feldman "his prime minister for Israeli affairs," promised to sell Israel tanks and Skyhawk jets and, before parting, told Eshkol: "I look you in the eyes and I tell you that we will protect Israel."[4]

The emphasis on the "I" was not accidental. Johnson gave Eshkol a list of tasks to help himself win the presidential election. Eshkol wrote Frankfurter: "I go back to Israel confident and cheered by the knowledge that the man in the White House is a friend of our cause." Johnson told his ambassador to Israel, Walworth Barbour: "I don't care a thing about Israel, but your job is to keep the Jews off my back." The strategy worked. NSC advisor McGeorge Bundy noted: "1964 was the first election year on record in which there was no trouble over Israel pressure on the American government."[5]

The 1965 decision to escalate the Vietnam War ended the triangular honeymoon by endowing Israel and American Jewry with strategic importance. To make sense of this unintended consequence, it is necessary to examine some of the assumptions and strategies chosen to secure American goals in Southeast Asia: The choice of Vietnam as a central battlefront in the Cold War reflected the conviction that the consolidation of Western Europe, the Soviet–Chinese rivalry, and the post-Cuban missile crisis Soviet–American detente meant that the containment of the Soviet Union had essentially been achieved. Hence, Washington could redirect containment towards the newly nuclearized People's Republic of China which Johnson believed was involved in a "brazen Communist attempt to conquer Asia." The NSC man responsible for the Third World Robert Komer wrote: "I favor a more flexible China policy and eventual US disengagement from over-commitment around the Chicom periphery, but this is achievable only *after* (as was the case in Europe) we have established unquestionably that this is leading from strength to strength."[6]

"Every President who has surveyed the situation," wrote Lyndon Johnson, drew the line in Vietnam because Communist control of all of Southeast Asia would inevitably affect the security of India and would "run perhaps all the way towards the Middle East."[7] Thus, the American goals included: avoidance of a "domino effect" in Southeast Asia and keeping South Vietnamese territory from "Red hands". Still, the primary goal was "to protect US reputation as a counter subversion guarantor" because as Assistant Secretary Paul Warnke explained, covert rather than "overt aggression" was the "gravest threat in an era in which the shadow of nuclear strategic weapons inhibited major military action by superpowers."[8] South Vietnam was chosen as the proving ground of American ability to thwart a "People's War."

Both the Chinese and the Soviets, who were vying for the leadership of the Afro-Asian world, advocated the use of national liberation movements, previously successful in undermining colonial regimes, to undermine pro-Western ones. Following the Cuban missile crisis, Soviet support for such movements declined, but not so the Chinese. The latter blamed the Cuban fiasco on Soviet "adventurism" and "capitulationism" as the Soviets first provoked the Americans needlessly, and then withdrew meekly. In Vietnam, as in China, the war should be fought and won by the Vietnamese people themselves with only material and technical allied support. "The whole cause of international Proletarian revolution," China contended, hinged on the outcome of "revolutionary struggles" rather than, as the Soviets maintained, on the world system of socialism and "proletarian internationalism."[9]

"Limited War" was the military strategy designed by Kennedy's "Best and Brightest" to frustrate such attempts to redraw the political and economic map of the world without endangering it through nuclear annihilation. Logistic capabilities (later known as the Rapid Deployment Force), counter insurgency techniques, and "nation building" programs were developed to cope with Third World originated crises. Indeed, "Operation Hard Surface" in 1963 and a parachute landing in 1964 successfully turned back a Nasserite challenge to the Saudi regime.[10]

However, by 1964, it had become clear that these techniques were insufficient to deal with the National Liberation Front's (NLF) challenge to South Vietnam. Washington, therefore, decided to use the proven Cuban missile crisis technique of gradual force application to induce a revolutionary Third World country (in this case, North Vietnam) to halt its aid to a national liberation movement. Absent outside assistance, the NLF would realize the futility of its efforts and collapse. Thus, incremental escalated bombing, rather than the quick massive air campaign preferred by the military, was the method chosen for Vietnam.[11]

The proponents of "gradualism" understood that such a course of action was "inherently likely to stretch out and to be subject to major pressures both within the US and internationally" but they also believed that to succeed the US had "to emerge from crisis without unacceptable taint from methods."[12] Tainting the US was precisely the Chinese intention as Premier Zhou Enlai told Egyptian President Gamal Abdel Nasser:

> We are going to escalate the Vietnamese War and to force the United States to accelerate in turn until the number of US troops reaches 700,000 . . . This will automatically increase the hostility of the American people to the US Viet Nam policy. Further, the United States will commit large scale atrocities against North Vietnam and this will prove to the yellow race that the US is waging a major war to liquidate all colored people whether yellow or black. . . . We are hindering Soviet aid to North Vietnam because we want nations to know . . . that we have no partners.[13]

After all, the war was also a contest between Beijing and Moscow. Moscow was pleased to see American attention diverted from Europe, but the bombing of North Vietnam confronted it with a difficult dilemma: "A communist country was exposed to open Western aggression, and the Soviet Union – the leader of the communist camp – does not openly interfere to save her. However, open interference would lead to the curtailment of the policy of 'peaceful coexistence' which is a Chinese goal."[14] Peaceful coexistence, or détente, was also essential to the American ability to keep Vietnam a one front war.

The Truman administration had financed the Marshall Plan, and built NATO, while fighting a war in Korea. However, the Johnson administration assumed it could avoid such an expensive two front strategy because "the USSR would be sufficiently concerned over the prospect of escalation of the crisis and of possible general war that it would not risk trying American temper by provoking major crises in Berlin, Cuba, or elsewhere." US analysts maintained that fear of "nuclear retaliation" would even deter China from creating "any major diversions outside Southeast Asia." However, by March 1965, these same analysts changed their minds and listed "sympathetic fires over Berlin, Kashmir, Jordan waters" as one of the "major risks" the US ran if it bombed North Vietnam.[15]

The change might have been attributable to the demise of Nikita Khrushchev, to the realization that there were "enough potential Vietnams" in the developing world to give any American official "gray hair," to the recognition that determination to prevent the US from focusing solely on Southeast Asia would cause Beijing to aid and abet as "many Vietnams" as it could or, probably, to all three. In any case, this understanding did not cause the administration either to curtail the Vietnamese escalation or to increase resources "elsewhere." It did lead to the development of a three prong strategy to protect US interests without getting directly entangled in another front.[16]

The first, and most crucial, prong was the establishment of indirect cooperation with the new "tougher" Soviet government. After all, since factors such as "strategic inferiority to the West," "economic faltering," and "the dispute with China" (which had undergirded Khrushchev's detente policy) had "not lost their force," Leonid Brezhnev and Alexei Kosygin, too, might be persuaded "to avoid sharp crises on two fronts simultaneously." As National Security advisor McGeorge Bundy informed Johnson, both Dean Rusk and Ambassador to Moscow Llewelyn Thompson agreed that "because of Vietnam" the US should maintain "a clear signal" of its "interest in improved peaceful relations with the Soviet Union and the European Block." It did.[17]

The second prong involved getting American NATO allies to share the burden of protecting the Western position around the globe. Germany was pressured to help financially, and, as British Defence Minister Denis Healey observed, "after trying for forty years to get Britain out of Asia, the Middle East and Africa," Washington began "trying desperately" to keep it in. Indeed, Johnson made it plain to Treasury planners that supporting the pound sterling in order to prevent "the danger" of British disengagement East of Suez or on the Rhine was a "major" American foreign policy concern.[18]

The third prong was a new Johnson, or regionalist, doctrine outlined in a March 1965 paper written by the head of the Policy Planning Council, Walt Rostow. Its goal was to reduce the developing world's "direct dependence" on the US while leaving it "open to cooperative military, economic and political arrangements with the United States." Its success depended on "a systematic policy designed to strengthen the hands of moderates in the regions and reduce the power of extremists – whether those extremists are Communist or ambitious nationalists anxious to take over and dominate their regions."[19]

Hence Washington would rely on her regional allies, not only to take care of themselves but also to protect her own interests. "Moderate" countries like Morocco, Saudi Arabia or Kuwait had become strategic assets while "extremist" countries like Egypt, Ghana and Algeria had become strategic liabilities. "Moderate" Israel emerged not merely as a regional strategic asset, but a global one, for she could also help sell the Vietnam War.

THE SELLING OF THE VIETNAM WAR

Clearly the administration's success in Vietnam depended on its ability to sell a multi-faceted and, at times, even contradictory policy. This task was particularly daunting because, as Dean Rusk explained, "limited wars" could not be sold by creating a war psychology based on enemy vilification. Such a traditional sale could lead "public opinion" to "get out of hand" and demand the use of nuclear weapons.[20] To remain limited, the Vietnam War had to be sold as it was supposed to be fought, in a sophisticated, calm and deliberate manner. It is possible to argue that wars could not be sold that way. It is not possible to argue that such a sale could be effective without the support of the intellectual community, whose vital function is to interpret and promote governmental policy.[21]

Moreover, since American war goals were defined in abstract terms such as "reputation" and "commitment" they inevitably fell into the domain of intellectuals who were defined by their "obsessive preoccupation with the question of end and means." Enlisting intellectuals to fight the public relations contests thus became as important as enlisting soldiers to fight the actual battles. No one understood this better than Hanoi which in December 1963 listed winning international sympathy and support amongst other Third World countries, and amongst "the masses" in the US, Britain and France, as one of its eight specific objectives.[22]

As the obvious underdog, Hanoi enjoyed the propaganda advantage not to mention the fact she was led by the much admired nationalist, the kindly "uncle Ho." The US, on the other hand, was no longer headed by a handsome stylish young man from "Camelot," but by a politically astute "Texas ruffian" who failed to appreciate the crucial role intellectuals played in the ultimate success or failure of his vietnamese policies. Consequently, the President treated intellectuals with a mixture of curiosity, unease and suspicion; they returned the favor.[23]

Still, neither the shortcomings of liberal intellectuals, who were the only ones who counted in the mid-Sixties, nor those of the President, adequately accounts for the breakdown of their relationship. That breakdown stemmed from more fundamental differences. Politicians Lyndon Johnson remembered "the loss of China" and assumed that retreat from Vietnam would present the right with an excuse to terminate his domestic reforms. Liberals remembered Woodrow Wilson, Franklin Roosevelt and Harry Truman, and "saw the cycle of reform, war and then cessation or slowing of efforts for social improvement about to occur once again."[24]

Intellectuals also concluded that the ultimate Cold War victory would belong to the power most successful in harnessing the inevitable revolutionary transformation of the developing world. To have a fighting chance, Americans had to align themselves with the Third World progressive forces. Nations went through various stages in their development, explained the modernization theorists, and any attempt to force them to adopt the liberal democratic model prematurely would only serve to push them into eagerly awaiting Communist arms.[25]

Liberal intellectual regard for John Kennedy was not based solely on his "style," but also on his "New Frontier" policies. Liberals heartily endorsed his creation of the Peace Corps and concurred with his support for Algerian independence and aid to such Third World leaders as Nasser, Nkrumah, Nehru and Sukarno. This became apparent when Kennedy shifted course. James Reston wrote: "President Kennedy's liberal intellectual supporters are beginning to sound a little sad and disillusioned about the administration. . . . There are a number of reasons for this feeling, beginning, of course, with Cuba."[26]

The Johnson doctrine, which viewed nationalists like Ho as extremists, struck liberal intellectuals as silly. It was absurd, argued Arthur Schlesinger Jr., to treat "ragged bands of guerrillas in black pajamas without heavy artillery or air power" as able to present a serious "challenge" to the US. It was much more important to end the specter of whites killing non-whites on their own land. Johnson was placing the US on the losing side of history.[27]

Many of these intellectuals were also Atlanticists. They knew that to keep costs manageable and to pacify Moscow for the abrasions of Vietnam, Washington had to soften its positions on issues dear to European hearts. Europeans were even asked to help finance the Vietnam War by accepting large quantities of American treasury bills at the same time that the US downsized its NATO forces. De Gaulle's France was the only European country to rebel actively, but American insistence that it could no longer carry the Cold War burden "alone" led NATO to the verge of collapse.[28]

Administration Pacificists, led by Dean Rusk, insisted that failure to honor commitments to Saigon would bring into question "the fidelity of the United States under its security treaties all over the world." Unlike Berlin, South Vietnam was a military keystone, and US forces in Vietnam were "a strategic reserve in respect to Europe." Atlanticist willingness to abandon Southeast Asia to communism, while protecting Europe from it, Dean Rusk added, reflected the subtle form of racism of men such as Dean Acheson and George Ball who "looked at yellow and brown men as peripheral." Atlanticist William Fulbright had opposed civil rights as well as the Vietnam War.[29]

This highly damaging intellectual opposition to the War was buttressed by an unusually determined religious leadership. In 1965, a questionnaire on Vietnam was sent to 100,000 clergymen. It found that 80 percent of them were unqualifiedly opposed to the war, 10 percent accepted it as a necessary evil, and 10 percent did not regard themselves competent to judge. Clergymen opposed to the war formed ecumenical *ad hoc* groups. Best known was the Fellowship of Reconciliation, which placed an ad in prominent newspapers calling on the President to stop the war. It was signed by 2,500 clergymen. Later, the number of signatories reached 16,000.[30]

Johnson knew that religious leaders possessed both moral authority and direct access to the voting public. He also thought he knew a foolproof way to control at least the restive Jewish leadership: He would enlist Israel's help. For just as the influence of Jewish intellectuals far exceeded their number, the influence of Israel in the international community bore no relationship to her size. Abba Eban recalls:

> Japanese statesmen and media did not quite know what to make of Israel and the Jewish People. When I told them that Israel's population was less than 2.5 million and that there were some 13 million Jews in the world, they burst into polite laughter and said that it was well known that Abba Eban has a good sense of humor, but how many are there really?[31]

Third World countries considered Israel a "model nation" which had been a "victim of racial discrimination" and "had to fight for . . . liberty."[32] In short, Israeli support could be invaluable in American efforts to sell the war both at home and abroad.

NOTES

1. JTA, Nov. 25, 1963.
2. Michael Bar Zohar, *Ben Gurion* (New York: 1986), 274–5. Eshkol became prime minister on June 21, 1963.
3. "Dear Mr. Justice," July 7, 1964, WHCF, Ex Co 126, box 42. LBJL; and interview with a source close to Eshkol.
4. Ibid.
5. Ibid.; Yitzhak Rabin, *Pinkas Sherut* (Tel Aviv: 1979), 127; Eytan Haber, *Hayom Tifroz Milchama* (Tel Aviv: 1987), 56; Johnson–Eshkol meeting, June 1, 1964, NSF, Israel, Box 138; Seymour M. Hersh, *The Samson Option* (New York: 1991), 161; and "US Foreign Policy since Nov. 1963," Jan. 12, 1965, NSF, Memos to the President, box 1, 95, LBJL.
6. Carl T. Rowan, *Breaking Barriers* (Boston: 1991), 238; and Komer to Bundy, March 11, 1964, NSF, Komer Memos, box 6, 176, LBJL.
7. Lyndon B. Johnson, *The Choices We Face* (New York: 1969), 25.
8. *The Pentagon Papers* (Boston: 1971), Gravel ed., III, 598–9; and Morton A. Kaplan *et al.*, *Vietnam Settlement* (Washington: 1973), 87.
9. Isaac Deutscher, "Russia vs. China, Clash Over Vietnam," *Nation* (July 5, 1965), 3–4; and Ilya V. Gaiduk, *The Soviet Union and the Vietnam War* (Chicago: 1996), 8–9 and 16–8.
10. Robert Attwood, *The Twilight Struggle* (New York: 1987), 266.
11. *The Pentagon Papers* (New York: 1971), *NYT* ed., 335.
12. *Pentagon Papers*, III, 599 and 617.
13. CIA Report, May 12, 1966, NSF, UAR, box 159, LBJL.
14. Anatoly Dobrynin, *In Confidence* (New York: 1995), 136; and Radio Cairo, Sept. 10, 1965, DCSS.
15. *Pentagon Papers*, III, 597 and 698.
16. Robert Komer to McGeorge Bundy, Oct. 4, 1964, NSF, Komer, box 6, 153, LBJL; and Yitzhak Shichor, *The Middle East in China's Foreign Policy* (London: 1979), 118.
17. Memorandum to the President, July 1, 1965, NSF, Files of McGeorge Bundy, box 18, 113, LBJL.
18. Denis Healey, *The Time of My Life* (New York: 1990), 280; and Lyndon B. Johnson, *The Vantage Point* (New York: 1971), 598.
19. W. W. Rostow, *The Diffusion of Power* (New York: 1972), 427.
20. Dean Rusk, LBJ-OH, tape I, 42.
21. Harry C. McPherson to the President, May 14, 1967, President's Appointment File, box 65, LBJL.
22. J. L. Talmon, "The Jewish Intellectual in Politics," *Midstream* (January 1996), 62; and R. B. Smith, *An International History of the Vietnam War* (New York: 1985), II, 221.
23. Interviews with Zbigniew Brzezinski (July 29, 1991) and John Roche (July 22, 1992).
24. Arthur Schlesinger Jr., letter to the editor, *NYT Book Review* (March 29, 1992), 31; and Eric F. Goldman, *The Tragedy of Lyndon Johnson* (New York: 1969), 441.
25. William B. Quade, "The U.S. and Wars of National Liberation," in

Richard A. Falk, ed., *The Vietnam War and International Law* (Princeton: 1968), 102–26.
26. *NYT*, Oct. 8, 1961.
27. Arthur Schlesinger Jr., *The Bitter Heritage* (Greenwich: 1967), xi–xii; and Healey, 280–1.
28. Wolfram F. Hanrieder, *Germany, America, Europe* (New Haven: 1989), 46–50, 182–5 and 192–3.
29. Dean Rusk, LBJ-OH, tape I, 4; Charles Frankel, *High on Foggy Bottom* (New York: 1968), 201; and interview with Dean Rusk (Aug. 2, 1991).
30. *Congressional Record – Senate*, June 7, 1965, 12719.
31. Abba Eban, *Personal Witness* (New York: 1992), 344.
32. A. Savant, "Rivalry between Egypt and Israel in Africa, South of the Sahara," *International Studies* (April–June, 1978), 312.

2 The Vietnam War's Effect on Israel

JERUSALEM AND SAIGON

On March 2, 1965, Dean Rusk instructed his embassy in Tel Aviv to request Israel's assistance in alleviating the critical shortage of medical surgical personnel in South Vietnam. A similar appeal was also made to Iran, India and Greece. It reflected the "very high priority" the President placed "on maximum free world support" in the Southeast Asian conflict. This novel inclusion of Israel in the "free world" did not escape Jerusalem's notice. Fearful of offending the Arabs, Washington had been keeping Israel at bay and advised her allies to do the same. As late as 1963, Saigon with American "knowledge and encouragement" rebuffed Israeli suggestions that they establish diplomatic relations.[1]

The two countries did have informal contacts, with Israel sending South Vietnam $5000 worth of pharmaceutical supplies to aid flood victims in 1964. However, the 1965 escalation of the War was accompanied by South Vietnamese and American entreaties that the two countries formalize their relations and that Israel provide Saigon with assistance which, as Johnson wrote Eshkol, would "give a clear signal to the world" of Israeli "support for resistance to aggression in Vietnam". Eshkol assured Johnson of his "full understanding" of the US "decision concerning South Vietnam," and expressed his hope that the decision would "have the desired effect and that the tragic conflict may yield to peaceful settlement." He avoided the subject of aid, but it refused to die.[2]

In July, the South Vietnamese representative in Bangkok presented the Israeli ambassador with a long wish list. He received no answer. In September, Saigon's ambassador in Manila asked that Israel receive an official delegation of youth workers. Israel agreed but South Vietnam dropped the matter. In October, the White House demanded to know the precise manner in which Israel would express "its solidarity" with Saigon. In November, South Vietnamese officials in Bangkok and Washington informed their Israeli counterparts to expect an official Vietnamese request to formalize their countries' ties. In December, the South Vietnamese ambassador to Thailand repeated his appeal for Israeli aid but added that, for the time being, diplomatic ties between the two countries should remain secret. Israel agreed to accept fifteen South Vietnamese for a week of agricultural training.[3]

Officially, Israel argued that she could not establish diplomatic ties with Saigon unless she would also do so with Hanoi. She had advanced the same argument during the Korean War. Then she had succumbed to American pressure, established diplomatic relations with Seoul but not Pyongyang, and abandoned planned diplomatic ties with Beijing. This time, as Dean Rusk commented, she maintained her position "rather stubbornly."[4] Why? The answer can be found in a combination of domestic, Jewish, regional and international factors which together illuminate not only Israel's response to the Vietnamese conflict, but also the conflict's effect on Israel.

During the mid-sixties, Israel was a thriving social democracy. Her population reached two and a half million, her economy enjoyed double digit growth, she was fifth among all nations in the proportion of university-level students to population, and the Israeli team won the 1964 Asian Soccer Cup. Her international cooperation activities embraced 90 countries, and were surpassed only by Britain and the US. In 1964, even Pope Paul VI came to visit.[5]

Still, the elite worried. Israel, it believed, was at a crossroads. The era of refugee settlement was over, anti-Semitism posed little threat, few Jews were knocking on her door, and the young saw the state simply as their birthplace. Did the great Zionist dream spawn only a small, insignificant Levantine state? And, if so, how would Israel hold on to its best and brightest?

The battle for Israel's future direction raged within the leadership circles of MAPAI, the party which had dominated Israeli politics throughout the country's existence. It led to the 1963 resignation of David Ben Gurion as prime minister. Ben Gurion was a brilliant, charismatic, intellectual elderly statesman who believed that only an Israel which fulfilled the messianic dream of molding "a society of righteousness" would exert "a moral influence among peoples of the world" and attract "Jewish youth as immigrants." "In a world split up into states and blocs" this mandated avoiding the clutches of the Cold War through "diligent efforts to preserve" Israeli "independence in security affairs" through a nuclear "force de frappe." Nuclear force also held the key to peace since it would convince the Arabs of Israel's indestructibility. In any case, Egypt too was developing "nuclear capabilities and trying to build missiles and aircraft."[6]

Ben Gurion's chief rival was Levi Eshkol, an affable, pragmatic politician who shared Abba Eban's view that the value of the Jewish state lay in its factual existence. Peace would come when the Arab states shed their strong ideological moorings and recognized the unique value and divergent interests of each of their separate thirteen states. Meanwhile, a well equipped conventional force, American guarantees, a Soviet commitment to the "status quo," and wide-ranging Third World ties sufficed to deter any Arab onslaught.[7] Nuclear weapons were expensive and Egyptian capabilities were such that Israel could afford to delay the actual manufacturing (but not researching) in return for American guarantees and arm sales. After all, France's wish to improve relations with the Arabs in the aftermath of Algerian independence reduced her reliability as Israel's chief arms supplier.[8]

The decision to delay going nuclear contributed significantly to Ben Gurion's decision to split MAPAI. But given the Israeli taboo on the nuclear issue, all he could tell the public was that Eshkol was "endangering the nation's security."[9] Ben Gurion and his disciples, Moshe Dayan, Shimon Peres and Teddy Kollek established a new party, RAFI. Eshkol with yet another labor party joined to create (the Alignment) MAARACH and the 1965 election battle was underway.

The campaign focused on the possibility that somehow, somewhere, Israel had missed an opportunity to reach an accommodation with her neighbors. All the parties placed their peace initiatives at the top of their agenda. The voting turnout was high (83 percent), and the leftist parties increased significantly their representation in the Knesset. The new left of center Eshkol-led coalition included MAPAM, a Marxist party strongly opposed to American policy in Vietnam. Israeli "stubbornness" increased exponentially.[10]

Thus, on August 29, 1965, the *Jewish Telegraphic Agency* (JTA) reported that Israeli officials had disclosed that the US had chartered "The *first* Israeli ship" to transport materials to South Vietnam. Israeli media reported the story only after the election, whereupon two Knesset members (one from MAPAM) presented outgoing foreign minister Golda Meir with the following official query: Did the story mean that Israel decided to take sides in Vietnam? Meir denied any connection between the government and the private chartering company, and emphasized (twice) that it was a *one time* deal. Hence, Eshkol could claim that his coalition would not withstand an open pro-American stance in Vietnam.[11]

Moreover, Eshkol won the election battle, but the war with RAFI raged on. Particularly damaging was RAFI's accusation that by, eschewing the nuclear option, Eshkol had given up Israel's independence in return for unreliable American guarantees. The fate of South Vietnam, Dayan warned, reflected the real price of such guarantees:

> By the way, in Israel, when one speaks of "American guarantees," it is important to know that the meaning of "American military aid" is not placing the Sixth Fleet at the disposal of the Israeli Defense Forces, but on the contrary, passing Israeli sovereignty into the hands of American forces. To protect the independence of an ally, first they take it away as collateral.[12]

Resisting American pressure to plant Israel's flag in Vietnam helped Eshkol demonstrate the country's independence. By December 1965 the Vietnam War had also emerged as a "hot" political topic, and there were anti- war demonstrations in Jerusalem and Tel Aviv.[13]

Eshkol also knew that Vietnam was a "hot" topic in American Jewish politics, and that Israel could not afford to alienate the war's opponents. Jewish youth's disinterest in Israel was already troubling, especially when compared to its enthusiastic response to the Peace Corps, the civil rights struggle, and the anti-war movement. Economic assistance notwithstanding, the diaspora helped improve the unfavorable numerical balance between Israel and her enemies. There were few on Israel's side, Abba Eban noted, but "not as few as Israel's limited population might indicate. There are millions of Jews across the world for whom Israel's security, welfare and honor are worthy of every effort and sacrifice." But for how long?[14]

Israelis knew that American and Arab officials were not only aware of the diaspora's political and economic power, but tended to exaggerate it. State officials constantly complained that Jews were "pushing" American officials to act against "the long-term interest of the United States."[15] The reality was different. Following a pre-election meeting with Jewish leaders, John Kennedy publicly promised "to waste no time" before using his Presidential authority "to call into conference the leaders of Israel and the Arab states to consider privately their common problems."[16]

However, once in office, Kennedy immediately accepted Nasser's request to put the Arab–Israeli issue "in the refrigerator." In fact,

Washington was directly responsible for the defeat of the December 1961 African sponsored UN resolution calling for direct peace talks between Arab states and Israel under UN auspices. Veteran Journalist William S. White observed: "Any notion that our foreign policy in the Middle East is run with special tenderness for Jewish feelings is one of the special idiocies of our time."[17]

Even so, it was a useful idiocy which Israel enjoyed milking for all the deterrence it was worth. After all, the Arab media never tired of decrying the inordinate "influence of international Zionism."[18] It is impossible to ascertain the degree to which sophisticated Arab leaders shared this popular perception though they certainly found it effective in putting American officials on the defensive, and in justifying the inability of one hundred million Arabs to defeat two million Jews.

One thing is certain, Johnson sought to change the traditional rules of the game by insisting that Israel control the Jewish response to his policies. In 1965, he conditioned military sales to Israel on her promise to help sell the arming of Jordan and Saudi Arabia to the American Congress and people. Eshkol hesitated: "How can I as the Prime Minister of Israel tell American Jews what they should or should not say in matters concerning citizens of the United States?"[19] After all, an American Jew who placed Israeli interests ahead, or even on par, with American ones could be accused of dual loyalty.

To prevent such an eventuality, Jacob Blaustein, the President of the American Jewish Committee (AJC), asked Israeli leaders to affirm that "Jews of the United States, as a community and individuals, have only one political attachment and that is to the United States." The 1950 Ben Gurion–Blaustein agreement formalized that principle. Ben Gurion reaffirmed it in 1961, and Eshkol in 1963 and 1964.[20]

Johnson's demand that Eshkol break the agreement jeopardized American Jews as well as Israeli–diaspora relations. When Ben Gurion, then a mere Knesset member, called for the "strengthening of the bonds between Diaspora Jewry and the State of Israel," his call was immediately brought to Blaustein's attention by none other than McGeorge Bundy. Ben Gurion did not "vitiate" their attached agreement, Blaustein wrote, though he went further than Blaustein would have liked. Bundy agreed and added: "Just the same, if there is a difference between Blaustein and Ben Gurion, I think I would be on the Blaustein side!"[21] The very existence of this exchange reflects the perils of the subject.

Since arms sales were crucial for Israeli security, Eshkol acceded to Johnson's demands. He promptly incurred the wrath of American Jewish leaders. One declared: "We as Jews are interested in American Middle Eastern policy – and as citizens of our country we have the right to try and influence our government to act according to our interests, that are also the interests of the state of Israel. When we try to do this – the Israeli embassy in Washington asks us to stop and thus stifles independent Zionist activity."[22]

Israelis knew that US requests for Israeli aid in Vietnam was intended in part to reduce Jewish opposition to the war. They also knew that an Israeli attempt to interfere would not only be resented, but might also prove futile. Such a public exposure of the limits of her influence on American Jews was not in Israel's interest, particularly at a time when Washington's overcommitment in Vietnam, and its inability to defeat the Vietcong, were beginning to have troublesome consequences for Israel in the Middle East.

THE REGIONAL AND INTERNATIONAL SCENES

Some Israelis studying the regional developments liked what they saw. Times were difficult for pan-Arab nationalists. The fact that Egypt was the single member of the United Arab Republic reflected the growing cohesiveness of individual Arab states. In 1964 President Nasser tried to unite the Arab world around opposition to the Israel's Jordan River project. He organized a series of summits of Arab kings and presidents to develop a joint anti-Israeli strategy. Their plan called for the establishment of a United Arab Command headed by an Egyptian officer, a major arms build up by the confrontation states to be financed by the oil-rich ones, and the creation a Palestinian entity. The traditional Arab demand for the "application of the UN resolutions on Palestine" i.e. the two-state solution, was replaced by a commitment to the "liberation of Palestine," i.e. the elimination of Israel. In September 1964 a Palestine Liberation Army (PLA), consisting of special Palestinian units within Arab armies, was created.[23]

Challenges to Nasser's bid for Arab leadership were partially responsible for the novel Palestinian focus. On the right, Tunisian President Habib Bourguiba argued that the Arabs were not a single nation, but an amalgam of nationalities each responsible for its own state's well-being. Arab states should reach an accommodation with Israel. The Palestinians should fight for their own independence and not expect other Arab states to accomplish that feat for them. Bourguiba campaigned hard for the creation of a Palestinian Liberation Front.[24]

On the left, the Syrian pan-Arabist Baath agreed with Nasser that the Palestinians were part of a single Arab nation, but asserted that procrastination was not a solution. Since the new Palestinian Liberation Organization was headed by the pro-Egyptian Ahmad Shukayri, had its headquarters in Cairo, and Radio Cairo broadcasted its programs, Syria threw its support behind a rival Palestinian organization named FATAH. It was headed by Yassir Arafat and was committed to immediate action. Arafat's friend was Ahmed Sweidani, the head of Syrian Military Intelligence and an admirer of North Vietnam's General Vo Nguyen Giap.[25]

The Syrian leadership was especially interested in applying Vietnamese tactics to the struggle with Israel. "The war itself will be carried on for all practical purposes solely on Israeli ground, as it is happening in South Vietnam. There the United States is unable to use her powerful weapons against the Vietnamese Liberation Front, because the front is fighting exclusively on the territory in which the Americans and their agents reside."[26]

At a closed Syrian foreign ministry briefing, Foreign Minister Ibrahim Machus illuminated the potential role of a Vietnam-style war in uniting the Arabs as well as fighting Israel:

> Independent North Vietnam did not pay any attention to her particular interest and is not surrendering a portion of her precious homeland, which is South Vietnam – for fear of her special position; . . . This is a living example, from which the Arab states – which are consumed by their own independence . . . should learn a lesson. . . . then we will no longer be afraid of Israeli retaliatory actions towards our semi-independent states, and the Arab land will necessarily become a battlefield, which will necessarily result not only in the liberation of Palestine, but in the Arab liberation everywhere and in their unification and once and for all liberation from all internal and external shackles.[27]

Israelis all across the political spectrum watched the attempt to transform the Arab–Israeli conflict into a war of national liberation, and to portray their own national liberation as a colonial venture, with unmitigated horror. Eban wrote:

> Sometimes our adversaries try to portray us as an expression of colonialism. There is no state in the world to which this definition is more incongruous. No state anywhere expresses the concept of nationhood more intensely than Israel. It is the only state which bears the same name, speaks the same tongue, upholds the same faith, inhabits the same land as it did 3,000 years ago. Israel is not alien to the Middle East; it is an organic part of its texture and memory. Take Israel and all that has emanated from Israel out of the Middle Eastern history – and you evacuate that history of its central experience.[28]

It was not easy to attach the colonialist stigma to the Jewish state, or to cover the Palestinians with the aura of national liberation warriors. Countries which possessed *bona fide* anti-colonial and pro-Arab credentials such as Yugoslavia and Cuba, and personages like Jean-Paul Sartre, refused to go along.[29] China was the only non-Arab country which accepted the colonialist argument, recognized both the PLO and FATAH, and agreed to provide them with ideological, political and practical support. In 1964 Arafat visited Beijing and received promises of support. To further convince the Chinese of their seriousness, FATAH began infiltrating units into Israel in January 1965. Bombs began exploding in residential compounds the following month. In March 1965 Shukayri too went to Beijing. Mao told him to follow Arafat's example: "There are many people studying military matters in China. . . . To go back and take part in fighting is more useful." Mao promised to supply Palestinian groups with the financial and military resources needed for such fighting.[30]

The Arab country most adversely affected by the new Palestinian movements was Jordan. Not only did the Palestinians claim the West Bank as part of their heritage, but Amman's long border with Israel and her large Palestinian population made her the natural candidate to fulfill the role of North Vietnam in a Palestinian people's war. Jordan opposed such a war, as much out of fear for the continued viability of the Hashemite kingdom as for fear of Israeli retaliation. The trouble was that her effective control of the West Bank was insufficient to prevent FATAH from using her territory for exit bases.

Jerusalem understood the Jordanian quandary, but she could not permit FATAH to have a free reign in the West Bank. To demonstrate her resolve to extract a heavy price, and to legitimize Jordanian opposition for a people's war Israel retaliated in May 1965 against three Jordanian villages which had served as FATAH exist bases.[31] The first to warn that a people's war had commenced on Israel's borders was a MAPAM Knesset member. Eshkol, himself, tried not to see: "I didn't want to give it that honor . . . and I really believed there was a difference between us and Algeria or Vietnam."[32]

Becoming identified with the American war in Vietnam could only serve to blur that difference. It would also counter Israeli efforts to improve relations with Asia, a continent teaming with Moslems but bereft of Jews. For as Daniel Levin of the foreign ministry's Asia desk explained, if Israel did "not belong in Asia," it did "not belong anywhere . . . there are international committees of the United Nations which decide and execute. Today, in every serious consultation, we are out."[33]

Israel used a highly effective technical assistance program to make friends and influence people in the developing world. Aid recipients often reciprocated by defending Jerusalem at international meetings where Arabs pressed anti-Israeli moves. However, Levin pointed out, there was a clear recognition in Asia that it had no room for an imperialist country. Israelis could come to Asia "as Asians" or – as the Arab propaganda claimed – as "representatives of American Imperialism." Already, a NLF delegation visiting Syria had told the press that the Arab struggle against Israel was similar to its own and that "the two peoples" faced "a mutual enemy."[34]

The Chinese role has to be understood in the context of the creation of the PLO and FATAH. On Dec. 31, 1963, Khrushchev proposed a worldwide agreement to eschew border changes by force. This led to an exchange of notes between Moscow and Washington in favor of solidifying "peaceful coexistence" through the maintenance of existing frontiers. The USSR, over strong Chinese objections, had joined the forces of the "status quo."[35] The notes did not include a specific reference to the Middle East, but Eshkol was amongst the heads of government invited to support the initiative. Indeed, in January 1964, Soviet ambassador to Israel Dmitri Chuvakhin told Eshkol that Moscow had informed the Arabs that it supported Israel's right to the Jordan waters and opposed the attempts to eliminate her because it would lead to a nuclear war.[36]

Egypt and Algeria protested that the principle was not applicable to Israel because she was "an imperialist base" designed to prevent the unification of the Arab world. Moscow published their objections without comment. Redefining the Arab–Israeli conflict as a war of national liberation prevented an Arab–Soviet collision. In the joint communiqué published following Khrushchev's 1964 visit to Egypt, Nasser expressed unqualified support for the peaceful settlement of territorial disputes. After all, he no longer defined the Arab–Israeli conflict as a territorial dispute even if the Soviets continued to do so.[37]

The Chinese argued that the appropriate way to defeat imperialism in Vietnam, or elsewhere, was "bit by bit." The Arabs were "the front gate" of the great Asian continent, and China was "the rear." It was important to engage the US on both fronts as China did in 1958. "Our forces shelled Quemoy," Mao told Shukayri, "to engage the imperialists during the revolution in Iraq and the American landing in the Lebanon." The strategy was not foreign to the Soviets. According to intelligence officer Pavel Sudoplatov, Moscow provoked the 1948 Berlin crisis to divert American attention from the imminent communist takeover of China. Nor did "peaceful coexistence" mean an end to "undermining imperialism from behind." That was the principle used to justify support for countries such as UAR, Syria or Algeria which were not communist but merely pursued a "socialist orientation." The argument was limited to the people's war tactic.[38]

Actually, the Vietnam War was but one manifestation of a new three-way rivalry for the Third World. In the fifties and early sixties, Britain and France represented the conservative powers, the USSR the radical ones, while the US straddled the middle with the help of nationalists like Nasser. Things shifted in 1965: The US joined Britain on the right, The PRC perched on the left, and the USSR straddled the middle. As the British ambassador to Washington warned the Egyptian UN representative in the presence of Adlai Stevenson, the American escalation in Vietnam had direct consequences for the Middle East. Since Johnson could not "ignore or dispense with the Middle East . . . he was leaving the reins to Israel."[39]

Nasser, who like other non-aligned leaders had benefited from active Soviet–American competition for his favors, understood that an American withdrawal from that competition would force him to choose sides and that whichever side he chose would get him cheaply. Since he correctly blamed the Vietnam War for the American policy change, he tried to mediate a settlement in Vietnam. He was rebuffed by both Washington and Beijing. So, to prove his destructive potential, he embarrassed both Washington and Bonn by publicizing West Germany's role in secret American arms sales to Israel. When Bonn responded by replacing clandestine weapons' transfers with open diplomatic relations with Israel, Egypt cut her ties with Bonn and demanded that other Arabs states follow suit. Egypt also became the first non-Communist country to invite East German President Walter Ulbricht for an official visit, and it demanded that Jordan buy arms from Moscow.[40]

An enraged Congress insisted on decreasing food aid to Egypt. The administration had no choice but to implement the Johnson doctrine in the Middle East with great dispatch. In February 1965, Averell Harriman and Robert Komer flew to Israel to finalize a deal to bolster the military capabilities of American allies (Israel, Jordan and Saudi Arabia) in order to enable them to withstand *alone* the expected Egyptian retaliatory onslaught. Israel was most reluctant to accept the deal which involved her in an expensive arms race, strengthened Jordanian military capabilities, and limited her freedom of action. But Harriman warned that the US was prepared to leave the region. After much haggling, a "regionalist" deal was struck and a "tacit alliance" was created between the countries supplied with Western arms, including Israel. They were to be buttressed by Britain, which was fighting a liberation war in Aden, the large oil companies, and the CIA.[41]

Nasser retaliated by denouncing US involvement in Vietnam, permitting the NLF to open an information bureau in Cairo, and supporting "Arab revolutionary action" against Israel, Aden and the Arabian peninsula monarchies. Zhou Enlai spent weeks in Cairo trying to translate Nasser's new radicalism into support for Beijing's effort to exclude Moscow from the upcoming Second Afro-Asian (Bandung) conference in Algiers and to insure the passage of a resolution containing a sharp condemnation of the American role in the Vietnam War.

Informed that the "need for US aid to solve the bread problem" restrained Nasser, Zhou offered to supply Egypt with wheat. But Nasser, who viewed both the Sino-Soviet dispute and the Vietnam War as damaging to the non-aligned movement, decided to side with the Soviets. The overthrow of Ben Bella, and the subsequent cancellation of Bandung II, convinced China of its inability to compete with the superior military and economic resources of Washington and Moscow. Hence, Beijing opted for ideological radicalism and support for Syrian-Palestinian belligerency in the Middle East.[42]

The wish to secure continued Soviet opposition to Arab belligerency, and non-recognition of the PLO, added to Israeli determination not to support the US in Vietnam. After all, at a conference on behalf of an independent Aden, the USSR and its allies opposed Arab efforts to add a call for the "liberation of Palestine" to the resolution. China, Indonesia, Albania, Japan and North Korea backed the Arab position and carried the day.[43] Israel also knew that Soviet Middle Eastern influence was rising geometrically. That was the reason that Eshkol was in Paris in March 1965 when NATO's European ministers interrupted their discussions on Vietnam to voice their objections to the planned American "withdrawal" from the Mideast which they expected to precipitate another Arab–Israeli war.[44]

Israel found superpower behavior during the 1965 India-Pakistan War most telling. The arms embargo the US slapped on both countries despite Pakistani membership in both SEATO and CENTO convinced Chief of Staff Yitzhak Rabin and others that the US "didn't come through" on its "commitments." American support for Moscow's mediation effort, regardless of its unrealized hope that the Soviets would "break their lance" in South Asia, further demonstrated America's single-minded concentration on Vietnam. US allies swiftly adjusted to the new reality.[45]

Israelis ignored Robert Komer's argument that the embargo reflected American anger with lack of Pakistani prior consultation or that the India-Pakistani War proved that air forces were of "marginal value." Instead, Jerusalem like Teheran, began to prepare for an American embargo during a future regional conflict, found hope in the fact that Moscow had at times "a quarrel" with Israeli policies but "not with its existence" and tried not to run afoul of the new regional superpower, the USSR.[46] Only the Saudis followed the American advice and increased their reliance on London. The American ambassador to Saudi Arabia reported: "Saudi–UK political cooperation is increasing which is largely consonant with US aims . . . On three separate occasions during the past twelve months the Saudi Government felt itself in danger of imminent UAR attack from the south. . . . in March and August 1965 his government appealed to the USG for military assistance while in February of 1966 it sought the aid of the UK."[47]

After all, the UK had already reevaluated her "commitments and objectives in the Middle East" and set a date for a final exit from

Aden. Even her Commonwealth brothers understood as much and preferred Soviet to British mediation.[48] In short, helping America to sell the Vietnam War was hardly the best way to curry Soviet favor, buttress the Israeli position in the international arena, refute Arab charges, or capture the imagination of the diaspora.

NOTES

1. Dean Rusk to Amembassy Tel Aviv, March 2, 1965; and Secretary of State to the Vice President, March 15, 1966, NSF, Israel, box 138 and 143, LBJL.
2. Lyndon Johnson to Levi Eshkol, July 26, 1965; and Levi Eshkol to Lyndon Johnson, July 28, 1965, Israeli–American relations, Yad Eshkol.
3. "Israeli Relations with South Vietnam," Dec. 1965, Israeli Relations with Asia, Vietnam, Yad Eshkol.
4. Interview with Rusk.
5. Misha Louvish, "Israel," in the *American Jewish Yearbook: 1964* (Philadelphia: 1964), 450–65.
6. David Ben Gurion, "The Facts of Jewish Exile," *Harper's Magazine* (Sept. 1965), 51; and Mohamed Heikal, 1967: *Al Infijar* (Cairo: 1990), 110.
7. *JTA*, Jan. 15, 1964; and Victor Cygilman, "Can Israel Go Neutralist?" *New Outlook* (Sept. 1964), 5–9.
8. Hersh, *The Samson Option*, 136–9; and Shlomo Aronson, *Conflict and Bargaining in the Middle East* (Baltimore: 1978), 44–5.
9. Ibid., 139; and Shimon Peres, "Kosher Dimyon Vekosher Peula Medini," *Mabat Hadash*, Oct. 13, 1965, 5.
10. Ze'ev Katz, "The Election – A Defeat for Activism," *New Outlook*, (Nov.–Dec. 1965), 13–17.
11. *Maariv*, Nov. 11, 1965; *Divrei Haknesset*, 29 Dec. 1965, 279.
12. Moshe Dayan, *Yoman Vietnam* (Tel Aviv: 1979), 59.
13. *Haaretz*, Dec. 29, 1965; and *Zo Haderech*, Dec. 30, 1965.
14. Abba Eban, "Israel Looks Outward," *Jewish Frontier* (Dec. 1966), 6.
15. "Discussion at Committee on Israel Meeting," Nov. 20, 1963, AJC, box 105, FAD-1, YIVO.
16. "Kennedy, election speech," 1960, AJC, Box 105, FAD-1. AJCL.
17. Mordechai Gazit, *President Kennedy's Policy Towards the Arab States and Israel* (Tel Aviv: 1983), 68.
18. *Al-Achbar* (UAR), Sept. 21, 1964; and *Al Jandi* (Syria), June 9, 1964. DCSS.
19. Etta Z. Bick, "Ethnic Linkages and Foreign Policy," unpublished Ph.D. dissertation (CUNY: 1983), 210–11.
20. Jacob Blaustein to McGeorge Bundy, Nov. 3, 1965, WHCF, Ex Co 125, box 42, LBJL.

21. Ibid.; Ben Gurion, 49; and Mr. Blaustein from McGeorge Bundy, Nov. 6, 1965, WHCF, Ex Co 125, box 42, LBJL.
22. *Hayom*, Sept. 12, 1966.
23. Hashim Behbehani, *China's Foreign Policy in the Arab World* (London: 1986), 37.
24. L. Kadi, *Arab Summit Conferences and the Palestinian Problem* (Beirut: 1966), 160–5.
25. "Ashaf," *Maarchot* (Oct. 1968), 24.
26. *Al Hayat* (Lebanon), June 17, 1965; *Al Baath* (Syria), Nov. 1 and 26, 1965, DCSS.
27. Captured Syrian documents quoted in Abraham Ben Tsur, *Gormim Sovietiim Lemilchemet Sheshet Hayamim* (Tel Aviv: 1975), 99–100.
28. Eban, "Israel Looks Outward," 6.
29. Jean Daniel, "An interview with President Bourguiba," *Midstream* (June 1965), 42–4.
30. Shichor, *The Middle East in China's Foreign Policy*, 118.
31. "Week's Developments in the Near East," Oct. 7, 14, 1965, NSF; Files of McGeorge Bundy, box 19, 8 and 9, LBJL.
32. *Maariv*, Oct. 4, 1967.
33. Aryeh Levin, "Hartzaa Biyshivat Hamachlaka Hamedinit," May 30, 1965, printed in H. S. Aynor, S. Avimor and N. Kaminer, eds., *Trumat tnuat Haavoda Beysum Kishrei Hachutz Shel Medinat Yisrael Beafrika Veasia* (Tel Aviv: 1989), 22–3.
34. Yehoshafat Harkavi, *Emdat Yisrael Besichsuch Yisrael-Arav* (Tel Aviv: 1967), 57; and *Near East Review* (Nov. 30, 1965), 95.
35. Abba Eban, "Reality and Vision in the Middle East" *Foreign Affairs* (July 1965), 626–38.
36. *Al Mukaf al Arabi* (Syria), June 24, 1965; and "Khrushchev-Eshkol letters," April 3, 1964, PM office, Israeli–Russian relations, box 809/00, ISA.
37. *Izvestia*, Feb. 13, 1964; *Soviet News*, Nov. 10, 1965; Arthur J. Klinghoffer with Judith Apter, *Israel and the Soviet Union* (Boulder: 1985), 27–57.
38. Shichor, 73 and 115–18; Pavel Sudaplatov and Anatoly Sudaplatov, *Special Tasks* (Boston: 1994), 210; and Alexei Vassilliev, *Russian Policy in the Middle East* (Reading: 1993), 62–3.
39. Heikal, *Al Infijar*, 114.
40. *Radio Cairo*, Sept. 9, 1965, DCSS. Documents on the mediation efforts are found in NSF, UAR, box 158, LBJL.
41. Rabin, *Pinkas Sherut*, 128–30; and "Recommendations on Near East Arms," (undated) NSF, Near East, box 116, 10a, LBJL; Heikal, *Al Infijar*, 110–15. On oil companies' discomfort with American Mideast policy see "Memorandum of Conversation," Jan. 13, 1965, NSF, Near East, box 116, 8-b, LBJL.
42. Chen Yi on Sept. 29, 1965, printed in Singh Karki, *China and Non-Alignment* (New Delhi: 1980), 91; Cairo to Secstate, June 24 1965; and *Communist China and the Arab World*, CIA report, Sept. 17, 1965, NSF, UAR, box 158, LBJL.
43. *Moscow Radio*, April 4, 1965, DCSS.
44. *Al Gumhuria* (UAR), March 30, 1965; and Thomas J. Schoenbaum, *Waging Peace and War* (New York: 1988), 423.

45. Robert J. McMahon, *The Cold War on the Periphery* (New York: 1990), 328–35; Amembassy Iran to Sectat, Nov. 28, 1965, NSF, Iran, box 136, 5; Memo for the President, Sept. 16, 1965, NSF; Files of McGeorge Bundy, box 19, 11, and Memo for the Record, Oct. 8, 1965, NSF; Komer, box 6, 131, LBJL.
46. Memorandum of Komer–Eban Conversation, Oct. 5, 1965, Israeli–US relations, 804/71, ISA; and Memorandum for the Record," Oct. 18, 1965, NSF, Komer, box 6, 120.
47. Department of State from Amembassy Jidda, March 30, 1966, NSF, Saudi Arabia, box 155, 35, LBJL.
48. Healey, *The Times of My Life*, 280.

3 On the Front Line of the Peace Movement

AMERICA'S JEWS ARRIVE

On January 15, 1966 the Synagogue Council of America (SCA), the coordinating agency for six organizations representing 3.5 million Orthodox, Conservative and Reform synagogue affiliated Jews, issued a plea to President Johnson to resist pressures to escalate the war in Vietnam even if his peace offensive should fail. "The appeal to President Johnson marked the *first time* that the *entire Jewish religious community* took a position on an *international issue* going beyond immediate Jewish concern," reported the major source of the Anglo-Jewish media, the Jewish Telegraphic Agency (JTA).[1]

The appeal raises three interrelated questions: Where did this leadership acquire the confidence needed for such a stand? Why were the Jewish religious leaders so supportive of the infant antiwar movement? And why did they care so deeply about the war in Vietnam?

First and foremost, the willingness of Jewish religious leaders to take such a strong stand demonstrates that they, along with their congregants, regarded themselves as "an indigenous, thoroughly acculturated community in a rapidly changing democratic society." Their high level of political participation, both in terms of voting and fund raising, had made them a powerful electoral force. Jews perceived their role in electing John Kennedy as a pivotal moment in their history. They had helped elect a chief executive and he knew it.[2]

The appointment of Arthur Goldberg as the American ambassador to the UN, seemed to prove that America was a meritocracy in which a Jew could affirm his origin, announce with pride "I am a Zionist," and still be judged qualified to represent his country in the highest international forum. When Goldberg promised that his sympathy for Israel would not affect his impartiality, he was believed. The Senate confirmed him unanimously.[3]

It would, indeed, have been a mistake to doubt the deep gratitude, love and loyalty American Jews felt for their country. Much of their opposition to the Vietnam War originated in their belief that the US was losing its way, that it was their obligation to save it, and that they had the power to do so! Arthur Goldberg told Yale University chaplain William Sloane Coffin that it was his "national duty" to resign from the Supreme Court because Johnson was "going to get enmeshed in Vietnam" and he had "the egotistical feeling" that he would be able not only to "influence the President not to get overly involved" but to use the UN to diffuse the situation.[4]

Similar self confidence was reflected in the assertiveness with which the community sought to remove the last barriers to Jewish advancement. It demanded that Jewish soldiers should have the right to serve anywhere, including Saudi Arabia; that governmental agencies should stop using responses to assertions such as that "Christ performed miracles" as a way to ascertain an applicant's religious faith, and that immigration laws should disregard national or religious origin.[5]

This muscle flexing extended to Israel. The President of the assertive American Jewish Congress Joachim Prinz, insisted that American Jews not only had "a distinct right to speak out on Israeli issues of concern to Jews as a whole," but should be invited to help Israel deal with church and state issues. The same did not hold true for Israel. Prinz informed the Israeli consul that American Jewry's commitment to Israel was not strong enough to persuade it to take Jerusalem's interests into account in matters concerning Vietnam.[6] American Zionism no longer even assigned a superior value to living in Israel.

American Jews really believed that anti-Semitism was dead, that their Judaism had become inconsequential, and that they had "made it" on their own. These fallacies led Goldberg to give up a position of real authority to become a salesman of policies over which he had no control, and little input. Granted that Johnson made the UN ambassadorship seem "almost tantamount to a second Secretary of State," but Goldberg should have known better. It was no secret that the President sought to replace Stevenson with "a known liberal" able to sell "unpopular American policies in Viet Nam and the Dominican Republic."[7]

Nor was Goldberg's Jewishness irrelevant. When Dean Rusk asked Joseph Sisco whether he foresaw "any overriding problem" with appointing a Jew as UN ambassador, Sisco intimated that UN diplomats would understand the political nature of the selection and know the limits of the position's influence on actual policy. In fact,

Sisco remembers that whatever influence Goldberg did have emanated from Johnson's conviction that "Goldberg knew what the thinking of the Jewish community was" and that "anything that would be acceptable to Goldberg would be acceptable politically in the country," especially "to the domestic supporters of Israel." After all, what could be more politically acceptable than having a self-professed Zionist represent the US at a time when Washington wanted to condemn Israel at the UN?

Sisco was right. Even Arab ambassadors remarked privately that "United States policies were made in Washington not at the United Nations," even if publicly they delighted in calling his choice "extremely logical" since "Zionists" directed American policy. Israelis knew not to expect Goldberg "to alleviate" Israel's position, and were careful not to embarrass Goldberg by focusing on his Jewishness.[8]

Justifiably or not, this self assurance led Jews to jump with both feet into the political fray. Their commitment to civil rights was astounding: Jews made up two thirds of the white Freedom Riders in the summer of 1961, and almost half of the 1964 Mississippi Summer volunteers. In the 1963 march on Washington, a rabbi walking hand in hand with Martin Luther King was at the head of the parade. Arthur Goldberg not only invited black leaders to his Passover Seder, but chose Dr. James M. Nabrit, President of Howard University, as his UN deputy. Jews voted overwhelmingly against ordinances designed to keep blacks out of white neighborhoods.[9]

Still, there was also an element of concern in this frantic political activity. American civil society was so welcoming and Jews so willing and able to take advantage of its opportunities, that the total assimilation of American Jewry seemed but a matter of time. Having "become part and parcel of the life of other people," many Jews, especially young ones, explained World Zionist Congress president Nahum Goldmann, were "threatened by an anonymous process of erosion, of disintegration, not as a theory or as a conscientious ideology but by the facts of this day to day life." They were about to vanish, elaborated novelist Herman Wouk, "pleasantly" "down a broad highway at the wheel of a high-powered station wagon with the golf clubs piled in the back." The phenomenon of "the vanishing Jew" filled the media. Some intellectuals enjoyed the relief of not having to be "special" but Jewish leaders, especially Conservative and Reform rabbis, were determined to arrest the erosion of their constituency.[10]

Analysts agreed that the young, who had "inadequate and sometimes distorted ideas" about Judaism, often considered themselves as "Americans who happen by accident of birth to be Jewish," an attribute they considered to be devoid of serious consequences. But liberal Jewish leaders found hope in the high degree of social and political activism amongst the over 300,000 Jewish students, who constituted 90 percent of college age Jewish males and 70 percent of Jewish females, because it proved that though not "Prophets," they were "yet the descendants of the Prophets." Twice as many Jewish as non-Jewish students participated in political campaigns or civil rights demonstrations, and four times as many Jewish students protested American military policy.[11]

These activists were often raised in well educated, politically aware, liberal families which encouraged their egalitarian, anti-authoritarian and self-assertive impulses. As an astute Israeli commentator wrote, it was an upbringing which replaced "outdated physical isolation" with a kind of "mental one" based on "a degree of alienation, of non conformity, of doubt and of willingness to challenge the conventional wisdom."[12] The question facing the Jewish community was how to make these children aware of the Jewish roots of their activism and, consequently, of the unique value of their heritage?

To Nahum Goldmann, the answer seemed simple: Jews had to recapture their "historical position of being among the pioneers of all progressive movements in history" instead of being satisfied with "the maintenance of the social and political status quo." Jewish institutions, seconded Prinz, should join in the struggle for racial justice and the war on poverty "because brotherhood and equality and care for the poor are among the great values of our faith. *These values must be rediscovered by a Jewish generation that is hardly conscious of them.*" Similarly, religiously based opposition to the Vietnam War demonstrated Judaism's attachment to peace and further proved Jewish uniqueness and mission.[13]

Thus, if Jewish students' "de-identification" with their community stemmed from the community's "overly narrow and parochial" ethnic concerns, synagogues and federations had to become involved with the national and international scene. After all, the urgent tasks of securing the physical survival of the remnants of European Jewry, settling the vast number of immigrants to Israel, and assuring the safety of that infant state had been successfully accomplished.[14]

The task of preventing the Department of State's Middle Eastern policy from tilting entirely away from Israel remained. American

Jews had helped secure Truman's recognition of Israeli statehood, and block the efforts of Eisenhower and Dulles to impose economic sanctions on Israel in 1957. They had even used the polls to punish the Republicans. In 1956 only 60 percent of the Jews voted Democratic; in 1960, 82 percent did so and, in 1964, 93 percent voted for Johnson.[15] Could Jewish youth not be galvanized against President Nasser, the PLO or Al FATAH? And what about the plight of Soviet Jewry?

VIETNAM AND ETHNIC PREROGATIVES

In 1960, Kennedy rewarded Jewish contributions to his election with the appointment of Myer Feldman as his special adviser on the Middle East. Jewish leaders "found from years of experience and personal contact" that there was "a psychological if not pathological tendency in the [State] Department to underestimate the villainy of the Arabs and overestimate the deceitfulness of the Israelis." They tried to circumvent the Department by using their constituency's influence on Congress and the American public. Kennedy's institutionalization of this Jewish interest removed the need for such grassroots mobilization.[16]

The foreign policy establishment struck back in the summer of 1963. The American Assembly is a yearly gathering of that establishment; of its 70 participants only three or four were sympathetic to Israel. Their report urged the US "to work to bring about greater public awareness, especially in this country, of the realities of the present relationship between the Arabs and Israel with particular reference to the refugee problem." The words "especially in this country" replaced the phrase "especially among the Jewish community of the United States" in the draft report.[17]

Clearly, the Assembly hoped to drive a wedge between Israel and American Jewry. The Senate Committee on Foreign Relations had provided it with ammunition. A few months earlier its chairman J. William Fulbright, under the guise of a hearing on "Activities of Agents of Foreign Principles in US," embarrassed American Jews by focusing on the close ties between Israel and the publications of the American Zionist Council. No one mentioned CIA covert subsidies to the pro-Arab American Friends of the Middle East. Nothing illegal was uncovered, but the limelight was disturbing.[18]

The 1964 selection of Barry Goldwater as the Republican candidate, and the absence of any reference to Israel in the Republican platform for the first time in twenty years further diminished Jewish bargaining power. The results were immediate. In December 1963, Abe Feinberg had told Eshkol that Johnson was worried about the upcoming elections and unsure about his ability to carry New York. But, by August 1964, Democratic party activist Philip Klutznick reported that overconfidence in the Jewish vote was reducing Johnson's interest in Jewish issues, and undermining Myer Feldman's influence.[19]

Klutznick proved right. Lyndon Johnson received a huge Jewish vote, but did not owe it his election. Feldman lost his running battle with Robert Komer over Middle Eastern policy in January 1965, and resigned. When Jewish Congressmen went to Komer's boss, McGeorge Bundy, to inquire about a replacement for Feldman, Bundy told them "that in default of a better watchman" for Israel, he "was doing this job." Bundy told Johnson that the Congressmen left reassured.[20]

Others, like Senator Abraham Ribicoff would have preferred to see Washington sign "a mutual assistance pact with the state of Israel." Such a pact, Ribicoff wrote Johnson, was in his interest since Israel was a country on which the US could "rely." Short of an American–Israeli security treaty, peace in the Middle East, he added, depended on Soviet–American cooperation. The escalating Vietnam conflict did not bode well either for Israel or for Soviet Jewry.[21]

Secularization threatened the continued existence of both the American and Soviet Jewries. The difference was that American youth chose to ignore their ethnic heritage, while Soviet youth's access to it was limited. During the mid-Sixties, young Soviet Jews began to rediscover their roots and the authorities responded with a contradictory policy. They published anti-Semitic tracts but permitted limited contacts between Soviet and Western Jews, and even some Jewish emigration (under the rubric of family reunification).[22]

Strong condemnation of Soviet anti-Semitism, and support for cultural and religious rights of Soviet Jews, soon united Israel and the diaspora (including Jewish communists). It also found a receptive audience in the international intellectual community, and amongst students and academicians normally alienated from organized Judaism. The unexpected success of a New York youth rally served as proof of the cause's enormous galvanizing potential.[23] However, Jewish leaders worried that concern for Soviet Jews, like concern for Israel, could push American Jews into the anti-communist camp. Moscow even accused Americans of using Soviet Jewry as a smokescreen for their own activities in Vietnam. Indeed, Barry Goldwater was quick to jump on the Soviet Jewry bandwagon.

Jewish leaders asked Washington to raise the issue of Soviet Jews with Moscow. But the administration argued that "formal government to government protests" were not "in the best interests of the Soviet Jews." At the same time, the administration made sure that news of the Jewish agitation would reach the Russians. USIA director Leonard Marks wrote to McGeorge Bundy: "In response to a request from your office, I am enclosing translations of the two items about this [Soviet Jewry's] rally broadcast in Russian to the USSR on Sept. 19 and 21." Someone handwrote on it "good."[24]

Goldmann asked people with friendly ties to Moscow to "bring even more pressure to bear" in support of Soviet Jews, but warned that "the impression that Israel and the Jewish people" were "an anti-Soviet factor" had to be avoided. After all, the USSR was not defenseless. An attempt to include a condemnation of anti-Semitism in the UN declaration against "racial discrimination" led Moscow to propose the condemnation of "Zionism, Nazism, Neo-Nazism and all forms of policy and ideology of colonialism, national and race hatred and exclusiveness." Both proposals had to be dropped. Accommodation with the Communist superpower seemed a much safer tactic.[25]

However, enlightened self-interest alone fails to explain the intensity with which men like Abraham Heschel, a professor of Jewish ethics and mysticism, opposed the Vietnam War. William Sloane Coffin describes how during a meeting with Secretary of Defense Robert McNamara "Heschel interrupted, or rather erupted. Out of control he poured forth his anguish, his hands gesticulating pathetically." Heschel explained: "I have previously thought that we were at war reluctantly, with sadness at killing so many people. I realize that we are doing it now with pride in our military efficiency."[26]

Holocaust survivor Heschel knew that efficiency and pride in military might were features of the Nazi war machine. Premier Nguyen Cao Ky seemed to prove that the Nazi experience was indeed applicable to South Vietnam. He told a British reporter that Hitler was his only hero, and that Vietnam needed "four of five Hitlers." At Harvard, peace activists distributed copies of the interview.[27]

Jewish students compared their own predicament with that of the Germans. "They, too," one remarked "watched helplessly while their government incinerated men, women and children." "In a free society," Heschel warned the students, "some are guilty but all are responsible." Rabbi Robert Goldberg of New Haven told draft resisters: "You may go to trial but never to a future Nuremberg." Nuremberg was also on the mind of radical intellectual M. S. Arnoni, who suggested that Bertrand Russell organize an international war crimes tribunal on the Vietnam War. Ralph Schoenman, Russell's Jewish assistant, compared South Vietnamese "strategic hamlets" to Nazi concentration camps. The tribunal proceedings were published under the title *Against the Crime of Silence*.[28]

Collective guilt for their relative silence during the Holocaust haunted Jews. "Everything in our tradition prompts us to believe that there are times when silence is immoral," asserted Rabbi Arthur Lelyveld, the head of the national Jewish students organization and SNCC member. "We know that American Jews showed great courage in their struggle against Johnson's policy," said Hanoi's ambassador to France, "and it is natural. Who suffered like the Jews from the terrible war crimes in our generation?"[29]

Finally there was concern that, as Rabbi Jacob Weinstein wrote upon his return from a 1965 fact finding mission in Vietnam, "whatever else may survive the war towards which our present policy seems directed, faith in God and man will not survive."[30] Religion barely survived one Holocaust, it could not survive another. This conviction haunted liberal Christians as well as Jews, and spurred their leaders into unprecedented political activism.

By November 1965, the entire biennial of the Reform movement's Union of American Hebrew Congregation (UAHC) focused on "A Call to Action on World Peace." Subsequently, its Commission on Social Action put together a program of study, publication and action to promote peace in Vietnam. Rabbis throughout the country received packets which included the biennial resolutions, *New York Times*, and *Christian Century* editorials, and an admonition to undertake a series of educational actions in the congregation and interreligious initiatives in the community. An attachment of recommended "Discussion Issues and Socio-Dramas on Peace" sheds light on the questions which would dog the rabbis: Can a Jew, who acknowledges that he would have fought against Nazi Germany, be considered a conscientious objector on Jewish grounds? Won't the synagogue involvement in such a divisive political issue be "harmful" to the community? Should synagogues try to protect peace activists from local draft board retaliation?[31]

Rabbis lobbying for a unified Jewish anti-war position had to have answers to this questions. If they succeeded it was because of fortunate timing. After all, the SCA statement was issued in the midst of Christmas bombing pause while the president's personal emissaries were encircling the globe asserting his desire for peace in Vietnam. Moreover, Goldberg had personally assured the rabbis that Johnson would welcome their statement. The pronouncement praised Johnson's peace initiative as "a convincing demonstration" of presidential integrity and "willingness to negotiate unconditionally" and only sought to aid him oppose "new pressures for unlimited escalation of the war resulting from impatience and disappointment." The rabbis even acknowledged that those seeking to check "Communist subversion by military means" were "no less dedicated to the cause of just world peace." However, they did declare that "the imperatives of our religious commitment call for the recommendations we prayfully put forward and commend to the attention of our synagogues throughout the land."[32]

The statement represented the high water mark of Jewish unity on the war. Within a month, orthodox rabbis not affiliated with the Synagogue Council began to voice their objections and the patriotic Jewish War Veterans (JWV), warned that the rabbis were giving the "wrong impression" that Jews opposed American policy in Vietnam. JWV commander Milton Waldor had just returned from a tour of South Vietnam where he met not only with ambassador Henry Cabot Lodge and General William Westmorland, but also with Jewish chaplains and veterans participating in the war effort.[33]

A year earlier, on December 16, 1964, Chaplain Meir Engel was killed in Vietnam. He was born in Israel, educated at Hebrew University and ordained as a rabbi at the Jewish Theological Seminary.[34] Engel was probably the first, but certainly not the last American Jew to be killed in the jungles of Vietnam nor the last Israeli to be killed because of the conflict that raged in it. American Jews may have differed as to the best way to minimalize that and other body counts, but not in their commitment to do so.

NOTES

1. *JTA*, Jan. 17, 1966.
2. Thomas B. Morgan, "The Vanishing American Jew," *Look* (May 5, 1964), 64; and Arthur Hertzberg, *The Jews in America* (New York: 1989), 347.
3. "Address by Arthur J. Goldberg," May 3, 1965, Goldberg, AJCL; and *Time*, July 30, 1967, 11.
4. Arthur Goldberg, LBJ-OH, Tape 1, 1–2; and William Sloane Coffin, *Once to Everyman* (New York: 1977), 207.
5. *National Jewish Post and Opinion*, June 14, 1963; *JTA,* August 25, 1964 and April 1, 1965.
6. *JTA,* April 15, 1964 and April 7, 1967; and Bick, "Ethnic Linkages," 208.
7. Interview with Joseph Sisco (Oct. 22, 1991); and *JTA,* July 21, 1965.
8. *JTA*, July 21, 22, 1965; *NYT*, July 22, 1965; *Al Gumhuria* (UAR) July 28, 1965; *Maariv*, July 21, 1965; and Harman to Bitan, July 21, 1965, Israeli–US Relations, 809/71, ISA.
9. Hertzberg, 348; and Nathaniel Weyl, *The Jew in American Politics* (New Rochelle: 1968), 167–8.
10. *American Jewish Yearbook*, 1965, 311; Sam Welles, "The Jewish Elan," *Fortune* (Feb. 1960), 137; and Hertzberg, *The Jews in America*, 379.
11. *Jewish Exponent*, July 1 and Nov. 3, 1966; Stephen D. Isaacs, *Jews and American Politics* (New York: 1974), 9–10; and *JTA*, May 25, 1964, Nov. 4, 1965.
12. Richard Flack, "Social and Cultural Meanings of Student Revolt," *Social Problems* (March 1968), 348; and Yitzhak Sharav, "Emdot Yehudiyot Leumat Interesim Yehudiyim," *Molad* (June 1967), 609.
13. *NYT*, Aug. 1, 1966; *JTA,* Oct. 22, 1964, Nov. 4, 1965, April 27, 1966.
14. *JTA,* May 25, 1964, Nov. 4, 1965; and *Maariv,* Feb. 2, 1966.
15. Isaacs, *Jews and American Politics*, 152.
16. Interview with Myer Feldman (Oct. 15, 1991); and "Excerpts from Discussion at Committee on Israel Meeting," Nov. 20, 1963, AJC files, mideast, box 105, YIVO.
17. Ibid.
18. Ibid.; U.S. Senate, Committee on Foreign Relations, the 88th Cong., 1st Sess., 12, 1 Aug., 1963; and I. E. Kenen, *Israel's Defense Line* (Buffalo: 1981), 109–10.
19. Interview with a source close to Eshkol.
20. Memorandum to Mr. O'Brien from McGeorge Bundy, April 6, 1965, NSF, Israel, box 138, 173, LBJL.
21. Jonas Abrams to the President, Feb. 17, 1965, WHCF, ExCo 126, box 43; Abe Ribicoff to the President, Jan. 15, 1965, WHCF, ExCo 126, box 42, LBJL; and *JTA*, Jan. 8, 1965.
22. Klinghoffer, *Israel and the Soviet Union*, 31–3; and *Davar*, April. 29, 1966.
23. *Davar,* April. 29, 1966; *JTA,* April 1, July 31, Aug. 3, Oct. 7, 1964, March 31, Oct. 21, 1965
24. *JTA,* Oct. 7, 1964; *Zo Haderech*, Sept. 30, 1966; interview with Nicholas deb. Katzenbach, July 15, 1991; and USIA, Sept. 23, 1965, WHCF, RM3-2, box 6, 4, LBJL.

25. *American Jewish Yearbook: 1966,* 458–63.
26. Coffin, *Once to Everyman*, 258; and *Newsweek*, Nov. 15, 1965, 78.
27. *Sunday Mirror*, July 4, 1965; *JTA,* July 16 and Aug. 8, 1965.
28. *The Jewish Exponent*, March 8, 1966; Coffin, 258; *NYT,* Feb. 19, 1967; *JTA,* April 7, 1967; and Ronald W. Clark, *The Life of Bertrand Russell* (New York: 1975), 624–7.
29. *The Jewish Exponent,* March 8, 1966; *Kol Haam*, March 29, 1966; and *Haolam Hazeh*, Oct. 10, 1966.
30. *Congressional Record – House*, Aug. 10, 1965, 19883–4.
31. "Discussion Issues and Socio-Dramas on Peace", AJC, the Vietnamese War, 1966; AJCL.
32. *JTA,* Jan. 17, 1966.
33. *JTA,* Feb. 23, 1966; and Jan. 17, 1966.
34. *JTA,* Dec. 17, 1964.

Part II
The Collision

4 Washington as a One Crisis Town

LEANING ON ISRAEL

In 1964, American policy makers studied their options in Vietnam; in 1965, they reached decisions; by 1966, they began confronting the domestic and global ramifications of those decisions and Washington became a "one crisis town". In 1964, administration analysts had predicted that "the US would probably find itself progressively isolated in the event that US sanctions did not soon achieve either a Communist reduction of pressure on South Vietnam or some progress toward meaningful negotiations."[1] By 1966, it became clear that the sanctions had not worked, there were no negotiations, and American allies and clients were distancing themselves from Washington in general and the Vietnam War in particular. This distancing helped harden Hanoi's heart, radicalize the Soviet position, and undermine public support for the War.

To reverse this trend, Washington embarked on an elaborate peace offensive in early 1966. It also increased its pressure on Israel to provide Saigon with "on the scene aid." "Given its resources Israeli contribution obviously could not be massive but fact that Israel helping would be significant contribution to world public opinion on Vietnam issue," Ambassador Barbour told Abba Eban on January 18, just six days after his appointment as the new Israeli foreign minister. Barbour, like his fellow ambassador to Egypt, Lucius Battle, discovered that Eban's ability to point to the divisions in "US opinion" made a hard sale harder.[2]

At the early February Honolulu Conference Lyndon Johnson specifically included Israel amongst the countries whose flag he wanted to see flying in Vietnam. Humphrey was so "enthusiastic" about the idea that he flew to Bangkok to expedite the negotiations personally. On February 9, the President met with Eban to finalize the sale of Skyhawk aircraft and used the occasion to emphasize that "US commitment to Vietnam was not without relevance for other areas." Indeed, "Israel would rightly be the first to be frightened if the US were to 'out [*sic*] and run' in Vietnam."[3]

Johnson would repeat that argument indefatigably. Washington was the ultimate guarantor of continued Israeli existence. If the US was forced to abandon Saigon, it would be in no position to stand by Jerusalem. Eban retorted that, unlike South Vietnam, "Israel had a stable government" and "had developed ability to look after herself." He promised nothing.[4] On February 23, Rusk informed Barbour that Humphrey's effort had bore fruit and Saigon had "officially conveyed to Israelis" its request for full diplomatic relations and "on the scene aid." Barbour was to remind the Israelis of the President's comments to Eban. Washington was "being most helpful to Israel," and would appreciate a "reciprocal gesture."[5]

"In an effort to reduce" Israeli leftist opposition, Washington brought to Jerusalem's attention a February 26 Radio Hanoi broadcast which supported the PLO and attacked American tank sales to Israel. Also, an unofficial Jewish emissary conveyed to Eshkol Johnson's personal request that "Israel do something to help Vietnamese refugees." However, the Israeli Cabinet decided to delay diplomatic ties with South Vietnam to the end of the war.[6]

Washington tried to appeal directly to the Israeli public. The American embassy organized a press conference for an American rabbi who stopped in Tel Aviv on his way back from Saigon. The rabbi said that there were 700 Jewish fighters in Vietnam, and he criticized the peace movement for undermining army morale. The embassy also sponsored a fact finding tour to Saigon for senior Israeli newsmen.[7]

These efforts suffered a serious set back in mid-March. The trouble began with South Vietnamese ambassador Vu Van Thai's unguarded remarks that Arab pressure caused his government to keep its distance from Israel. When "rumors" of these remarks reached Humphrey, he went directly to Johnson to suggest that Saigon preempt them by promptly recognizing Israel. Johnson suggested he get in touch with Rusk "at once." Humphrey wrote Rusk that, given the "disaffection on the Vietnamese issue in the Jewish community," Saigon's recognition of Israel was "needed and very soon." Rusk promised to consider a unilateral gesture, expressed his preference for a reciprocal deal, and warned that an attempt to force Jerusalem's hand might backfire.[8] Inaction surely did.

In a follow-up interview with *JTA* reporter Milton Friedman, Vu Van Thai confirmed that fear of Arab recognition of the NLF caused him to visualize "a formula for diplomatic contacts between South Vietnam and Israel that would fall short of full recognition." The ambassador revealed Johnson's and Humphrey's direct involvement in the bilateral negotiations and Saigon's interest in receiving Israeli paramilitary agricultural instructors. American officials, Friedman reported, confirmed both revelations.[9]

It took Washington a mere twenty-four hours to convince Vu Van Thai to announce that his government had decided to enter into a full *de jure* diplomatic relationship with Israel. State spokesmen tried to keep up appearances by noting that the matter involved two sovereign states alone, but the White House let in be known that the President would "welcome" a more active Israeli "role in supporting the Saigon regime" and in defeating "the Communist Chinese 'wars of national liberation.'" Rusk instructed Barbour to contact Israeli officials "as soon as possible," and "at appropriate high level," to say that Washington saw "no reason" why Israel could not send "a survey team" to Vietnam. The "highest levels" of his government, Barbour was to emphasize, were following the "developments with closest interest and attention."[10]

Rusk explained that in addition to "the international political advantage in having Israel active in Vietnam . . . the importance of the American Jewish community was very significant." It was the administration's hope that Israeli activity in Vietnam "would have direct influence" on the community's attitude towards the war.[11] Instead, *The Jewish Exponent* reported that "a new diplomatic accord" had "been urged upon Israel with a country whose leader publicly proclaimed his admiration for Adolf Hitler" and advised Jerusalem "to proceed with caution and not place too high a premium on expediency." In Israel, Eban denied having ever considered sending paramilitary personnel to South Vietnam or any immediate plans to formalize relations with that country.[12] Reports that the Israeli decision had been influenced by the Soviet ambassador were particularly alarming. If American pressure on Israel could no longer outweigh the Soviet one, then the rise of Soviet regional might indeed had concrete meaning.

In April, Raymond Hare, the head of State's Near East Agency (NEA), met with Eshkol and Eban in Tel Aviv. He told them that the "Vietnam problem" was "the touchstone of American foreign policy," and Israeli responsiveness on this issue was "important" to the development of closer American–Israeli relations. Eban retorted that his government's efforts to improve relations with Moscow and the developing world "would be adversely affected by a show of support for Vietnamese." Barbour noted that this was the first time a "responsible" official openly admitted that relations with Moscow were a "factor" in the Israeli decision.[13]

This turn of events was discussed at the annual US ambassadors' meeting in Beirut as symptomatic of the post-Tashkent decline of American regional influence which also had led Iran to purchase Soviet weapons and Turkey to restrict American naval operations in the Black Sea. The British decision to leave Aden in 1968, and the French partial withdrawal from NATO, did not help either. Nor did Washington's paltry efforts to calm jittery allied nerves by exercising US rights to train in the Black Sea; increasing the air force capacity to deploy B-58 bombers and KC tankers in Spain; homeporting a navy seaplane in Bahrain; or conducting combined CENTO air defense exercises, officer training programs and morale raising visits of allied leaders to the White House.[14]

In fact, these developments, along with the growing strain on American and South Vietnamese economic and political life, led Walt Rostow, Robert McNamara and Lyndon Johnson "to consider seizing on the troubles (with Buddhists in South Vietnam) as a vehicle for US disengagement." After all, by the spring of 1966, a distraught Beijing had given up on inter-state diplomacy, recalled its Third World ambassadors, and embarked on a self-destructive Cultural Revolution. However, a precipitous forceful suppression of dissent by Saigon prevented Washington from cutting its losses in Vietnam and the issue of Israeli support of American policy in Vietnam therefore remained alive.[15]

The State Department wanted to send Israel a strong letter citing the "President's disappointment over Israel's failure to make any gesture towards Vietnam." Walt Rostow discussed the subject with Israeli Ambassador Avraham Harman, but refused to approve the letter before Hare had the opportunity to "settle down." Rusk so notified Barbour, adding that the Department finds it "difficult to believe Israel means curry favor with the USSR on a matter of such vital concern to the US."[16]

Rostow may have been influenced by a letter from Humphrey. Washington's and Saigon's continued adherence to "on the scene" aid as a condition for diplomatic ties with Israel, and the unfortunate Vu Van Thai interview, argued Humphrey left the impression that relations between Jerusalem and Saigon were "not too good" and had a negative "bearing on some of the reactions of the leaders of the American Jewish community towards our policy in Vietnam."[17] State insisted that "the Israelis were the ones dragging their feet." Indeed, on June 2, an Israeli spokesman did announce that the time was still "inopportune" for the establishment of diplomatic ties with Saigon.[18]

Of course, a less rigid posture along the lines recommended by Humphrey might have forced Israel's hand. Nevertheless, some State officials were happy with the impasse because they feared that Israeli and American Jewish support "might be exploited by Arab propaganda and Hanoi sympathizers to depict the war as 'backed' by Zionism, reaction, colonialism, and imperialism." Walt Rostow suggested that Johnson use the matter as a bargaining chip by reminding the Israelis that, on this "very important" issue to the US, they saw "their interest differently."[19]

LEANING ON AMERICAN JEWRY

With the mid-term election fast approaching, Johnson and Humphrey had little choice but to deal with American Jewry directly. On June 4, 1966, Hubert Humphrey described the Israeli stake in Vietnam to members of the American Jewish Press Association in an "unusually frank" manner:

> When I hear about what is called the Palestinian Liberation Organization and I read and know that Communist China seeks to infiltrate, to assist, to generate more trouble in this organization, then I say that this is not unrelated to some of the problems we and the South Vietnamese confront in Southeast Asia.[20]

Assuming that trouble in the Middle East would "send cold shivers down the backs of the Americans in the White House," China did its best to stir the simmering regional pot. Palestine Day was celebrated in Beijing on May 20, 1966; China trained and armed PLO and FATAH members and a general even suggested that their guerrillas use the Galilee as a base of operations for its proximity to vital Israeli positions and accessibility to Syrian and Lebanese rear bases.[21]

However, State immediately announced that it had no evidence that the PLO was receiving *substantial* Chinese support. Acknowledging the similarity between the American and Israeli problems meant condoning an Israeli reprisal policy which, as Walt Rostow wrote Johnson, might result in "a major Mid-East fracas" which the US could not "afford" while it was "pushing ahead in Vietnam."[22]

The announcement undermined the effectiveness of Humphrey's argument by refocusing Jewish attention on the war's corrosive effect on the American commitment to Israeli security.

Just days following Humphrey's address, *Newsweek* notified its readers that a "FOUR-STAR CORRESPONDENT" would be joining the press corps in Vietnam. General Moshe Dayan would "move about freely and give and take advice in actual operations" in order "to learn the latest tactics and developments in guerrilla war." Washington (AID financed his sojourn) might have hoped to unsettle Eshkol by providing his charismatic rival with a valuable public forum. It certainly expected the popular general to help reduce Jewish peace agitation.[23]

However, once in Washington, Dayan turned down direct requests by Abe Feinberg and Robert Komer that he express Israel's special interest in the war and refused to comment on Vietnam before he had a chance to examine the battlefield in person. He did promise to stop again in the US on his return home, and Walt Rostow even offered him a quiet place to write his articles. Still, media coverage of his meetings with McNamara and Rostow served the administration's cause, as did pictures of the photogenic one-eyed general running around South Vietnam dressed in army fatigues.[24]

Even these dubious political benefits carried a strategic cost. Cairo retaliated for what it considered to be American "activation" of Israel outside its regional arena by permitting the NLF to open an office in Cairo. Furthermore, Shukayri announced that he would send officers to Hanoi not only to train "for the inevitable battle for the liberation of Palestine" but to fight alongside the Viet Cong in order "to demonstrate the Palestinian people's solidarity with the Vietnamese nation in its great war of liberation."[25]

Several Congressmen had been demanding for some time that UNRWA, the UN Relief and Works Administration, cut its support for PLO members or, at least, not use American funds for such support. State had opposed these demands, but Shukayri's announcement had pulled the rug from under its position. Attempts to erase PLO members from UNRWA rolls led to rioting in Gaza and the West Bank in which Palestinians expressed their eagerness to fight for the Viet Cong. Jordan accused Washington of "surrendering" to the Zionists.[26] Finally, UNRWA officials arranged for special Arab donations for PLO members. Washington publicly objected to this solution, but tacitly accepted it.[27]

Neither the American trepidation about a Middle Eastern "fracas," nor the potential NLF–PLO connection, escaped Soviet notice. So when Washington informed the President of the Security Council of its intention to step up its bombing of the fuel installations around Hanoi and Haiphong in response to NLF "aggression," Moscow used a Syrian–Israeli border incident to serve notice that it might respond to further escalation in Vietnam by causing trouble in the Middle East.

On July 13, two Israelis were killed when their vehicle struck an anti-tank mine. It was the latest in a series of sabotage and mining incidents carried out by FATAH. The Israeli air force retaliated. On July 18, both Israel and Syria notified the Security Council of the episode. All appeared routine when on July 21, Damascus suddenly requested an urgent Security Council meeting to deal with the incident; Jerusalem quickly followed suit.[28]

At the Security Council meeting, Nikolai Fedorenko declared that "the activation of the forces of aggression in the Middle East" was part of "a policy designed to thwart by the use of force, the national liberation movement of peoples" as "exemplified in the expansion of the criminal war waged by United States imperialists against the Viet-namese people." Fedorenko added that it was "significant" that the Israeli retaliation occurred while Assistant Secretary of State of International Organizations Joseph Sisco was in Israel, and warned that Moscow could not "remain indifferent" to "attempts to destroy peace" in an area "*in the immediate vicinity of its frontiers*."[29]

Prior to 1964, Washington opposed reprisals. However, when the Security Council considered a Yemeni complaint of British bombing of its territory in response to cross border infiltrations into Aden, a debate developed within the administration. Adlai Stevenson argued that the US should condemn both the British action and the provocations. Dean Rusk disagreed because "the U.S. itself" might have "to respond to provocations of a more serious but technically similar sort either in Cuba or in Vietnam." A compromise was reached. The US abstained, but did not encourage others to do so; the resolution passed.[30]

If the Soviets expected a repeat scenario, they were quickly disappointed. Joseph Sisco, who took Goldberg's place for the duration of this debate, was defiant: He deplored the Israeli retaliatory action, denied any inference that Washington was consulted or had prior knowledge of it, and called on both sides to respect the armistice agreement and make use of UN machinery. Britain followed the American line but, in a pointed reference to Vietnam, France deplored the Israeli operation "because it condemns all reprisals and all so-called 'punitive' operations."

American efforts notwithstanding, the Security Council debate was conducted in the shadow of Vietnam as the Soviets insisted on severing the ties between the provocations and the reprisal. Sisco lamented that "no serious attempt was made to produce a resolution which might represent broadly the Council's views." Finally, a resolution dealing with the Israeli action "as if it happened in isolation" was put to a vote. No country opposed it but, since Washington and all of its allies including France abstained, it failed to receive the nine votes needed for passage.

Meanwhile, mere references to the American bombing in Vietnam in July turned into a full fledged debate on the war in August. Fedorenko charged Israel with "following the illegal course charted by some of its protectors." The "criminal nature" of her action was apparent "in the barbarous war waged by United States imperialists in South-East Asia." Sisco tried to side-step the Vietnamese issue by noting that Moscow had in January opposed an American call for a Security Council debate on Vietnam. Fedorenko agreed that he did not wish "to enter into polemics on the question of Vietnam in the Council."

The following day, in an obvious effort to point out similar Soviet vulnerabilities, Britain asked for a Security Council debate on a UAR retaliatory bombing in Aden on behalf of Yemen. The Yemenis argued that they had "the same justification to strike against Saudi 'bases of aggression' as the US has in bombing NVN." The British request led to yet another "bitter exchange" between Sisco, Fedorenko and Tarbanov of Bulgaria. Tarbanov modified his previous position by stating that in the case of Israel, "as in the case of the United States aggression in Viet-Nam," the Council was not faced with "reprisals" but with "aggression pure and simple."[31]

Sisco reminded Tarbanov of his past opposition to a Security Council debate on Vietnam, and called on Moscow to reconvene the Geneva Conference. Fedorenko then attacked the American efforts to use the Security Council "for the unseemly purpose of concealing the ever-increasing escalation of its dirty war against the Viet-Namese People." The US should relinquish the "role of world policeman" and withdraw its troops from South Vietnam.

Sisco accused Moscow of shirking its "responsibilities as a great power by disclaiming any direct involvement in the Viet-Namese war," while supplying Hanoi with the means to prolong that war. Ridiculing Sisco's assumption of a "didactic role," Fedorenko reiterated his government's intention to continue its support for "the Viet-Namese people." The exchange ended when the representative from New Zealand moved to formalize the debate as one on Vietnam rather than on the Middle East, and the Security Council president ruled against it.[32]

If, as *The Washington Post* suggested, both the US and the USSR were determined to "persuade" the other that their future relations were "mortgaged" to Vietnam, and the bombing of Haiphong had been designed to tighten "the diplomatic screws on Moscow," then the Security Council debate signaled that Moscow's response to such tightening would come in the form of a diversionary "second front," possibly, in the Middle East. After all, noted columnist James Burnham, the US was "so heavily committed" in Southeast Asia that it "would have unusual difficulty in counteracting even a modest move in another theater; at the least, a diversionary move would have an automatically depressant effect on the Vietnam effort."[33]

At the very least, American officials told Jewish reporters, Moscow had signaled its determination to stand by Syria at all costs; Israeli reprisals might give Syria "a pretext to demand a Soviet security guarantee against Israel." Such a guarantee might tempt "irresponsible" Syrian leaders to ignite a war and "cause an East-West confrontation in the Near East" at a time when the US "concentrated on Viet Nam." Israel therefore had to avoid reprisals, and analogies between Palestinian and Vietnamese liberations movements had to be actively "discouraged." Indeed, in his August 25 address to the JWV convention, Humphrey did not repeat the "detailed and poignant analogy between the communist-inspired threats facing both Viet Nam and Israel" but focused on the dangers of "Neo-isolationism."[34]

Congressman Herbert Tenzer, who offered to publicize the NLF–PLA analogy because it "would have a tremendous impact on Jewish people," was similarly "discouraged." It was true that Shukayri "clearly envisages the PLA as a force which should be developed along the lines of the Viet Cong" and that the analogy made sense "from the viewpoint of persuading American Jews" to support Johnson's policy in Vietnam. But, Walt Rostow asserted, since it was not in American or Israeli interests "to play up" the comparison publicly, it should only be used privately. The only analogy fit for public consumption was the one made by the President that both Israel and South Vietnam were "small countries with general need for US support against aggression." It found few Jewish buyers.[35]

THE PRESIDENTIAL WARNING

By the fall of 1966, Lyndon Johnson's patience with what he considered an ungrateful, inconsistent and vociferous constituency was fast running out. Already in June, at a meeting with state legislators, Johnson had complained about the lack of Jewish support for the Vietnam War adding: "The American Sixth Fleet is the best guarantee to the continued existence of Israel. Israel, with her limited forces would not be able to stand alone against potential conquerors if we . . . ran home, surrendered or waved the white flag."[36]

Abe Feinberg undertook "his own campaign within the Jewish community on Vietnam." Feinberg wanted Jews to understand, Dayan noted skeptically in his diary, "that the welfare of Israel (and A. Feinberg thinks that she is amongst the countries the United States promises to come to their aid if they were attacked) demands that the US fulfill its obligations in South Vietnam and fight the attacking Viet Cong."[37]

When Israeli President Zalman Shazar visited the White House in the midst of the Security Council debate, Dean Rusk reminded Johnson that "Israel's influence in world affairs belies its small size and newly independent status. The voice of Israel is respected in world councils."[38] But Johnson was interested in Israel's American friends:

> U.S.G. did not want troops or money from Israel. . . . What we wanted was a sympathetic understanding of the principles involved . . . If, because of critics of our Vietnam policy, we did not fulfill our commitments to the 16 million people in Vietnam, *How could we be expected to fulfill our commitments to 2 million Israelis?* Yet some friends of Israel in the United States had publicly criticized US policy in Vietnam.[39]

In other words, "once the American people dump one place, they'll drop another." Therefore, it was in Israel's interest to warn Jews not to stoke the fires of traditional American isolationism.[40] Johnson even told Shazar that "Jewish support for the Vietnam involvement was his due in light of his record of support for Israel," and Israel had better let Jews know that. The notion that American Jews would, and should, reward Johnson for his support of Israel was nurtured by his close Jewish friends. Arthur Krim, Abe Feinberg, David Ginzberg and Ephraim Evron, who had all functioned as his emissaries to the Israeli and Jewish leadership, participated in American–Israeli aid negotiations and encouraged him to secure Jewish electoral support through a series of carefully spaced "pro-Israeli gestures."[41]

Special interest politics are as American as apple pie, but the preoccupation with the Jewish vote led Dayan to wonder whether Johnson's men were "aware how disproportionate – though understandable – is their awareness of the American domestic opinion (Brooklyn Jews – because they will determine the election results here)" as compared to their total disregard for European opinions.[42] But foreign, rather than domestic, concerns underlay this preoccupation. The administration believed that the Vietnamese were "watching the elections in November," and that they would "*not agree to peace talks*" if it seemed that the Americans had "deserted the President." Moreover, American diplomats reported that "the rising level of public controversy and debate in the United States" contributed to foreign governments' reluctance to display their "sympathy" for the American Vietnamese policy "in public."[43]

Shazar issued a statement praising American efforts "to achieve a world" in which every nation's "independence and integrity" would be "respected." It was useless. Campaigning in Ellensville, New York Johnson appealed to Jews directly:

> And if you turn the other cheek in Vietnam and you look the other way – because the price is heavy, and unpleasant, and ugly – . . . What do you do when little Israel calls on you for assistance?[44]

Johnson also tried to find out: "Who's who in the American Jewish community?" He approached American Jewish Committee president Jacob Blaustein, but Blaustein insisted that the Jews were just like everybody else and wrote a memo analyzing "the public opinion question in relations to Vietnam." A frustrated Johnson continued "to badger everybody."[45]

Finally, on September 6, following an "animated and pointed" discussion concerning the "unusually vociferous opposition" of the "majority" of the Jewish leadership's to the war, Johnson and the Jewish War Veterans embarked on a high risk strategy: JWV commander Malcolm Tarlov called a press conference to report that

Johnson urged him to explain to other Jewish leaders that, if forced to abandon SEATO 'commitments' in Vietnam, "*the less explicit* American 'commitments' to Israel would be jeopardized." The report received international coverage and was universally interpreted as a Presidential threat that, if Jews "didn't support him in Vietnam, he wouldn't support them in Israel," To counter that impression, Johnson told B'nai B'rith representatives:

> I never said that, I never meant that. I think the United States ought to defend Israel, period, . . . I hope you'll help me get off this, because I don't want it thought that my support for Israel is conditioned on their support for Viet Nam.[46]

But Johnson also told them that he was personally "disappointed" because "anyone who gave so much support to Israel as he did was *entitled* to a little consideration on another matter – Vietnam." In short, Johnson's supposed "indiscretion" seems to have been a carefully planned "warning" to an ethnic group which seemed to have forgotten the rules of the game. How else does one explain Johnson's steadfast refusal to offer, or permit, any member of the administration to present even a hint of public disavowal of the alleged statements for a full month? When Walt Rostow related the President of the Zionist Organization of America's (ZOA) suggestion that "a personal appearance before an enthusiastic Jewish audience . . . would end the matter," Johnson not only refused but scribbled "forget it" on the memo and made sure Bill Moyers and Harry McPherson received copies of it.[47]

On October 6, McPherson was finally permitted to answer one of the letters of concern which flooded the White House. He wrote that "any inference in the news stories that the President linked American Jewish support in Viet Nam with continued United States support for Israel is wholly fanciful." Also, on the eve of the Congressional elections, a press release on a US loan to Israel included a statement that the loan was intended "to prove that the President's unhappiness over Jewish attitudes towards the war in Vietnam did not affect his commitment to Israel."[48]

Johnson was gratified when he received a JWV report that, "on balance," the results of the "warning" were "advantageous" as they had brought about a Jewish community "reexamination" of the issue. Harry McPherson notified Bill Moyers:

> Evron, my friend at the Israeli Embassy, called to say that the National Council of Churches had approached the Synagogue

Council of America over the weekend to ask the Synagogue Council's concurrence in a Vietnam statement – generally slanted against the US position. The Synagogue Council turned NCC down.[49]

Barbour also reported "signs of shift" in Israeli policy and that he expected the "Israelis to be reasonably helpful on Viet-Nam in UNGA" debate. Rusk tried to encourage these trends by being especially friendly in his pre-debate meeting with Eban. He compared Nasser to Nkruma, Ben Bella and Sukarno and revealed that American representatives had been telling Nasser to learn from the fate of other leaders who neglected their countries' problems for "regional and international adventurism." Rusk cancelled a post-debate meeting, but asked Barbour to communicate his gratitude "for the constructive contribution" Eban had made to the UN debate and his approval of the Israeli decision to bring the ongoing Palestinian "terrorist" raids to the Security Council's attention.[50]

In reality, the American inspired Israeli effort to use the Security Council as an alternative to military retaliation collapsed when the Soviets vetoed a heavily watered down resolution they were expected to support.[51] An angry US let it be known that its efforts to restrain Israel were terminated. But Moscow demonstrated its own style of restraint, warning Jerusalem that it would view any reprisal against Damascus as designed to serve American regionalist interests and convincing Egypt to sign a mutual defense treaty with Syria. Consequently, when Israel did retaliate, she did not strike at Syria but at Jordan. Moscow got "bouquets for having, in Arab eyes, effectively safeguarded Syria" while King Hussein's American supported throne teetered.[52]

Washington decided to teach Israel a lesson, and chose Arthur Goldberg to administer it. It was Goldberg who issued the statement deploring the attack. It was Goldberg who blamed Israel not only for the raid, but for the subsequent Palestinian riots. It was Goldberg who cast the vote in support of a blanket condemnation of Israel reminiscent only of the one condemning China's entry into the Korean War. And it was Goldberg who concurred "word for word" with a memo detailing the "massive" weapons airlift to Jordan which, according to Rostow, was part of the "sharp" American reaction to the raid.[53]

The *New Republic* complained that while "consistency is not to be expected of nations," the bombing of Vietnam "must have become world history's longest retaliatory raid." Abe Feinberg warned that administration failure to find a balanced way of handling the Arab–Israeli conflict could lead the Jewish community into Republicans arms. Johnson asked his friends to diffuse the Jewish resentment in return for a sympathetic Presidential consideration of Israeli defense needs. They did so loyally.[54]

Within months, Johnson also renewed the pressure for an "Israeli gesture towards Vietnam." Thus, in March 1967, David Ginsberg told Israeli officials that Johnson had initiated a conversation in which he assured Ginsberg that he remembered that 95 percent of the Jews voted for him and asked Ginzberg to prepare a detailed plan of things he, as US President, could do for Israel. To compete, the NEA updated a memo entitled "What we have done for Israel" to which it added the question, "Is it a one way street?" Rostow gave it to Johnson prior to his meeting with Feinberg, along with the suggestion that it be used to "lay the groundwork for a slim response" to the Israeli aid request. But Johnson told Feinberg and Ginzberg that Israeli humanitarian aid to South Vietnam would help disprove the implication that American–Israeli relations were a one way street.[55] The story typified his, and his men's, reluctance to entertain the possibility, indeed the probability, that their one front war was in serious jeopardy.

THE SHADOW OF A SECOND FRONT

Washington virtually ignored the Middle East during the winter of 1967. The post of the head of the NEA was left vacant for six months, the State Department Policy Planning Council did not have a member assigned to the area and, after months of delay, the new ambassador to Egypt was a diplomatic novice. Talented individuals were routinely transferred to Vietnam. Robert Komer left his position as the NSC point man for West Asia to head the Vietnam pacification program. William Porter, the ambassador designate to Saudi Arabia, became the Deputy Ambassador to Vietnam and Ellsworth Bunker left the desalinization program to become the ambassador to Vietnam.

Ambassadors became reluctant to bother the President with their concerns. Thus, when Ambassador Armin Meyer requested that Johnson intervene to prevent Iran from concluding another arms deal with Moscow, he wrote: "Knowing how heavily beset you and our colleagues are with the problem of Vietnam, I regret having to bring this matter to your personal attention." But the Shah is "deeply impressed by Vietnam situation," and insists that "self reliance" is consistent with both the American and Iranian interests.[56]

Iran, like other American friends and foes, understood that the neglect reflected US determination not to "take over any new commitments east of Suez" because, as Rusk told concerned Israelis, "its involvement in Vietnam was engaging all its strength and national attention" and "causing enormous internal strains and external stresses." All Washington was prepared to do for its regional clients was to build up their "defensive strength." American weapons sales to the Middle East increased from $44.2 million in 1963 to $995.3 million in 1968.[57]

This regionalist strategy ultimately depended on Soviet restraint. American allies might be able to handle their regional enemies, but not the USSR. The efficacy of Arab nationalism as a barrier to Soviet expansion was also brought into question. Saudi fears of a "coordinated" Egyptian–Syrian "strategy with Soviet support" to gain control of oil facilities, Suez and Bab al-Mandeb were not without merit. Indeed, following a regional fact finding tour, the new Under Secretary of State Eugene Rostow suggested that "there should be a strategic study of the military, political and economic implications of the entire area from Morocco to Iran" because "the threat to the oil resources" was as great in Libya as in the Arabian Peninsula, and Morocco was "on the right flank of the Sixth Fleet in the Mediterranean."[58]

Johnson appointed the former ambassador to Iran, Julius C. Holmes, to head a special Defense-State study group on the issue. The North Atlantic Command (which included France) planed a special meeting to discuss extending NATO's reach at least to North Africa. Greater European regional involvement might save Washington from having to choose between reordering its Pacificist priorities and, as the military advocated, increasing its resources to a level adequate for a two front war. In the meantime, the question whether the Arabs would use American preoccupation in Vietnam to attack Israel was openly discussed in UN corridors.[59]

Worried Republicans called on the US, Britain and France to reaffirm the 1950 Tripartite Declaration guaranteeing the region's borders. Rusk retorted that there was no need for a new declaration because he was "not aware of any change in the positions of either the British or French Governments" which would "cast doubt on their adherence" to the principles of the original declaration.[60]

On October 7, 1966, Johnson suggested renewing the spirit, and improving the substance, of détente in Europe. Moscow retorted that Americans were laboring "under strange and persistent delusion" if they thought that it was possible to improve bilateral relations despite the Vietnam War." Yet Soviet concern with China's Cultural Revolution (thirteen Russian divisions were transferred to the Far East) led the administration to hope that not only could the Soviet–American "implicit alliance" be renewed, but the Russians might be induced to help end the war. Indeed, by the end of 1966, Moscow had indicated an interest in the reduction of Middle Eastern tensions, agreed to negotiations on a Non Proliferation Treaty, and had used Hanoi's own concern with the effect of the Cultural Revolution on the flow of aid to encourage her to enter into negotiations with the US. This resulted in the Wilson–Kosygin mediation effort of January/February 1967.[61]

The collapse of that effort precipitated a quick deterioration of superpower relations. Its extent can best be demonstrated by events in the Black Sea. The American Sixth Fleet, and the fast-growing Soviet so-called "Red fleet," had been keeping an eye on each other for at least two years without, as the navy reported, the occurrence of any "embarrassing or dangerous incidents." However, a February 1967 US destroyer's transit of the Black Sea produced an "almost continuous surveillance and/or harassment by Soviet ships and aircraft" which reached its peak when "a Soviet oiler attempted to create a collision situation by maneuvering into the path of one the destroyers." *The Economist* editors at least understood the hint. On March 25, 1967 they led with an article entitled "A Triangle to Watch" which predicted that the Morocco–Somalia–Iran area would become the center of the Cold War during the summer of 1967 due to the change that took place "in the relationship between Russia and America in other parts of the world."[62] They proved correct.

NOTES

1. CIA*DIA*INR Panel Draft, Nov. 6, 1964, *Pentagon Papers*, III, 598.
2. From Amembassy Tel Aviv, Jan. 19, 1966. NSF, Israel, box, 139, 53; and From Amembassy Cairo, May 13, 1966, NSF, UAR, box 158, 55, LBJL.
3. *JTA*, March 21, 1966; *Yediot Aharonot*, March 23, 1966, and Dept. of

State to Embassy Tel Aviv, Feb. 23, 1966; NSF, CF, Israel, box 138. 63, LBJL.

4. Department of State to Amembassy Tel Aviv, Feb. 19, 1966, NSF, Israel, box 139, 7, LBJL.
5. Sec. Rusk to Amembassy Tel Aviv, Feb. 23 and 26, 1966, NSF, Israel, box 138, 11 and 15, LBJL.
6. Interview with a source close to Eshkol.
7. *Hayom*, March 16, 1966.
8. *Yediot Aharonot*, March 18, 1966; letter from the Vice President to the Secretary of State, March 15, 1966; and Letter from Secretary of State to the Vice President, March 31, 1966, NSF, Israel, box 139, LBJL.
9. *JTA* and *Yediot Aharonot*, March 20, 1966.
10. *JTA*, March 22, 23, 66; *Haaretz*, March 22, 1966; Department of State to Amembassy Tel Aviv, March 23, 1966, NSF, Israel, box 139, 17, LBJL.
11. Interview with Rusk.
12. *The Jewish Exponent*, March 25, 1966; and *Haaretz*, March 23, 1966.
13. *NYT*, March 23, 1966; Department of State to Amembassy Tel Aviv, May 9, 1966 and Amembassy Tel Aviv to Department of State, April 26, 1966, NSF, Israel, box 139, 32 and 32e, LBJL.
14. Weekly Report, DoD, Jan. 18 and 25, March 29, May 10 and 24, 1966, LBJL.
15. Robert McNamara, *In Retrospect* (New York: 1994), 266; *Pentagon Papers*, III, 690; and Ben Tsur, *Gormin Sovietiim*, 56–75.
16. *Kol Haam*, May 13, 1966, Saunders to Walt Rostow, May 2, 1966; and Department of State to Amembassy Tel Aviv, May 9, 1966, NSF, Israel, box 139, 32 and 32a, LBJL.
17. The Vice President to Walt Rostow, May 1, 1966, NSF, Israel, box 139, 28d, LBJL.
18. Memorandum for Bromly Smith, May 2, 1966; and Note for Bromly Smith, May 6, 1966. NSF, Israel, box 139, 128b and 128f, LBJL; *Divrei Haknesset*, June 1, 1966, 1588–9.
19. *JTA*, Sept. 12, 1966; W. W. Rostow, July 30, 1966, Memos for the President, box 7, 5, LBJL.
20. *Jewish Exponent*, June 24, 1966; *Haaretz*, June 5, 1966.
21. Behbehani, *China's Foreign Policy in the Arab World*, 48–9; and *New China News Agency*, May 4, 14, 15, 1966.
22. *Maariv*, Aug. 5, 1966; and W. W. Rostow, NSF, Memos for the President, box 8, 33, LBJL.
23. *Newsweek*, June 13, 1966.
24. Dayan, *Yoman Vietnam*, 40–1; and *Washington Post*, Nov. 12, 1966.
25. *Radio Cairo*, June 10, 1966, DCSS; and *Haaretz*, June 10, 1966.
26. *Davar*, June 17, 1966; and Michael Elkins, "Ahmed Shukayri, Arab Dissention and the Viet Cong," *Midstream* (Oct. 1966), 14–22.
27. *Near East Review*, June 12, 1966; and *Congressional Record*, March 10, 1966, 5552 and June 23, 1966, 14082.
28. *Security Council Official Records*, Supp. for April, May and June 1966, doc. S/7391; Supp. for July, August and Sept., doc. S/7401; and 1293rd Meeting: 1 Aug. 1966, 18.

29. *Security Council Official Records*, 1288th Meeting, July 25, 1966, 44.
30. For the President from McGeorge Bundy, April 9, 1964, NSF, Memos for the President, box 8, LBJL; and *UN Monthly Chronicle*, May 1964, 14–20.
31. *NYT*, Aug. 4, 1966; and "Vietnam and Public Opinion," A USIA report, Aug. 1966, HHH Papers, 23E 6 4F. MSA.
32. *Security Council Official Record*, 1290th meeting: 28 July 1966, 4 and 8; 1293rd, Aug. 1, 1966, 24–5; 1295th Meeting, Aug. 3, 1966, 1–21; and Supp. for July, Aug. and Sept., 1966, S/7391, S/7401; and *NYT*, July 30, 1966.
33. *The Washington Post*, July 25, 1966; and James Burnham, "The Kremlin Move?," *National Review* (Aug. 23, 1966), 822.
34. *The Wisconsin Jewish Chronicle*, Sept. 16, 1966.
35. Memo to "Lois" and Henry Wilson to Walt Rostow, Sept. 14, 1966, WWR from Hal Saunders, Sept. 19, 1966; and Henry Wilson from W. W. Rostow, Sept. 19, 1966, NSF, Middle East, box 140, 141, LBJL.
36. *The Los Angeles Herald Express*, June 23, 1966.
37. W. W. Rostow, June 10, 1966, NSF, Memos for the President, box 9, LBJL; and Dayan, *Yoman Vietnam*, 29.
38. "Talking paper for the meeting with Israeli President Zalman Shazar," Memos for the President, undated, box 9, 5b, LBJL.
39. Memorandum of Conversation, Call on President Johnson by President Shazar, Aug. 2, 1966, NSF, NSC History of M.E. box 21, 46 (underline in original), LBJL.
40. Interview with Roche.
41. Bick, "Ethnic Linkages," 206; Memos for the President, Aug. 30, 1966, box 10, 13, LBJL; and W. W. Rostow, July 29, 1966, NSF, Israel, box 138,9, 153a, LBJL.
42. Dayan, *Yoman Vietnam*, 44.
43. Kathleen J. Turner, *Lyndon Johnson's Dual War* (Chicago: 1985), 162 and 290n; "Vietnam & World Opinion," USIA Report, Aug. 1966, HHH papers, 23E 6 4F, MSL.
44. *Kol Haam*, July 19, 1966; and *The Public Papers of Lyndon B. Johnson, 1966*, 855.
45. *Haaretz*, Sept. 23, 1966; LBJ to Jacob Blaustein, Sept. 19, 1966, The files of Harry McPherson, WHCF, box 42, 54; and interview with Katzenbach.
46. *JTA*, Sept. 7, 1966; and Harry McPherson, LBJ-OH, tape 4, 37. For details see Chapter 7.
47. Bick, 205; *Haaretz*, Aug. 2, 1966; and W. W. Rostow, Memos to the President, Sept. 19, 1966, box 10, 92, LBJL.
48. *American Jewish Yearbook, 1966,* 80.
49. Harry McPherson, LBJ-OH, tape 4, 37; Felix M. Putterman to Marvin Watson, Nov. 7, 1966, WHCF, ND19/Co 312, box 268; and For Bill Moyers, Oct. 4, 1966, office file of Harry McPherson, box 51, LBJL.
50. Dept. of State to Amembassy Tel Aviv, Sept. 20, and Oct. 18, 1966, NSF, Israel, box 140–1, 144a and 73, LBJL; and Eban's report to foreign ministry department heads, Oct. 31, 1966, 7227/55, ISA.
51. *Haaretz*, Aug. 24, 1966; and Gideon Rafael, *Destination Peace* (London: 1981), 130–1.

52. Moshe Zak, *Arbaim Shnot Du-Siach im Moskva* (Tel Aviv: 1988), 142–3; and *The Economist*, Nov. 26, 1966.
53. W. W. Rostow, Nov. 14 and Dec. 12, 1966, NSF, Memos for the President, box 11, LBJL.
54. *New Republic*, Dec. 10, 1966, 7; and W. W. Rostow, Dec. 10, 1966, Memos for the President, box 11, 32, LBJL.
55. IGD; "U.S.–Israel Relations," Feb. 8, 1967; and "Subject 1968 – American Jewry and Israel in Preparation for the 1968 elections," April 20, 1967, NSF, Israel, box 140, 1, 113b; and "Your Talk with Feinberg," Feb. 13, 1976, NSF, Memos to the President, box 13, 145, LBJL.
56. Steven L. Spiegel, *The Other Arab–Israeli Conflict* (Chicago: 1985), 119–20; *The Baltimore Sun*, Aug. 4, 1967; Incoming Telegram from Amembassy Jiddah, Sept. 2, 1965, NSF, Saudi Arabia, box 155, 45; "To the President from Ambassador Meyer," July 28, 1966, From Amembassy Teheran, May 23, 1966; and Memorandum for the President, May 17, 1967, NSF, Iran, box 136, 256a, 119 and 245, LBJL.
57. Rafael, *Destination Peace*, 130; and Spiegel, *The Other Arab–Israeli Conflict*, 135.
58. Ibid.; Dept. of State to Amembassy Jiddah, Dec. 30, 1966, NSF, Saudi Arabia, box 155, 111; and Eugene Rostow, Nov. 22, 1966, Memos for the President, box 11, 15m, LBJL.
59. John M. Leddy, LBJ-OH, tape I, 13–14, LBJL; interview with Eugene Rostow (Oct. 15, 1991); and *El Hawadat* (Lebanon), Dec. 2, 1966.
60. *American Jewish Yearbook, 1967*, 154.
61. *Pravda*, Oct. 16, 1966; Spiegel, 135; Memorandum of Conversation, Dec. 20, 1966, NSF, France, Box 173, LBJL; and Schoenbaum, *Waging War and Peace*, 455–6.
62. Weekly Report, DoD, Feb. 28, 1967; and Walt Rostow to the President, May 29, 1967, NSF, M.E. Crisis, box 17, LBJL.

5 Israel Veers Towards Neutralism

THE TASHKENT SPIRIT

"Leave us alone, we have enough troubles of our own," was the essence of the Israeli response to the relentless American pressure that she place her flag on South Vietnamese soil. In fact, Abba Eban made the refusal to do so a cornerstone of his new "neutralist" foreign policy with which he hoped to secure a solution "in the spirit of Tashkent" for the Arab–Israeli dispute. Specifically, Israel hoped to see the defunct 1950 Tripartite Declaration replaced with a four-power one guaranteeing the region's borders and limiting its arms build up. Assuming that Israel lacked the bargaining chips for a comprehensive peace, Eban even appreciated the fact that the January 1966 Tashkent conference did not seek to terminate the conflict between India and Pakistan, but only to freeze it.[1]

After all, there was a marked resemblance not only between the regional causes of the disputes, but also in their relationship to the Vietnamese conflict. India and Pakistan, like Israel and the Arabs, were involved in a lengthy territorial dispute. Pakistan, with Chinese encouragement, tried to get her way by supporting a "people's war" in Kashmir; India responded with a conventional war. Close Soviet–American cooperation resulted in the reestablishment of the *status quo ante* and produced an Indian–Pakistani commitment to solve future differences exclusively through peaceful means. Since the Arabs (especially Syria), with Chinese backing, were embarking on a similar venture, Eban hoped to induce the superpowers to extend their cooperation to the Middle East without the advent of an actual war.[2]

Levi Eshkol congratulated Alexei Kosygin on his successful mediation effort and suggested that he undertake a similar initiative in the Middle East, adding: "The face to face meeting of two countries which only a short time before were facing an international conflict and their joint declaration fill our hearts with hope that it won't be long before we, too, sit at a joint negotiation table with our neighbors."[3]

In a series of public pronouncements, Soviet and East European officials confirmed the applicability of the Tashkent solution to the Arab–Israeli dispute and expressed their willingness to guarantee the regional status quo provided that "other nuclear powers" join it. Privately, they demanded a price and urged Jerusalem to pay it in a hurry since though "its 'specific gravity' in the Soviet–American equation was significant . . . The USSR and the US would make a deal on Vietnam, and after that the significance of Israel's policies would diminish markedly."[4]

What was the price? First, the answer came, "active opposition to German rearmament." Second, "cessation of the public campaign on behalf of Soviet Jewry." Third, "Israel would have to persuade the US to withdraw its nuclear forces, including those of the Sixth Fleet, from the entire region." How could "little Israel" induce the Americans to undertake such a radical measure?, asked an Israeli official. "You should tell the Americans you'll not make nuclear weapons if they accept our conditions. Then we can help you with your problems," was the Soviet answer.[5]

Moscow might have settled for less. On February 18, their political counselor in Tel Aviv suggested that the US make specific proposals concerning a possible superpower agreement to diffuse the regional arms race and prevent nuclear proliferation. Ten days later, the first secretary of the Romanian embassy in Tel Aviv presented his American counterpart with the following proposal:

> One would be a declaration by Israel denying any intention to acquire nuclear weapons and renouncing what he called "a nuclear policy." The second step would be a guarantee by the US, USSR, UK and France in a single document that they would oppose by all necessary means any aggression in the Middle East. . . . in case it proved impossible for the US and the USSR to sign the same document, the French and the British could do so on the basis of side agreements to include the Soviets and Americans.[6]

A disconcerted Arab commentator asked: "Is the rumor that the Soviet Union and the United States agreed to divide the world into spheres of influence in order to destroy the People's Republic of China correct?" Another assured his readers that "If there was room for the Israeli proposal [on the subject of Tashkent] then there would be room to ask why didn't the Soviet Union apply the Tashkent-route also to the Vietnam conflict." If Moscow did cut a deal with the US, wrote yet another, France might be persuaded to become an alternative to the USSR.[7]

Consternation about potential Soviet–American collaboration dovetailed with a debate over the appropriate response to a nuclearized Israel. The Egyptians held that "preventive war" was the only solution to an Israeli bomb which would freeze the status quo. The Syrians retorted that conventional warfare was too expensive and that Vietnam had demonstrated the efficacy of people's war against nuclear powers.[8]

The ball was in the American court, but the players "suddenly remembered that Tashkent was situated in the Soviet Union." In fact, The Department of State had concluded that Moscow wanted "*to promote Arab unity in the direction of unity against the West*" and that it "advocated "*a peaceful solution to the Arab–Israeli quarrel*" in the hope of turning both against the West. The US saw no reason to cooperate.[9]

Israel protested that it was not fair to force her "to pay indirectly for the strengthening of Western positions in the area." Jordan was supplied with modern tank and artillery units, and the Saudis with British aircraft designed solely for NATO use. Israel had little choice but to embark on an expensive modernization of her own armaments. The US even shifted from grant aid to credit sales for countries "like Iran and Israel" which could "afford to buy" the weapons as the US tried to "bolster" its balance of payments.[10]

Unlike Iran, Israel could not threaten to purchase cheap Soviet weapons, but it knew that Washington was so unhappy with any weapons sales to Israel that Johnson literally asked Eban "to enter the Pentagon by a side door." So, it hoped the American discomfort over weapons sales to Israel would persuade Washington to cooperate with Moscow.[11]

On March 2, 1966 Arthur Goldberg told reporters in London that the US was willing "to join with the Soviet Union . . . in any common agreement to halt the flow of weapons to the Middle East." But a savvy Soviet official was quick to remark, "Goldberg is only a UN man. What he says at a press conference does not necessarily represent official American policy. Now if Rusk were to say it, that would be different." Washington, indeed, informed Harman that past American "experience indicates that the Soviets are prepared to discuss area arms controls only in a context unacceptable to us (Sixth Fleet, Turkey, etc.)." State officials told inquiring

American Jews that, "fruitful negotiations between Israel and the Arabs will have to await a further 'cooling off' period of Arab emotional hostility to the fact of Israel's existence."[12]

Congressional friends tried to help. Senator Wayne Morse asked: "How long can a new arms race go in the Middle East before the entire region is embroiled in combat?" Jacob Javits repeatedly called on the administration to end the Middle Eastern arms race before it was "faced with a second front." Johnson asked Goldberg to come up with an American sponsored solution. Goldberg suggested pulling "the political sting" out of the Arab–Israeli conflict by tackling the refugee problem. Rusk hoped Israel would reject the idea, but Rostow informed him that "the President understands that Goldberg's approach will not appear to the Israelis as an attempt to push them into something they are not prepared to accept." Either paralyzed by the Vietnam War, or using that war as an excuse, State insisted on trying to keep the Middle East on the back burner while the Soviets increased their "wide-ranging activities from Kashmir to Algeria – but including Syria, Iraq and Egypt."[13]

Under such circumstances, Israel could afford to alienate neither Moscow by planting her flag in Vietnam nor Washington on whose weapons she relied. During a January meeting with Barbour, Eban promised to raise the issue of Israeli aid to Saigon in the Cabinet, but warned that the "presence of left-wing MAPAM in the new government would make it even more difficult to secure approval for Israeli presence in Vietnam." Had Eban wished, the matter could have been treated as a routine ministerial decision. Making it a cabinet decision, conveniently shifted the blame to MAPAM.[14]

Eban delayed the matter until after he had a chance to meet with Johnson and finalize the Skyhawk deal. Then, he told the Cabinet that he supported diplomatic ties with South Vietnam, "but only after peace would be established in the area." He did propose sending medical equipment and personnel as a humanitarian gesture, sponsored by the non-governmental Red Star of David. After much debate, it was decided to send a physician on a survey mission but the MAPAM health minister was unable to find a suitable one.[15]

In response to the March 1966 Vu Van Thai media uproar, Ambassador Chuvakhin met with Israeli officials to express Moscow's opposition to Israeli ties with Saigon. Deciding that silence was golden, Eban refrained from even mentioning the subject in his yearly foreign policy address. The subsequent public outcry, however, compelled him to return to the Knesset podium the very next day, deny any Israeli intention to establish diplomatic ties with Saigon, and promise to consult with all the coalition members prior to any change of policy. In other words, MAPAM could veto any change. Hence, Eban was in a position to drop hints about a possible Israeli change of heart, knowing full well that he could not follow through.[16]

For once, the media united behind the government. Israel's socialist elite felt closer to Ho Chi Minh than to General Ky. In 1946, Ben Gurion and Ho Chi Minh had lived in the same Paris hotel and had become friends. Ben Gurion revealed that, after hearing about the "Jewish problem," Ho suggested that he proclaim a Jewish government in exile, headquartered in Hanoi. When asked about Vietnam, Ben Gurion said: "If I were the American President, I would have pulled out the American army from Vietnam, even though such a move might possibly have grave consequences."[17]

Some analysts argued that silence was the least Israel owed the US, especially, given the personal stake Johnson had in Vietnam and the importance of his role in balancing a chronically Arabist Foggy Bottom. Others retorted that American support for the Arabs was at least as great as its support for Israel and that Johnson's preoccupation with Vietnam meant that decisions concerning the Middle East were left to the hostile NEA. Some even suspected that the unwanted publicity was directed at Jewish peace activists and was being used to convince the American public that Israel was not so "pro-Western."[18]

The issue also had a moral dimension which was best summed up by radical editor and Knesset member Uri Avnery: "We blamed the whole world for standing aside when six million Jews were slaughtered. Americans, Britons and others had very good reasons to keep quiet and not disturb Hitler's murderous project, reasons of high policy, propaganda, and military strategy. And still we say: They should have gone beyond all those considerations and put an end to the horror. And how can we say such things, when today we behave exactly like them?"[19]

Avnery represented leftist intellectuals; most Israelis were happy to note that, for once, "there was no contradiction between utilitarian interest and moral stand." A public opinion survey conducted in November and December of 1966 revealed a high level of interest in the war: 50 percent thought it was "essentially a North Vietnamese expansionist war against South Vietnam," 43 percent thought it was "essentially an American attempt to establish in Vietnam a governmental system they could control." Only 7 percent believed it "was essentially a civil war in South Vietnam."[20] This response reflected popular awareness of the wider origins of "local" disputes. After all, the country was in the midst of an intense partisan debate concerning Dayan's decision to visit the Vietnamese battlefields.

THE DAYAN DECISION

To his close friend, Gad Yaakobi, Dayan explained: "My main specialty is security. Just as an expert on plant diseases travels to see them and how they are cured, so I want to see and study the war in Vietnam, and its possible implications on war in our area."[21] Critics maintained that the trip would "serve the interest of the American and Palestinian propaganda machines and give credence to their effort to place the US and Israel on one side of the fence and the Viet Cong and the Palestinians on the other." Nor was it in Israel's interest to offend Jewish leaders who played such "a central role in the intellectual opposition movement." Dayan was a symbol of the Israeli military, and he should not be allowed to think or pretend otherwise. His defenders replied that Israel was a democracy and Dayan was no less entitled to do what he thought was right than the left was entitled to participate in Soviet sponsored gatherings. Indeed, the personal contacts forged on such occasions served Israel well.[22]

Dayan rejected these arguments, in part because he had underestimated his own aura especially following the publication of his book on the Sinai war. The book received rave reviews and established him as a military thinker and a major celebrity. His diary and letters reflect his amazement at the red carpet treatment he ended up receiving. In any case, he hoped that his request to visit North Vietnam would help alleviate whatever public relations problem he might cause Israel and that benefits would accrue to the Israeli army from the lessons he was bound to learn in Vietnam.[23]

More serious was the strategic argument against his trip: The Israeli steadfastness on the Vietnamese issue, which functioned as proof of her independence, would lose credibility if the Soviets concluded that Dayan served as an unofficial emissary to compensate the US for the failure to send an official one. But in May, even that argument seemed moot to Dayan and his RAFI colleagues. Kosygin had visited Cairo, met with Shukayri and *Pravda* began again to refer to Israel "as the strategic base of imperialism." The fact that the Soviet change of heart occurred while Israel's European ambassadors were meeting in Warsaw proved that Soviet attitudes towards Israel had nothing to do with Israeli actions or inactions. Dayan's ally, Shimon Peres announced that "the Tashkent spirit" was over because Moscow had decided to establish a new pro-Soviet Arab bloc as a "new phase in the Cold War."[24]

Eban refused either to disavow his "new" foreign policy for which Israel received accolades in Europe and the Third World or accept that his domestic critics were right all along. He saw Dayan's Vietnamese study tour as a manifestation of the broader RAFI challenge to his foreign and nuclear policy. Dayan was not permitted to wear his Israeli army uniform or be hosted by any Israeli embassies.[25]

Some worried that Eban's unrestrained opposition would alienate Washington. Eshkol characterized the relations between the two countries as "half a chicken – half a horse." There was no equality, but "there was respect."[26] His government believed that Israel was quite safe in an era in which she had access to arms; Egyptian troops were busy fighting a counter-revolutionary insurgency in Yemen, and the Arabs were quarrelling over the appropriate policy towards Israel. Even regionalism had its advantages. Eban remarked:

> It used to be said: a small country is incapable of securing its own defense, it has to rely on outside factors, friends, world opinion, allies, the heavens – all the exhortations, except the advice that Israel should rely on herself. This time we heard, for the first time, that it is good for a small country, regardless of her being tied to big countries, that as far as possible she should use her own defensive and deterrent capabilities.[27]

Perhaps this equanimity was responsible for Eshkol's decision to forgo a unique opportunity to cut a deal with an Egyptian president made desperate by cuts in American foreign aid. In 1962 Washington had started to supply Egypt with surplus wheat. By 1965, six out of every ten loaves of bread eaten in Egypt were made with American grain. In 1966 Washington curtailed these wheat shipments in part as a response to Nasser's provocations; in part because provisioning Vietnam had dwindled the wheat surplus; and in part because "hawks" wanted to cut "back elsewhere in order to support Vietnam" and "doves" to prove that Vietnam was undermining "other programs."[28]

Following secret mediation involving a Jewish businessman, MOSSAD chief Meir Amit and Deputy Foreign Minister Zvi Dinstein were invited to Cairo to meet Egypt's number two man, Ab'd al Hakkim Amer. Egypt wanted Israel's help in getting the food aid renewed. In return, Egypt would relax the Arab boycott and permit limited Israeli use of the Suez Canal. Eshkol hesitated, and was eventually persuaded to turn down the offer. There are those who believe Eshkol did so because of the opposition of Issar Harel, his former MOSSAD chief.[29]

Sending Amit was obviously risky. Eban opposed the idea. Perhaps he doubted Israel's ability to extract American food aid at a time when his own country was told to "bear in mind heavy demands from Vietnam," and "not make aid level a measure" of her relationship with Washington. Either way, the termination of the food aid meant increased Egyptian dependence on Moscow, i.e., the forging of closer Egyptian–Syrian ties at a time when Damascus insisted on actively backing a Palestinian people's war.[30]

THE SYRIAN PROBLEM

In his address to the American Legion, Johnson warned that if a "war of liberation" succeeded in Vietnam then, as Marshal Lin Biao said, "The people in other parts of the world will see that what the Vietnamese people can do they can do, too." The fallacy in his argument stemmed from the "if." As 1966 unfolded, so did Vietnam inspired guerrilla warfare in the Middle East. Bombs exploded in Aden, Jiddah, Riyadh and along the ARAMCO pipeline and there was unrest in the Persian Gulf area.[31]

Pivotal was the February 1966 Syrian coup perpetrated by a narrow based radical faction called the "Neo-Baath" and headed by three young Arab intellectuals.[32] The strategy of this Syrian "troika" was to attach itself to the Soviet Union, while executing a Chinese inspired foreign policy. The crucial negotiations took place in March during a Neo-Baathist delegation visit to Moscow. The Soviet government refused to support a Palestinian "people's war." However, the Soviet military appreciated the delegates' willingness to place Syrian naval facilities at the disposal of the Soviet Mediterranean fleet, and Moscow decided to adopt the new regime. Yassir Arafat's friend Ahmed el Sweideni was the new chief of staff, and, within mere months the number of FATAH raids doubled.[33]

This radical regime was anathema not only to Israel but to the Arab kings who began, with the help of internal Syrian opponents, to plot promptly its overthrow. The Arab kings response fit a pattern. In 1965, Lin Biao had spoken of wars of national liberation but, in May 1966, he spoke of Mao's fear of coups. Mao, Lin Biao reported, had counted 64 "counter revolutionary coups d'etat" in Asia, Africa and Latin America since 1960, 59 of them successful. Third World regimes began to question the safety of non-alliance or, in Soviet terminology, independence in international affairs.[34]

Moscow blamed both the coups and the Vietnam War on "certain forces" (a combination of the CIA, oil companies and the military-industrial complex?). *Pravda* wrote that the US and Saudi Arabia had budgeted 250 million dollars for the overthrow of the Neo-Baathist. In any case, to scuttle what she perceived as an American instigated frontal attack on the forces of national liberation, and to prove that her protection was worth having, Moscow resolved to defend the new Syrian regime at all costs. She sent hundreds of officers and advisers to fortify, stabilize and moderate it and told Israel that any anti-Syrian act regardless of motivation or provocation would be interpreted as one undertaken on behalf of those "forces." If Israel did not wish to find herself "at the bottom of a volcano," she had better hold her fire.[35] Eshkol found himself in an impossible situation:

> Do not tell me stories that we, Israel, are being pushed by Imperialism. . . . I was told . . . that, with the visit of a particular person from the United States, we certainly arranged our actions against Syria – and this at a time when I did not know yet of any problem with Syria and then happened what happened, to my great sorrow, with Jordan, and after a very short time I heard the second version, that Israel has a special interest in Syria, because of her ties to this great power. Soon it would be said that we are asking Syria to place mines and kill the two young men from Rosh Pinah, and now we are waiting for a third mine.[36]

His sarcasm reflected his helplessness. What was he supposed to do when the third, fourth or fifth mines exploded? RAFI demanded that Eshkol demonstrate that Israel would "not put up with any attempt to conduct either the Cold War or the intra-Arab war" on her "back." The left condemned the FATAH attacks, but, like Moscow, blamed them on US efforts to instigate an Israeli attack on Syria in the hope of toppling the radical regime and undermining Soviet–Israeli relations; perhaps Israel would then even establish ties with South Vietnam.[37]

In May, Syrian imprisonment of Arafat had raised Eshkol's hopes that Moscow would succeed in restraining the Damascus regime. Would Moscow telegraph its support for the regional status quo by improving relations with Jerusalem? He asked De Gaulle to find out. The answer was negative, though Moscow promised to avoid increasing Middle Eastern tensions. Arafat was soon released, and FATAH activity renewed.[38]

Following four terrorist incidents, which caused the death of two civilians and the injury of two others within a 24-hour period, Israel unleashed its air force. The diplomatic fallout was a total surprise. The Syrian complaint to the Security Council was unexpected but Israel, with the help of the Israeli–Syrian armistice commission report, made a strong case for Syrian culpability and American support prevented the passage of an anti-Israeli resolution. The price was an emotional debate held "in the shadow of Vietnam." The Israeli representative protested vainly that her refusal to acquiesce to Palestinian attacks had "nothing to do with allegations of imperialist plots or with the events in South-East Asia."[39]

Even France, Israel's closest ally and chief military aircraft supplier, refused to listen. RAFI, a strong advocate of the "French orientation," blamed the government for permitting American inspections of the French built Dimona nuclear facility and for diminishing French interest in Israel by deciding to purchase Skyhawks in lieu of Mirages.[40]

Was Washington prepared to place itself in the Israeli camp and recognize Israel's right to an American style response to the "national liberation war" waged against her? Joseph Sisco implied not. He argued that since there was no UN machinery in Vietnam, American retaliatory bombing was permissible. But given its existence on the Israeli borders, such bombing was "deplorable."[41] In short, Israel found itself completely isolated on the subject of holding her neighbors responsible for Palestinian acts of sabotage.

It also found itself isolated on the subject of holding Syria responsible for living up to the armistice agreement. This became apparent when an Israeli patrol boat was grounded in the Sea of Galilee in August, and Syrian ground and air fire prevented its rescue for eleven days. Reporters asked State officials to express their opinion on the extraction of the boat, given the fact that the Sea of Galilee was Israeli territory. The officials, as an Israeli Cabinet member wrote to Eban, provided the Syrians with legitimizing arguments by pointing out that "the Sea of Galilee was in Israeli jurisdiction, but these were not Israel's final borders."[42]

Delighted, Syria pointed to the incident as proof of its vanguard role because "the strength of nations is measured by their faith and willingness to sacrifice, if this was not so, we would not have been watching the Vietnamese nation inflict daily blows on the American army." Buoyed by the admiration of the entire Arab world (including Bourguiba), the Syrian president and chief of staff announced plans to activate the Israeli Arabs.[43]

Not wishing to be left behind, Cairo adopted Damascus' line, at least verbally. Israel not only demanded "Arab acquiescence to its criminal existence," Radio Cairo complained, but also "their cooperation in prohibiting the freedom of movement of Palestinians and the prevention of their activity on behalf of regaining their stolen rights." By publishing a detailed account of American arms sales to Israel Eshkol hinted that renewal of Palestinian infiltration from Gaza would lead to war. Cairo retorted that since war would mean "Israeli defeat or a world war," a US "suffering under the yoke of the Vietnam war" would be sure to prevent it.[44]

Nasser's protege Shukayri announced the return of the first group of PLO trainees from China as instruction from the Chinese, Algerians and Syrians began to tell in the increasing daring and effectiveness of both PLO and FATAH operations. One of the areas most severely affected was Jerusalem. Bombs blew up in its residential areas, injuring citizens, and the railroad to the city was made unsafe. Domestic pressure for reprisal grew irresistible as the basic promise of the Jewish state was "Never Again." That did not mean that Jews would be safer in Israel, only that their blood would not be shed with impunity. No Israeli government could afford to ignore this promise for any length of time. Eshkol tried but his references to "an open notebook" in which he kept a running score of Damascus' transgressions only led to a widespread quip that an al FATAH unit had entered his office and stolen the open notebook.[45]

Earlier that summer, a foreign ministry study had concluded that "Israel formed a formidable obstacle" to Soviet plans to fill the strategic vacuum which British withdrawal was leaving in the region. If undeterred by a Western show of strength, Moscow "would within a year" provoke a war "to remove the Israeli road block." British and American experts shared the Israeli analysis, but Britain wanted the Americans to take over and the Americans claimed that Vietnam engaged all their resources.[46] Israel had to find a way to deal with the Soviet backed Syrian-Palestinian challenge without American support.

As Eban was preparing to speak at the annual General Assembly debate, one of his representatives in the US cautioned him: "One word of criticism on Vietnam and you can kiss off Johnson." Nor should he expect support from an increasingly isolationist US. Eban took these words to heart. He endorsed the Vietnamese elections, hinted that he might reconsider ties with Saigon, and prepared a speech on Vietnam so full of "creative obscurity" that it succeeded in pleasing both Rusk and Gromyko.[47]

However, it all seemed for naught. That September, world and American attention were focused on the Johnson–Jewish public brawl. Publicly, Eban insisted that the brawl was an internal American affair. Privately, he tried to address the effect of Jewish anti-war activism on Israel without alienating his touchy audience. He began by explaining that the Vietnam War was harmful to Soviet–Israeli relations, and to the cause of Soviet Jewry, because "when the co-existence is diminished as by the Vietnam crisis; then the Soviet Union becomes less interested in . . . world opinion and more interested in Arab votes to be mobilized against the United States in the Cold War." Only when asked specifically about the suggestion that Jewish attitudes on Vietnam hurt Israel did he say:

> From an Israeli point of view . . . small countries . . . must be interested in an America of commitment and responsibility . . . I read something of a sermon by a Rabbi who is saying that Vietnam was 9,000 miles away, what interest is that? Well, Israel is 6,000 miles away and this business about measuring your commitment by distance reminds me of 1939; Czechoslovakia, that little country far away of which we know nothing.

Still, the two commitments had to be separated, he added, before their glaring differences on the issues of political stability and self-reliance got blurred and undermined US support for Israel. So, what should Jews do?

> Now, I don't think it matters if a man . . . says what he thinks about Vietnam as an individual, but if a Conference of Rabbis

> or . . . the World Jewish Congress speaks out on Vietnam, the implication is that . . . there is such a thing as a Jewish attitude on Vietnam and there isn't. Therefore it would be better I think for citizens to speak on this question either as individuals or within groups which do not bear a collective Jewish connotation.[48]

Eban was much less successful in assessing the effect of Vietnam on Israel, or deciphering the meaning of his encounters with his fellow foreign ministers. Rusk seemed to have a dual purpose: (1) to prepare Eban for reduced American aid and (2) to reduce Israel's fear of a Moscow backed Arab onslaught. Rusk succeeded brilliantly. In a report to his staff, Eban called the sum of $25 billion, Rusk claimed Washington spent on Vietnam, "frightening" and justifying "cut backs elsewhere." Eban also seemed mesmerized by Rusk's display of "intimacy" towards Israel and "sobriety" towards Nasser. With American–Egyptian relations at such a low web, Jerusalem could trust Rusk's promise that Washington would stand by her side if she agreed to bring her complaints concerning Syrian backing of FATAH infiltrations to the Security Council.

Gromyko, too, tried to convince Eban that Israel had no reason to fear Moscow's increased regional influence. He called their bilateral relations "normal;" expressed his opposition to the destruction of "proper" states; and reminded him (for the first time in over a dozen years, Eban happily remarked) of Moscow's significant contribution to Israel's creation. Further "warming" of their relations depended on Israeli help in expelling foreign bases from the region and ending agitation on behalf of Soviet Jewry. After all, Israel was no longer a "small" but a "medium" country.[49]

French foreign minister Couve de Murville warned Eban that the Vietnam War had revived the Cold War. Moscow was no longer functioning as a responsible superpower but as a side in the Cold War, and her Middle Eastern policy was a direct consequence of that fact. However, Eban convinced Eshkol that Israel had nothing to lose by giving the Security Council a try. The results were disastrous: the Security Council deliberated for weeks while FATAH attacks continued as Syria refused "to hold back the revolution of the expelled and oppressed Palestinian people." Finally, a resolution "inviting," rather than "reminding," Damascus to prevent "incidents which constitute a violation of the General armistice agreement" gained majority support. The Soviets, who had played a key role in weakening the resolution, promptly vetoed it. "The

World is ready for an anti-Syrian action," Eban told his men.[50]

The opportunity came on November 11 when three Israeli soldiers died opposite Mt. Hebron and "it was clear to everybody," Avnery wrote, "that the Eshkol government would not be able to refrain from a military response. The political and psychological pressures were too strong."[51] Only Eshkol had second thoughts. Nasser had just signed a mutual defense treaty with Damascus, and Moscow had made it clear that it would treat any anti-Syrian operation as if it was undertaken on behalf of "oil companies and forces unknown to governments which are responsible for the Vietnam War and for events in the Middle East." In vain did Eshkol implore Chuvakhin to leave Vietnam and mysterious forces alone. The Soviets insisted that Israel had to take the long view and refrain from responding to FATAH provocations.[52]

When Harman suggested asking Johnson to appeal to Kosygin to restrain Syria, Eban turned him down for fear that Kosygin would argue that it was more important that the US be restrained in Vietnam than Syria on Israel's border. Harman retorted that precisely "because of Vietnam and the danger that the Russians would think that . . . the US was immobilized and will not interfere, that it was important to engage Washington in a discussion with the Russians . . ."[53]

A "tiny" reprisal against FATAH bases in Jordan seemed to offer Eshkol a way out. Former chief of staff Yigal Allon explained: "Israel cannot determine its security policy based on Arab ties to the superpowers, and if Hussein has no immunity – Who does?"[54] The plan to blow up a few houses of Samu villagers went awry when a Jordanian army convoy passed by and engaged the Israeli army in a day long battle. The West Bank erupted and bombs exploded in Jordanian government buildings. Palestinians carrying PLO and FATAH placards demanded weapons to protect themselves. Shukayri called for the overthrow of "the Hashemite harlot," and for a Vietnamese-style "people's war" against Israel. There were border skirmishes between Syria and Jordan. Within days, the Security Council passed a unanimous resolution condemning Israel, and Washington embarked on a massive arms airlift to Amman. Hussein made brutal use of his army and reestablished control over the country.[55]

The sharp American response surprised Israeli advocates of military reprisal. They had assumed that Vietnam had taught Americans to appreciate the destructiveness of armed infiltration. Samu proved them wrong. Rusk argued that the US had waited five years before she started bombing the North and, regardless of NLF use of Cambodia, the US had refrained from moving against Sihanuk. Eban countered that Israel could not be as patient because she had no hinterland and everything happened in her own "house." Walt Rostow complained to Evron and Feinberg that Jerusalem had failed to take into account the effect her reprisal would have on American global interests which mandated US deployment of "*static defense* in the Middle East."[56]

Eban blamed Eshkol for moving against Jordan instead of Syria, but Eshkol deduced that he should have cleared the operation with Washington. Arab and Western observers surmised that Israel was too "frightened" to choose war in the aftermath of the Egyptian–Syrian defense treaty.[57] After consulting with Secretary of Defense Shams Badran, Amer telegraphed Nasser: "We suggest the evacuation of the UN emergency force. There is no danger of Israel attacking soon and it is better to take the wind out of the sails of Hussein and his reactionary allies." But Nasser retorted: "that means war!" In Paris, Kosygin gave up publicly on a "Tashkent conference for the Middle East" because "both belligerents" refused to agree to such a conference.[58]

An isolated, moderate and poorly led Israel, argued an increasing number of Arab strategists, could be provoked with relative impunity. The fight should be confined to the Israeli and Palestinian people. Since the Palestinians had no territory or army, "armed struggle" Viet Cong style was their appropriate choice. Such an "armed struggle" would stunt the Jewish State's growth. It would not only burden its economy but create an atmosphere of fear which would decrease immigration and increase emigration. Concentration on counterinsurgency techniques would also damage her military preparedness. Already FATAH succeeded in getting Israel to increase her military budget and lengthen the compulsory military service.

Moreover, a combination of American restraint and Eshkol's moderation would ensure that Israel would refrain from starting a war as she did in 1956. Even the number and scope of her inevitable reprisals would be easily manageable, and even beneficial, as they would galvanize the Palestinian population; shame Arab states into improving their armed forces and responding more aggressively to Israeli reprisals; and provide Palestinians with the opportunity to prove themselves deserving of international support.

Palestinians should go to Vietnam to study methods of dealing with the defensive measures Americans developed there and which they planned to reveal to Israel.

Some Arab analysts contended that hopes of turning Jordan into a "second Hanoi" should be abandoned since Amman was more likely to turn into a "second Danang." Also, given the national cohesion of the Jewish state, Palestinian warriors could not melt into the population. Therefore, rather than trying to constrict the battlefield as in Vietnam, the Arabs should seek to widen it. This would frustrate American efforts to contain the war, and might even prevent American interference. If the US did interfere, the Palestinians would use guerrilla warfare against them. Widening the war would also undermine the logistical advantages enjoyed by Israel. Indeed, the Israeli army should be lured into the Sinai and the West Bank of Jordan and destroyed there. After all, Arab "admiration" for the Vietnamese people derived not from their specific tactics but "from their iron determination to fight and from their unusual willingness to withstand blows silently," which contrasted so sharply with their own "lack of response."[59]

The Israeli military intelligence assumed that war was unlikely as long as the superpowers were set against it, and Egyptian troops were stuck in Yemen. However, Eshkol surprised his top brass in February 1967 when he warned of an imminent war and demanded an updating of war plans. He had "a strong feeling" that American policy was "shifting" away from Israel, a situation which might tempt her enemies to go too far.[60]

NOTES

1. Interview with a source close to Eshkol; and Amnon Kapeliuk; "An Interview with Mr. Eban," *New Outlook* (July 1966), 11.
2. *Divrei Hakneset*, Jan. 12, 1966, 344.
3. Levi Eshkol to Alexei Kosygin, January 29, 1966, Israeli–Russian Relations, Yad Eshkol; and Eliezer Doron, *In Watch and Confrontation* (Jerusalem: 1978), 27.
4. *Al Hawadat,* March 25, 1966; DCSS; and Amembassy Tel Aviv to Department of State, March 11, 1966, NSF, Israel, box 139, 66, LBJL.
5. Ibid.
6. Secretary of State from Amembassy Tel Aviv, Feb. 23, 1966, NSF, Israel, box, 139, 59 and 62, LBJL.

7. *Al Hawadat*, March 25, 1966; Radio Cairo, March 5, 1966, DCSS; and *Divrei Hakneset*, March 16, 1966, 1014.
8. Y. V., "Atom and Middle East Tashkent," *New Outlook* (March 1966), 3–4; and *Haaretz*, June 20, 1966.
9. Secretary of State to Amembassy Tel Aviv, Feb. 22, 1966, NSF, Israel, box 139, 59; *Congressional Record – Senate*, March 15, 1966, 5988, and March 10, 1966, 5555; "Soviet and Chinese Communist Intentions in the Near East – Red Sea Area," (underline in original) June 13, 1966, NSF, Saudi Arabia, Faisal Briefing Book, box 155, 34, LBJL.
10. W. W. Rostow to the President, Nov. 8, 1966, NSF, Senator Fulbright, box 3, 11, LBJL.
11. *Al Zaffa*, Jan. 5, 1966, Jan. 25, 1966, DCSS; and Eban, *Personal Witness*, 340.
12. Amembassy Tel Aviv to Department of State, March 13, 1966; "Points of Discussion with Ambassador Avraham Harman," May 3, 1966, NSF, Israel, box 139, LBJL; and Sandy Bolz to Simon Segal, Feb. 15, 1966, Israel file, box 105, AJCL.
13. Arthur Goldberg to the President, May 19, 1966; W. W. Rostow to the President, May 31, 1966; W. W. Rostow to the Secretary of State, June 3, 1966, NSF, Israel, box 139, 152, 152a, 152c, LBJL; and *Jerusalem Post*, May 5, 1966.
14. Amembassy Tel Aviv to Department of State, Jan. 19, 1966, NSF, Israel, box 139, 53, LBJL; and *Kol Haam*, March 25, 1966.
15. Interview with a source close to Eshkol; and "Foreign ministry background paper: Vietnam," July 20, 1966, Israel–Asian relations, Vietnam, Yad Eshkol.
16. David Magen, "No Israeli Ties with Vietnam," *New Outlook* (May 1966), 17; *Haaretz, Yediot Aharonot*, and *Kol Haam*, March 22–5, 1966.
17. *Davar*, March 21, 27, 1966.
18. *Davar*, March 24, 1966; *Lamerchav*, April 18, 1966; and *Haaretz*, March 18, 1966.
19. *Haolam Hazeh*, Oct. 4, 1966, 13 and 24.
20. *Davar*, March 23, 1966; and Uzi Peled, "Hayisraelim Umilchemet Vietnam," *International Problems* (May 1968), 41–44.
21. Shabtai Tevet, *Medinai* (Jerusalem: 1969), 550.
22. *Haolam Hazeh*, June 5, 1966; and *Haaretz*, June 9, 1966.
23. Dayan, *Yoman Vietnam*, 7–45; and Slater, *Warrior Statesman* (New York: 1993), 237–9.
24. *JTA*, June 10, 1966, *Mabat Hadash*, May 17, 1966.
25. *Divrei Hakneset*, 1484–7; and Dayan, *Yoman Vietnam*, 28–9.
26. Interviews with a source close to Eshkol and an Israeli diplomat.
27. *Diyun Bachug Haraayoni: Mediniyut Hachutz Hayisraelit* (Tel Aviv: 1966), 30–1.
28. Walt Rostow from Komer, March 66, NSF, Files of Robert Komer, box 1, 2, 113a, LBJL.
29. Haber, *Hayom Tifroz Milchama*, 64–5; and interview with Yariv.
30. Amembassy Tel Aviv to Department of State, April 18, 1966, NSF, Israel, box 138, 9, 29, LBJL.

31. *NYT,* Sept. 2, 1966; and Intelligence Memorandum, May 21, 1966, NSF, Iran, box 136, 28c, 28d, LBJL.
32. All were in their thirties and forties and had doctorates.
33. Ben Tsur, *Gormin Sovietiim*, 56–75; Vassiliev, *Soviet Policy in the Middle East*, 63–4, 77; and Yaacov Bar Shimon, "Relationship Between Domestic and External Conflict Behavior," Ph.D. dissertation, Hebrew University, 1978, p. 288.
34. *Davar*, June 13, 1966; *Kol Haam*, May 29, 1966; and Jaap Van Ginneken, *The Rise and Fall of Lin Piao* (New York: 1977), 59.
35. *Pravda*, Oct. 3, 1966; and Zak, *Arbaim Shnot Du-Siach im Moskva*, 137–40.
36. *Divrei Hakneset*, May 17, 1966.
37. *Mabat Hadash*, May 17, 1966, 3; *Kol Haam*, May 3, 10 and 13, 1966.
38. *Maariv*, July 3, 1966; and *Davar*, June 27, 1966.
39. *Security Council: Official Records*, Doc. S/7411, S/7412 and S/7440, Supp. for July, Aug. and Sept. 1966, and Aug. 1, 1966, 27.
40. Ibid., July 29, 1966, 8; and *Haaretz*, Aug. 8, 1966.
41. *Security Council Official Record*, Aug. 3, 1966, 15.
42. Eliyahu Sasson to Abba Eban, August 23, 1966, Israeli–American Relations, Yad Eshkol.
43. Radio Damascus, Aug. 17, 1966; *Kol Haam*, Aug. 20 and 23, 1966; and *Al Ahram*, Aug. 20, 1966, DCSS.
44. *Roz al Yusuf*, Sept. 19, 1966; Radio Cairo, Sept. 20, 1966; and *Al Gumhuria*, Sept. 16, 1966, DCSS.
45. *Haolam Hazeh*, Nov. 16, 1966.
46. Rafael, *Destination Peace*, 130.
47. Shlomo Argov to A. Evron, Aug. 28, 1966, Israeli–US relations, Yad Eshkol and Eban's briefing of the heads of his department, Oct. 31, 1966, 210/09, ISA.
48. "Discussion Following Speech by Foreign Minister of Israel Abba Eban," Oct. 12, 1966, AJC, FAD-2, 59–66, box 43, YIVO.
49. Eban's briefing of the heads of his department, Oct. 31, 1966, 210/09, ISA; and Eban, *Personal Witness*, 347.
50. Ibid.; and *American Jewish Yearbook, 1966,* 113.
51. *Haolam Hazeh*, Nov. 16, 1966.
52. "Discussion Between Semyonov and Israel Katz," Nov. 9, 1966; "Discussion between Chuvakhin and Eshkol," Nov. 11 and 12, 1966. Israeli–Soviet Relations, Yad Eshkol.
53. Eban to Embassy Washington and Harman to Eban, Nov. 1966, Israeli–American Relations, 804/71, ISA.
54. Interview with a source close to Eshkol; and Moshe Gilboa, *Shesh Shanim-Shisha Yamim* (Tel Aviv: 1968), 77.
55. Samir Mutawi, *Jordan in the 1967 War* (London: 1987), 76–7; and *Al Yaum* (Lebanon), Nov. 24, 1966.
56. Report on Harman–Rusk meeting, Eban–Barbour meeting and Rostow's meeting with Evron and Feinberg, Nov. 1966, Israeli–American relations, 804/71, ISA.
57. *Maariv*, Aug. 5, 1966; Gilboa, 66; and Mutawi, 77.

58. *Jewish Exponent*, Dec. 9, 1966; Gilboa, 76, Sadat, *In Search of Identity* (New York: 1977), 172.
59. Salach Shaval, "New Strategy for the Liberation of Palestine", *Maarchot*, May 67, 26; *Al Dafah*, Nov. 15, 1966; "Flexible action plan – in light of experience," *Hedim Utguvot*, March 23, 1967; and *Al Charia*, Jan. 9, 1967, DCSS.
60. *Tmurot*, Jan. 1967, 19–22; and Haber, *Hayom Tifroz Milchama*, 133.

6 Jewish Leaders Clash with Lyndon Johnson

RABBIS ON THE OFFENSIVE

Jewish religious anti-war activists began 1966 with determined optimism. The Vietnam War was a moral outrage, stated reform rabbi Arthur Vorspan, but never before in human history had "Jews had the freedom and security and the access to the ears of the world to give universal meaning" to the prophetic and rabbinic demand that "Jews stand, as co-partners with God, in shaping the messianic vision of a time when nations shall beat their swords into plowshares."[1] Rabbis planned to stimulate a national "dialogue for peace" and, in the process, illustrate the pertinence of Jewish values to their cosmopolitan young.

They launched their campaign with an all-day study conference entitled "Judaism and World Peace." One hundred and fifty rabbis and lay leaders listened to a careful exposition of the history of the Vietnamese problem provided by Wolfgang Friedman of Columbia University. The professor concluded that, given the facts on the ground, "a stalemate from which negotiations can proceed" was the best possible solution and he recommended that concerned citizens focus on keeping the tragic conflict within physical, moral and legal bounds.

Then three rabbis, each representing a major Judaic strand, offered their interpretation of the "relevance of Jewish religious tradition" to the conflict. Jewish law, they reminded their audience, differentiates between obligatory war (Milchemet Chova), when idolaters attack, and permissible war (Milchemet Reshut), when the idolaters are preparing to attack. A Jew can object to fighting a permissible war, though not an obligatory one. Wars of conquest, aggression or expansion are forbidden. That means that, under Jewish law, it is possible to have a "conscientious objection to a specific war." But the rabbis differed on the appropriate category for the Vietnam War.

Irving Greenberg, of the Orthodox Yeshiva University, argued that Jewish morality justified the war as long as it was needed to block aggressive communism which denied basic human dignity. However, Jewish law demands the minimalization of evil and who, more than the Jews, were "shattered by the sight of burning children." Therefore, Jews ought to promote a "neutralist or Titoist solution for South Vietnam."

Seymour Siegel, of the Conservative Jewish Theological Seminary, acknowledged that it was easier for Jews to make "discriminate judgments" about the Middle East than the Far East. Still, those difficulties did not absolve teachers of morality and religion "from making agonizing decisions" or from giving "concrete and wise guidance" to those responsible for making "the practical arrangements which make life possible." He recommended holding the Vietnamese conflict "within controllable bounds," while searching to end it in a manner which would "preserve the dignity of our adversary."

Reform Rabbi Arthur Lelyveld presented the most pacifist interpretation of Jewish law. He emphasized how remarkable Biblical distinctions were in light of the fact that they were analyzing "wars of survival for the people of the Covenant, and hence for the Covenant itself." Indeed, Judaism decreed that life should only be taken to preserve life or human dignity. Since modern mass warfare "inevitably" depreciated life, it was forbidden. He demanded that Johnson "desist" in Vietnam and declared that, as it was the obligation of Jews "to perfect the world," no Jew could ask "What's Vietnam to me or I to Vietnam?".

During the discussion period, it became clear that the divisions were as intra-organizational as they were inter-organizational. When Greenberg dared to note that most Orthodox Jews supported the President, Orthodox rabbis begged to differ. Similarly, Lelyveld's bitter denunciation of Johnson's conduct led a participant to exclaim: "I refuse to believe that our soldiers in Vietnam are murderers. And I refuse to believe that the President does not tell the truth to the American people." The rabbi identified himself as the spokesman of "Young Israel." He was immediately rebutted by yet another rabbi from the same organization who agreed wholeheartedly with Lelyveld.

The conference did not receive universal accolades; some criticized organizers for their failure to achieve a consensus, while others questioned the propriety of religious organizations taking a stand on a complicated global issue. Henry Siegman, the Vice President of the Synagogue Council, retorted: "That we disagreed in our conclusions is hardly surprising nor terribly relevant. What is significant is that in joining in this common search for justice we give expression to the true vocation of the religious personality. We may be criticized for our political expertise; that is a risk we must run. But let us not be faulted for having abandoned our moral obligations." The conference proceedings were distributed to synagogues, and follow-up regional conferences took place around the country.[2]

The desired scenario, however, was the one which took place at a Conservative synagogue in Highland Park, Illinois. There, a symposium on Vietnam followed the Friday night service during a week when college students were home for the holidays. Students, armed with the conference booklet, presented papers and debated the war "in specifically Jewish terms" in front of an audience of 300. When the formal discussion ended at midnight, students and elders entered into an informal discussion until the early hours of the morning. Again, there was little effort to reach a consensus and students had difficulty in deciding whether the war was mandatory, permissible or aggressive. Many seemed more comfortable debating whether the war served the "bedrock vital interest of the United States." Still, they based their demand for an end to the "needless carnage" by either the American army or the Viet Cong on the Jewish belief in the sanctity of life.[3]

Thus the debate served to inform the young of their religion, its relevance to their lives, and their rabbis' interest in the issues that affect it. Just as importantly, it provided students with a potential Jewish justification for claims of conscientious objection to the Vietnam war. Indeed, an increasing number of Jewish rabbis supported such claims with mixed results, in part because the Court held in U.S. *v*. Kauten that judgments about the aggressiveness of a war were political rather than moral.[4]

Still the Jewish Peace Fellowship, which was founded in 1941 and supported conscientious objectors, boomed during the Vietnam War. Nevertheless, there were also cases like that of army private Robert Levy, who after eighteen months of voluntary service in the medical corps, decided that his religious conviction as an Orthodox Jew no longer permitted him to serve in "an army practicing violence" in Vietnam. He went on a hunger strike. The army placed him in a mental institution because "it was unfair to bring religion into it."[5]

In any case, galvanized by their success with religious organizations, the anti-war rabbis turned their attention to lay organizations in an effort to activate against the war the entire Jewish community as a community and not merely as "an assemblage of persons who happen to be born Jewish." The fact that they were part of a wider "clerical wave of protest" laid to rest their concern that they might reawaken the ever present anti-Semitic monster. After all, when a rabbi tolled the bell for peace in Vietnam, he did it jointly with a Catholic priest and a Protestant chaplain.[6]

Their first target was the American Jewish Congress, an activist organization dedicated to "full and frank discussion of issues affecting the Jewish community." During the January 1966 bombing halt, its governing council adopted a policy statement on "Viet Nam and Peace" which called for an immediate ceasefire, negotiations with both the NLF and North Vietnam, and free elections in South Vietnam. By the time the statement was published, the bombing had resumed and the organization was careful to mention that it had been adopted during the halt.[7]

Three weeks later, caution was thrown to the wind with an appeal to the President to suspend the bombing and negotiate with all parties concerned. In the months leading to its April 1966 biennial convention, the anti-war forces led by the women's division, worked hard to secure a strong resolution. At the convention, president Joachim Prinz questioned whether it was advisable for Jewish organizations to take a public stand on issues not directly related to Judaism. After all, the March Vu Van Thai fiasco had already revealed the administration's sensitivity to Jewish peace agitation. Prinz was forced to retreat in the face of Arthur Lelyveld's insistence that civil rights and Vietnam were purely Jewish matters. The anti-war resolution not only passed but the organization undertook to mobilize American Jewry against the war under the leadership of its new president, Arthur Lelyveld.[8]

New York Congressman William Ryan asserted approvingly that no religious group had been "more outspoken" in its opposition to the war than "the Jewish community." But the Jewish War Veterans (JWV) vehemently disagreed: organizations critical of the war represented "only a vociferous minority" and had no right to speak in the name of "the Jewish community." Connecticut Senator Tom Dodd concurred. JWV commander Milton Waldor personally assured Johnson that during a thirty-one state lecture tour, he had found "overwhelming grassroots" Jewish support for the President's policy and promised to continue to rally Jewish support for the war. Johnson was "very delighted."[9]

The anti-war forces knew that the easiest way to sway the Jewish community "as such" was to argue that the price of dissent was increasing. Not only had Jewish commitment to dissent extended back to Abraham, but the prevalence of Jewish youth in the anti-war movement led their elders to do their utmost to eliminate the price of dissent. The Vietnam War, warned reform rabbi Albert Vorspan, would produce such "a dark and dangerous era" as would "make the McCarthyism of the 50's look, in retrospect, like a mild national aberration." Already Attorney General Nicholas Katzenbach had threatened to investigate, and possibly prosecute, demonstrators and J. Edgar Hoover had advocated maximizing the penalty for draft card burning. "And perhaps the most ominous of all" were instances of cancellation of protestors' draft deferments.[10]

It was "deliberate nonsense" to claim that there were "dangerous indications of rising McCarthyism" trying "to repress and deter dissent over Vietnam," retorted JWV's Monroe Sheinberg. In fact, there had never been a "more uninhibited discussion and less repression on a vital issue of world concern." He granted that some "ill-advised counteraction" had occurred, but what many dissenters demanded was not merely "freedom from repression" but immunity from criticism.[11]

To prove that the dissenting rabbis did not speak for their congregations, Sheinberg emphasized his own membership in a Reform synagogue. Indeed, many congregants did demand that their rabbis stick "to religious matters and keep out of politics." The response to Vorspan's call for Jewish anti-war mobilization also revealed the deep schism on the subject even within Reform Jewry. Correspondents were especially critical of any attempt to refer to or claim the right to speak for "the (organized or not) American Jewish community."[12]

The Jewish press corps could not but be impressed by the depth of the White House resentment of the Jewish anti-war agitation revealed during their June 1966 convention. Johnson himself told the editors that he deserved Jewish support because he had appointed Jews like Arthur Goldberg (who was present at the meeting) to high posts and "we gave you Hawk missiles, we gave you planes." Humphrey appealed not to Jewish gratitude but to ethnic interests: Chinese "wars of national liberation" threatened Israel as well as South Vietnam. Shukayri's visit to China, and his announcement of a PLO decision to send troops to fight alongside the NLF, helped buttress Humphrey's argument. Humphrey's speech, and Shukayri's pronouncements, received wide coverage in the Anglo-Jewish press, but were they enough to halt the progress of the anti-war rabbis?[13]

The first skirmish came at the June CCAR convention. The rabbis acknowledged the problem, but refused to back off:

> Reports that the National Liberation Front (Vietnam) and the Palestine Liberation Army (Arab) are collaborating in anti-Israel activities disturb us greatly. Our position on the Vietnam war favors negotiations with the NLF. We continue to affirm that position, but . . . we condemn any action by the National Liberation Front calculated to impair the security of the State of Israel and endanger peace in the Middle East.[14]

A reporter remarked that this resolution tried to ignore the inconsistency between criticizing NLF–PLO collaboration and calling for talks with the NLF. However, the rabbis' request that their fellow peace activists urge the NLF "to desist from support of anti-Israeli aggression" indicated that future ability to maintain their difficult position would depend on the response of the NLF and their peace camp allies.[15]

The major battle began at the plenary sessions of the conference of the National Community Relations Advisory Council (NCRAC), a central advisory body of eight national lay organizations. Peace advocates again used the "right of dissent" issue to rally NCRAC behind a statement critical of the administration. The draft resolution acknowledged that "opposing views" were being expressed more freely "than in comparable war-time periods of American history." However, any attempts to stifle dissent was "deplorable" for they might revive "the hysteria of the McCarthy period" which proved particularly dangerous "to minority groups." Moreover, dissenters should enjoy special protection because, without them, "pressing issues" would not be subjected to "close examination."[16]

Activists should debate the war "on its merits" and not harbor illusions of immunity from criticism, retorted the JWV. Public criticism of minorities, as the dissenters admitted, could indeed lead to "lynch mob mentality, vigilante spirit, mindless name calling and irrational chauvinism." Organizations which gave the impression that Jews as such opposed the war were not only distorting facts, but endangering the Jewish community.[17]

The JWV found itself in a minority of one. When JWV vetoed its adoption as a NCRAC resolution, the rest of the members (the

American Jewish Congress, the Anti-Defamation League, Jewish Labor Committee, National Council of Jewish Women, American Hebrew Congregations, United Synagogue of America and the Union of Orthodox Jewish Congregations of America including the mainstream B'nai B'rith and the Anti-Defamation League) issued the statement under their own auspices. Waldor informed Johnson that the JWV had "blocked" a resolution which sought to "exploit" the "dissent" issue. Johnson thanked him, reaffirmed that "no American" should be denied the right of dissent nor should any minority "ever be muzzled," but added that "each" had to know "why" he protested and "what" he dissented from. The Presidential answer was timed to reach JWV just prior to its August national convention. The JWV published it, along with a news release rehashing the June controversy.[18]

Throughout that summer, the Jewish leadership was remarkably adept in keeping the news of Johnson's disaffection with the Jewish anti-war activism from reaching the public. Only the communist *Morning Freiheit* picked up Marianne Means's article linking American aid to Israel to Jewish dissent. Johnson's Ellenville speech, reports that Johnson had pressured Shazar to mute Jewish opposition to the Vietnam War, and a press briefing at which Johnson discussed "the Jewish interest" in Vietnam left almost no traces in the media.[19]

Instead, AJC president Morris Abram met with "one of the President's principal advisors and urged him that the President be cautioned against making any such statements." The aide promised Abram that Johnson would never do so "in a serious vein and certainly not for the press." Reassured, Jewish organizations even convinced the World Jewish Congress (WJC) to pass an anti-war resolution. Nahum Goldmann, who considered the war "a catastrophe," warned that "misplaced self-confidence is dangerous for both the diaspora and Israel." But Jewish leaders were in no mood to listen.[20]

THE TARLOV INCIDENT

On September 6, 1966 newly elected JWV commander Malcolm Tarlov met with Lyndon Johnson. Johnson derided the "unusually vociferous" manner in which "the majority of the leaders of the American Jewish community" opposed his "Vietnam policies" and asked Tarlov to make his feelings "known to the appropriate persons within the Jewish community." Tarlov immediately held a news conference at which he reported the gist of Johnson's comments and requested a meeting with the Presidents' Conference.

The choice of the Conference, a body created for consultations on Israeli–American relations, seemed to legitimize a connection Jewish leaders were determined to avoid. Indeed, members of the Presidents' Conference angrily charged Tarlov with a "lack of discipline" and a "disregard for the interests of the Jewish community." The commander retorted that "anyone selected as President Johnson's emissary would have had to make the same kind of report to the Conference." However, accusations did not emanate from the content of the report but from Tarlov's willingness to discuss the "Jewish position on the war," his promise to explain to the "Jewish community" how important their support for the war was to Jews in Israel and the Soviet Union and, most importantly, his holding of a press conference on the forbidden subject.[21]

First reports of the Tarlov press conference reached Jewish organizations on September 7. As AJC director of domestic affairs Nathan Perlmutter wrote Abram, the Tarlov statement remained even "after re-reading and re-reading, an extraordinary statement – both in its own terms and in terms of its source." Mistakenly assuming it to be a mere indiscretion, Perlmutter suggested that "a private meeting" with men known to Johnson as friends might "well move him to greater sensitivity – to his own as well as the Jewish community's interests." Abram promptly called Bill Moyers to offer his "assistance" in correcting "any false impressions" that might have arisen from the story which he "felt" had to be "incorrect, taken out of context or even distorted."[22]

He reached only White House aide Doug Cater who, after checking with Moyers, said only that Johnson had not spoken for publication. The Executive Director of the American Council for Judaism (ACJ), Elmer Berger, was similarly informed by the White House that it was "very difficult to 'track down'" the origin of the story since there was "no written record of the alleged conversations." Obviously, the President was not anxious to correct "false impressions."[23]

Two days later, "a *rumor*" that the White House had asked "Abe Feinberg to get together several leading Jews in order to discuss the implications of the statement" reached Perlmutter. Sensitive to organizational politics, Perlmutter suggested that since "the transmission belt for the presidential statement was a small and not very highly regarded Jewish agency, the transmission outlet for the denial" would be "a long established and highly regarded Jewish agency." In the meantime, Boris Smolar, the editor in chief of *JTA*; Joachim Prinz, the head of the Presidents' Conference; and John Slawson, the Executive Vice President of the AJC, decided to make use of a *Morning Freiheit* article stressing the blackmail aspect of the story. The communist outlet charged that Johnson valued Soviet Jews and Israel "only for the price" of "support of his reckless ventures," and accused him of playing into the "hands of anti-Semites." The three reasoned that if Johnson should become aware that the *Freiheit* was likely to be read by Soviet officials, "he would readily see that the Soviet Union could make considerable hay out of the statement" which provided it with "one helluva response" to "charges" that it was "anti-Semitic."[24]

The strategy was partially effective. Abram called McPherson and, the very next day, William Wexler and Jay Kaufman of B'nai B'rith were ushered into Johnson's office to discuss the "published reports." They found a defiant President who told them that he did not condition his support for Israel on the behavior of American Jewry, but that he thought Jewish leaders were not "repaying" him for that support in the expected manner. They promised "to release a statement" clarifying the issue.[25]

In the meantime, the media "accentuated the sense of anxiety and anger felt by many in the Jewish community" with erroneous reports that Israel supported Johnson's policies in Vietnam and opposed Jewish anti-war activities. Wexler and Kaufman tried to diffuse matters by issuing a statement expressing their belief that Johnson's words were "either misunderstood or poorly interpreted to the news media," that American Middle Eastern policy did not depend on the behavior of American Jews, and that they regretted that the "Right to Dissent" resolution had been "misinterpreted or distorted to imply a Jewish viewpoint on the Vietnam issue itself." As Berger noted, "in this embarrassing emergency," those who had regularly supported "Jewish unity," had reversed their position and begun stressing Jewish diversity.[26]

On September 13, Jewish leaders met with Goldberg and Feinberg to demand that the President "offer a public disavowal of these alleged statements." Goldberg countered that it would be "inappropriate" to ask Johnson to deny remarks he either did not make or did not authorize for publication. The President, Goldberg argued, was not trying to "blackmail" Jews but merely to predict the "ultimate impact" their anti-Vietnam activity would have on American Middle Eastern policy.

Encouraged by Johnson's firm stand, Tarlov reaffirmed the validity of his original report, adding that the JWV would build "grassroots support" for the war, especially within "those groups where organizational positions do not necessarily reflect rank and file attitudes." Finally, his advisors' pressure, and the avalanche of letters which inundated the White House and Congress, convinced Johnson to authorize McPherson to deny the connection between Jewish activism and American policy towards Israel. The vehicle was an October 7 letter to an Ohio college student.[27]

However, what worried and united American Jews was the revelation of the fragility of their own position. One constituent complained to Johnson: "I can't understand how you can single out one group of people because of their critical remarks and statements from various members of their clergy and organizations, since I hear no such comments from you or your office about members of your own party no matter what their religion." "By the bitter experience of their fellow-Jews in Germany and elsewhere" wrote columnist Max Lerner, Jews had learned that a "group label" led "to group libel." Few were amused by the button slogan: "You don't have to be Jewish to be against the war in Vietnam."[28]

A hastily conducted Gallup poll demonstrated that Jews were like everybody else. When asked whether they approved of Johnson's Vietnamese policies, 43 percent of all Americans as compared to 41 percent of the Jews approved. 40 percent of all Americans as compared to 41 percent of the Jews disapproved. The result might have been skewed by the question as some respondents advocating escalation of the war opposed the President's policies, and others who favored de-escalation supported him in the belief that he was doing his best to achieve peace. A lesser known 1967 survey later found that 48 percent of American Jews opposed US military involvement in Vietnam as compared to 29 percent of West European Catholics, 26 percent of Southern European Catholics, 17 percent of West European Protestants, 15 percent of Long-time American Protestants-Catholics and 7 percent of East European Catholics.[29]

THE RESPONSE

Two separate questions confronted the Jewish leadership: (1) Which organizational structure would best safeguard the community? (2) On which considerations should Jewish response to the Vietnam War be based?

Jewish opinion was decidedly mixed. Gilbert H. Liberman wrote: "Of course the Jewish community (most of it) is against your Vietnam policy. And why not? It's treacherous, murderous, futile, cynical, naive, blundering and aggressive. But then again, it's hard to find a non-Jew who feels otherwise." But the editors of the *Jewish Forward* were not alone in concluding that since anti-war activists had frequently made known their position "in the name of Jewish organizations," "it was only right that the other side also make its stand known and eradicate the false impression that most Jews opposed the administration policy." Indeed, many correspondents combined their objections to Johnson's remarks with expressions of support: "I am a Jew, and although I have substantial doubts about where our present policy in Vietnam would lead us, I do see the practical necessity and I do support it," wrote Harold Miller. Entertainer George Jessel sent Johnson an article describing Jews fighting and dying in Vietnam.[30]

One thing was certain. Plans for a fall Jewish anti-war conference were postponed "until the passing of the storm," as was a *NYT* ad circulated by Heschel stating that "As Americans and as Jews we call upon our government to stop the war and then make peace in Viet Nam." Jewish intellectual anti-war sentiment remained strong: A Boston area poll found that 73 percent of the Jewish professors opposed the war, as compared to 13 percent of the Catholic and 28 percent of the Protestant ones. Nor did organizations which were on the record as opposed to the war modify their stance because "after the threat it became important to stand up" and not "be intimidated." But no additional organizations joined their ranks, in part because constituents no longer accepted the leadership's right to speak for them but demanded that "as a matter of fairness and accuracy" the members be polled on any important controversial issue.[31]

Did the rediscovered Jewish vulnerability mandate a more or less cohesive organizational structure? The drive for a Jewish position on Vietnam was part of a larger experiment with Jewish ecumenism. In 1964, 25 leading Jewish organizations founded the American

Jewish Conference on Soviet Jewry. In April 1966, the Conference of Presidents joined the WJC and became a decision-making body whose members had the right to represent their organizations. The Tarlov incident certainly enabled Berger to argue that Johnson's warning proved yet again that claims of Jewish unity invariably led to expectations of payment for services rendered.[32]

Others drew the opposite conclusion. Rabbi Judah Cahn insisted that an "organized Jewish community" was "a necessary evil," and Philip Klutznick contended that Jewish divisions permitted Johnson to ignore the community during normal times and manipulate it during abnormal ones. He suggested that periodic meetings between a subcommittee of the Conference and a presidential representative replace *ad hoc* meetings of individual leaders with the President, Feinberg or Goldberg. Feinberg agreed, discussed the suggestion with Moyers, but it was decided to delay its implementation "so that it would not seem that the President succumbed to pressure." In December, the job of Jewish ombudsman went to Harry McPherson.[33]

Humphrey's confidant Max Kampelman remarked: "The Tarlov incident was a warning shot to the Jewish community to shut up. It could have been a warning shot from a friend. . . . and I did not think it had bad consequences."[34] Those consequences included an article by philosophy professor Michael Wyschogrod accusing American Jews of "moral dereliction" for failing to consider the "Jewish self-interest in the Vietnamese situation." "There cannot be a defensible notion of justice without the recognition of a legitimate self interest," he chastised.

Two aspects of the Vietnamese situation, argued Wyschogrod, interested Jews: First, a communist victory in Vietnam would enhance Soviet influence and Soviet communism carried the "danger of cultural extermination" as demonstrated by the fate of Jews living under communist rule. Second, both Israel and South Vietnam were created by artificial splits of a geographic entity. In both cases, only one side was "willing to abide by the *status quo*" and "the themes of national liberation" had been sounded. Also, "the sympathy of the world Communist movement" belonged to those who opposed the status quo and that of "the Western world" to those who supported it. In both cases, peace rested "on the aggressors resigning themselves to the existence of borders they" did not like.

That this parallel did not escaped the notice of Arabs or Israelis, but did not escape the notice of American Jews, meant that the community lacked "the almost instinctual reflexes that come into play when the vital interests of a group are threatened." If such was the case, it meant that many Jews "no longer identify as Jews on this visceral level" and that posed a danger which extended "far beyond any individual issue, be it Vietnam or anything else."[35]

In his response to Wyschogrod, Charles Liebman agreed that liberal Jews had indeed "lost a sense of visceral identification as Jews." But, argued Liebman, an NLF victory would strengthen Chinese rather than Soviet communism and Israel was not endangered by "internal revolution," or by "a Palestinian Liberation Front" but by the surrounding Arab countries. Nor were Shukayri, Nasser or Hussein restrained by American guarantees but rather by the strength of the Israeli army. American policy would be dictated by its national interests. In any case, the peace movement's motto was "stop the bombing," not "pull out of Vietnam."

The 1967 Middle Eastern crisis (though not the Six Day War) erupted before Liebman's finished his article. He therefore had the opportunity to raise an important question, the answer to which would have a profound effect on subsequent Jewish history:

> Events of the past few weeks only strengthen the argument against Wyschogrod. But advocates of peace in Vietnam also stand before a test. Will they demand American support of Israel in the current crisis, thus demonstrating that their concern in both the Middle East and Vietnam is a moral one? Or will they retreat to isolationism and indifference thereby suggesting that their stance in Vietnam was motivated by cowardice rather than morality?[36]

NOTES

1. Albert Vorspan, "Vietnam and Jewish Conscience," *American Judaism* (Passover, 1966), 9.
2. *Judaism and World Peace; Focus Viet Nam*, (New York: 1966), 38–41; *Jewish Exponent*, Jan. 31, 1966; *JTA*, Feb. 23, 1966.
3. "The Jewish Attitude Towards the Vietnam War," *Jewish Currents* (March 1967), 4–7.
4. Sherry Gershon Gottlieb, *Hell No, We Won't Go!* (New York: 1991), 166 and 245; and Berl Wein, "Jewish Conscientious Objectors and the Vietnamese War," *Jewish Life,* (Sept.–Oct. 1969), 24.
5. *JTA*, March 1, 1967.

6. Charles DeBenedetti, *An American Ordeal* (Syracuse: 1990), 145.
7. "Viet Nam and Peace," *Congress Bi-Weekly* (Feb. 7, 1966), 3.
8. *NYT*, Feb. 27, 66; and Diane Winston, "Vietnam and the Jews" in Jack Nusan Porter, ed., *The Sociology of American Jews* (Washington, 1980), 199–200.
9. *Congressional Record – Appendix,* April 7, 1977, A2065 and May 23, 1966, 11175; and *JTA*, Feb. 23, April 27, 1966 and May 27, 1966.
10. Vorspan, "Vietnam and the Jewish Conscience," 8.
11. Monroe R. Sheinberg, "Memo from National," *Jewish Veteran* (May 1966), 4.
12. Garfield I. Kass to Rabbi Maurice N. Eisendrath, Oct. 29, 1969 (it referred to a June 1966 letter of similar content), AJC, Vietnam, 68–9, YIVO; and "Letters to the Editor," *American Judaism* (Fall 1966), 4 and 41.
13. *Haaretz*, June 5, 1966; *JTA*, June 10, 1966; and *Near East Report*, June 14, 1966.
14. *Central Conference of American Rabbis Yearbook* (Toronto: 1967), 54.
15. Ibid. and *JTA*, June 23, 1966.
16. *Right of Protest and Dissent*, June 27, 1966, AJC, Vietnam, JSX 63–8, YIVO.
17. *JTA*, June 27, 1966. A similar argument was made by Ralph Bunche when he rebuked Martin Luther King for mixing up the civil rights and the peace movements. Brian Urquhart, *Ralph Bunche* (New York: 1993), 388–9.
18. *JTA*, June 27, 1966; and JWV, *News*, Aug. 21, 1966, AJC, Vietnamese War/J, AJCL.
19. "Johnson and His Jewish Critics," *The Nation*, Sept. 26, 1966, 268; and *NYT*, Sept. 16, 1966.
20. Minutes, AJC Bd of Governors, Oct. 66, AJC, Co/Vietnam, YIVO; *Maariv*, Aug. 10, 1966; and Harry McPherson to Morris Abram, Oct. 3, 1966, WHCF, RM3-2, box 7, LBJL.
21. "*A Statement by the Executive Committee of the Associations of the Jewish Chaplains*," Oct. 24, 1966, WHCF, ND 19/CO 312. box 268, LBJL.
22. Nathan Perlmutter to Morris Abram, Sept. 7, 1966; *Haaretz*, Sept. 23, 1966; and Morris Abram to the President, Sept. 14, 1966, AJC, F, Co/Vietnam, box 81, YIVO.
23. Minutes, AJC Bd of Governors, Oct. 66; and letter to the President from Richard Korn, the President of ACJ, Sept. 13, 1966, AJC, F Co/Vietnam, JSX 63–8, YIVO.
24. To Morris Abram and Nathan Perlmutter from Lucy S. Dawidowicz, "*Freiheit* on President Johnson's remark to JWV," Sept. 9, 1966, AJC, F Co/Vietnam, JSX 63–8, YIVO.
25. Bick, "Ethnic Linkages," 205; and President's Appointment File, Sept. 13, 1966, WHCH, box 44, LBJL.
26. *NYT*, Sept. 13, 1966; and "Can the US Rights of Jews be Traded for Aid to Israel?" Oct. 1966, AJC, Vietnam, AJCL.
27. *JTA*, Sept. 20 and Oct. 7, 1966.
28. Ira Dabrow to the President, Sept. 14, 66, WHCF, Gen ND19/Co312, box 267, LBJL; Max Lerner, "We're Caught in a Crossfire," *The Jewish*

Ledger, Sept. 23, 1966; and *American Jewish Yearbook, 1966,* 80.

29. *Near East Review*, Oct. 4, 1966, 79; and Isaacs, *Jews and American Politics*, 101.
30. The letters to the President, the White House responses, and Anglo-Jewish press coverage of the incident can be found in WHCF, ND19/Co312, box 267, LBJL.
31. David Ariel, Sept, 28, 1966, Israeli–Asian relations, Vietnam, Yad Eshkol; Abraham Heschel to John Slawson, Sept 9, 1966; and Nathan D. Shapiro to Benjamin R. Epstein, Sept. 20, 1966, AJC F Co/ Vietnam, JSX 63–68, YIVO, "Professors' Attitudes towards the Vietnam War," *Public Opinion Quarterly* (Summer 1967), 159–75; and Winston, "Vietnam and the Jews," 202.
32. Richard Korn to Rabbi Jacob Weinstein, President of CCAR, Sept. 22, 66, AJC F Co/Vietnam, YIVO.
33. *NYT*, Oct. 2 and Sept. 16, 1966; Philip Klutznick to Abraham Feinberg, Sept. 19, 1966, Abraham Feinberg to Philip Klutznick Sept. 28, 1966, CF, Israel, box 139, LBJL; and *JTA*, Dec. 10, 1966.
34. Interview with Max Kampelman.
35. Interview with Max Kampelman (Oct. 15, 1991); and Michael Wyschogrod, "The Jewish Interest in Vietnam," *Tradition* (Winter 1966), 5–18.
36. Liebman, "Judaism and Vietnam," *Tradition*, (Spring–Summer, 1967), 155–60.

Part III
Blow Up

7 America Rejects a Second Front

THE SOVIET CHALLENGE

On April 6, Johnson sent a letter to Hanoi via Moscow. It was opened, returned, but not acknowledged. It was too late. China had taken steps to reopen the arms supply routes to North Vietnam and Hanoi had regained her confidence in military victory. Concluding that the time had come to increase the pressure on Hanoi and her allies, Johnson cancelled the bombing prohibition within ten miles of Hanoi and Haiphong (where Soviet supply ships abounded). Brezhnev, however, was determined not "to sink in the swamps of Vietnam."[1]

On April 25, he told European communists gathered in Karlovy-Vary that peace in Europe could not be separated from the global struggle. Vietnamese patriots "were dealing telling blows" to the US by pinning "down" substantial American forces and undermining "the U.S.A.'s prestige and political positions throughout the world." The time had come to assist Third World "liberation struggles" by inflicting a defeat on imperialism "that would be felt everywhere." He then called "for the demand that the U.S. Sixth Fleet be withdrawn from the Mediterranean to ring out at full strength."[2]

Plans to integrate NATO navies in the Eastern Mediterranean under US command did not find favor in the Soviet military, especially after Brezhnev's man, Andrei Grechko, became Defense Minister in April 1967. Grechko had fought in the Northern Caucasus during World War II and possessed an acute appreciation of the strategic value of the Middle East.[3] At the end of March, Gromyko made a sudden visit to Nasser "to discuss also the problems of UNEF on the UAR–Israeli border." Their joint communiqué expressed the two men's concern with "the aggression against the Vietnamese people" and predicted that their determination to oppose efforts to "check" other national liberation struggles would "have an influence on events in Vietnam."[4] On May 9, Soviet news agencies reported an imminent "Zionist-imperialist-reactionary" threat to the Syrian regime. On May 12–13, Soviet officials began spreading false information concerning Israeli troop concentration on the Syrian border. In short, to take advantage of the American single front strategy, and/or relieve the pressure on Vietnam as Brezhnev reportedly told Polish and East German leaders Gomulka and Ulbricht, the Middle East was chosen as the location for a decisive "anti-imperialist blow."[5]

Retreating Atlanticists such as Brzezinski, and Defense experts like McNaughton and Nitze, warned that the intensified bombing of Hanoi "would lead to increased Soviet pressure on Berlin or even some kind of general war with the Soviet Union."[6] On April 13, ambassador Dobrynin was recalled because "his policy towards the United States was too soft." Then, he helped convince Llewelyn Thompson that Moscow had adopted a "new hard anti-U.S. line." The Hungarian charge d'affaires, Janos Radvanyi, got so agitated by prospects of a superpower collision that he asked for political asylum.[7]

The administration had expected the Soviet countermove to come in Berlin, where the Soviets could control the crisis better and where their conventional forces enjoyed a significant advantage. But this overlooked the damage such a move would do to Soviet–French relations, not to mention its potential in uniting NATO. A move against NATO's southern flank was bound to exacerbate the argument over the organization's relations with Mediterranean states and provide ammunition to Atlanticists who, as the President complained, were "saying that we are over-emphasizing Asia."[8]

When Eugene Rostow joined State, Rusk asked him to study the Korean settlement. He discovered Eisenhower's use of the nuclear card. On May 15, Washington decided to try it by publicizing a June 1965 remark Johnson had made to the effect that "he might go down in history as having started World War III." Moscow retorted that the story was obviously designed "to scare somebody" by implying that Washington was "ready to take any risk," and warned that "attempts to frighten the Vietnamese people" or "other people" would fail. The *Washington Post* carried the "World War III" story on the same page where it reported the Egyptian two-prong challenge to American Middle Eastern allies: A) Cairo not only bombed Yemeni guerrilla bases within Saudi borders but, for the first time, admitted doing so and B) Egyptian troops marched into the Sinai and Nasser demanded that UNEF withdraw from it.[9]

Not being "naive," the administration identified "the Soviet fingerprints" in Nasser's actions. It also recognized the similarity between Vietnam, the "wars of national liberation" raging on Israeli and Saudi borders, and the increased guerrilla activity in Latin America. Thus, Johnson's May 19 letter to Kosygin suggested that the superpowers undertake "concerted or parallel action" to contain "a series of situations" brought about by Hanoi's support for the NLF, Damascus's backing of FATAH, and Havana's aid to insurgents in Venezuela. For "taken together," they might seriously "impair" Soviet–American relations. Though the superpowers were not in full control of these conflicts, Johnson concluded, their joint influence was "formidable."[10]

To emphasize American steadfastness, Johnson hinted at a possible widening of the war in Vietnam and did not cancel the bombing of the Hanoi power plant. Similar motivations led sixteen "dovish" Senators to declare that Hanoi, Beijing and Moscow should know that they did "not favor unilateral withdrawal from Vietnam." They did favor bombing cessation and, that same day, McNamara joined their ranks. He presented Johnson with a "radical" memorandum which precipitated "an administration-wide" Atlanticist–Pacificist debate on "the fundamental issues" of American Vietnamese policy, a debate conducted in the shadow of the Mideast crisis.[11]

Unhappy with the terms of the debate, and anxious not to "commit American forces in the Middle East too," the administration hoped to separate Nasser from Moscow with promises of generous economic aid.[12] The first offer was carried by UN General Secretary U Thant, a man deeply resentful of "the white man's aggressiveness" in Vietnam whose response to Nasser's request for UNEF withdrawal reflected his sympathy for the Soviet and French positions connecting the two Asian crises. Without a critical word, U Thant had ordered the complete withdrawal of UNEF within hours of receiving the Egyptian request. He refused to invoke article 99 of the UN Charter authorizing him to bring to the attention of the Security Council any matter which might "threaten the maintenance of international peace and security," and even agreed to Nasser's request not to bring his *American* assistant Ralph Bunche to Cairo.

Lacking an ambassador in Cairo, Johnson had few alternatives. In the meantime, he refused Israeli requests to issue "unilateral United States assurances." Even Israeli warnings of the dire consequences of "any interference with Israeli shipping through the Gulf of Aqaba" were transmitted only to Jiddah and Amman. Eugene Rostow did tell the Soviet charge that Washington knew that Moscow was spreading "very dangerous and inflammatory" stories about

Israeli troop concentration on the Syrian border. But when asked "Is that a warning?," he answered "its just a friendly exchange."[13]

These moves backfired. They reflected, as Harold Saunders later wrote, an administration resolved to avoid involvement in "another war . . . *at all cost*" and determined to restrain Israel for fear that it might get "in over its head and ask for help in the middle of the Vietnam war."[14] So, on May 21, Nasser told his aides that he no longer believed that the expulsion of UNEF, or even the closure of the Straits of Tiran, would result in war: Israel knew that the United States was too deeply involved in Vietnam to come to her aid and she would not fight without US support because it feared the Soviet Union.[15]

Moscow agreed. For, on May 22, *Pravda* ended a week long silence with a front page article summarizing the official decision reached by both the Central Committee and Communist Party. "Events in the Middle East," wrote Victor Mayevski, were closely linked with the intensified US bombing in Vietnam, and with "the preparation by the USA of new provocations against Cuba." Moscow did not expect Israel to act without American support but, if she did, the Soviets would undertake the "necessary measures." To underline the point, the Soviets informed Turkey of their plans to augment their Mediterranean fleet.[16]

While U Thant was on his way to Cairo, Nasser announced the closure of the Straits. But even Goldberg advised him to ignore the snub and continue his mission. Once in Cairo, U Thant advised Nasser to present "the UAR case . . . in the light of the Big-Power play" and agreed to issue an appeal for a cooling off period on terms which, the horrified Bunche complained, placed him "in the position of effectively endorsing the blockade and fully implementing it without any further effort by Nasser."[17] Apparently, U Thant was amongst those who hoped that the crisis would provide both a spur and a cover for a superpower deal which would secure peace in both parts of Asia.

Suddenly, a May 20 JCS Worldwide Posture Paper including "reservations concerning the ability of the United States to meet worldwide military commitments and contingencies beyond" Vietnam acquired a new significance. Since deterrence had failed, there was no escaping a serious exploration of the military option. There was none, insisted the military. There was one, retorted McNamara, but it should not be used.[18]

The debate came to the fore during the May 24 NSC meeting.

Johnson asked McNamara to appraise the situation. The secretary insisted that there was "no substance" to the notion that the US could not "manage" both crises at the same time. But when asked for a "detailed rundown" of the military option, JCS chairman General Earle Wheeler, without overtly disagreeing with McNamara, explained that "it would be harder to open the Gulf of Aqaba" than had been assumed:

> We have a powerful naval force in the Mediterranean; that out [*sic*] land forces are few, limited to about 1400 Marines now in Naples, three days away; that our nearest ASW unit is two weeks away, since we cannot send one through the Suez Canal; that the UAR coastal battery and naval and air forces in the Red Sea will be the units employed to blockade the Gulf of Aqaba; that we will have trouble with overflight and staging rights in Turkey, Libya and Spain if we have to introduce our own ground forces.[19]

Nor was this assessment kept secret from either Congress or the public. The *NYT* reported that military leaders informed Congress repeatedly that the Sixth Fleet was "under strength in planes and pilots. In any protracted major shooting war, it would soon suffer from lack of ground forces, replacement aircraft, pilots, ammunition and in general the sinews of combat." The military blamed the failure to mobilize, and "McNamara's insistence on using up inventories of weapons and supplies and holding down production" for the absence of much of a "cushion." Israel, it insisted, could take care of itself.[20]

The crisis's depressant effect on the war in Vietnam was annoyance enough. Not only were requests for the expansion of the bombing, and the mining of coastal harbors and waters, turned down but the May 22 closing of the Straits brought a 24 hour complete bombing pause followed by the re-imposition of the 10 mile bombing exclusion zone around Hanoi. Complaints that just when the pressure on North Vietnam had been increasing, and weather conditions were "optimum," the military had to "back off" fell on deaf ears. In such a high risk global poker game, an American president lacking a crucial Mideast military high card, had to keep the stakes as low as possible, at least until the Soviets revealed their hand.[21]

BUYING TIME

Moscow had adroitly avoided clarifying the extent of its support for Egypt; Nasser showed no interest in a Western brokered deal, and Israeli warnings led to expectations of an immediate military action to open the Straits. Lyndon Johnson turned to his Jewish friends to help him buy time. He asked Feinberg and Harman (who was in Washington) to go to Goldberg's New York apartment and await his phone call. Feinberg recalled: "The President talked to us on the phone between 10 p.m. until 2 a.m. There were about half a dozen phone calls. He pleaded with Israel to give him time to organize the allies to break the blockade on the Straits. Harman called Israel. Military action was forestalled for a time, giving Johnson a chance to try." In return, Johnson promised to deliver a policy statement supportive of Israel and to release an aid package he had personally held up four days earlier.[22]

The statement afforded yet another demonstration of Johnson's political skills. John Roche recalled: "Here he [Johnson] called me up in the middle of the night and asked me to come in. . . . The State Department had prepared a draft for him which was the most incredible document. . . . It didn't cut ice at all." Roche revised the draft by eliminating "as much of the conditional-subjunctive" as was possible "short of issuing an ultimatum." Walt Rostow approved the redraft. But Johnson wanted to immunize himself from future criticism.

Throughout the day, callers were treated to a reading of State's draft, followed by "they think this is the kind of thing I ought to say. How does it sound to you?" Not good. Johnson delivered the Roche version. He declared the blockade of Israeli shipping to be illegal and "potentially disastrous to the cause of peace," expressed his opposition to any "overt" or "clandestine aggression," and reiterated his commitment to oppose aggression in Vietnam. Israelis and their friends issued a sigh of relief.[23]

No one dared point out its failure to balance the Soviet statement issued earlier that day. The latter blamed "imperialists" for "activating" Israel, expressed support for "the Arab countries in their just struggle for national liberation," and cautioned that whoever unleashed "aggression" in the Near East would "encounter not only the united strength of the Arab countries" but that of the USSR and its allies.[24]

Concern about the American "physical capacity to take on another major commitment in addition to Vietnam" dominated the May 23 executive session meeting between Dean Rusk and the Senate Foreign Relations Committee. Noting that "a two continent war" was even worse than "a two-front war," the Senators insisted that the administration chose between them. Pacificist Rusk tried to avoid assigning "a priority," but Fulbright urged Rusk to "try a unilateral and possibly unannounced cessation of bombing as a step towards gradual disengagement." Symington preferred to "prosecute the Vietnamese war to the fullest" in order "to bring it to an early conclusion." Escalate or de-escalate, but get the war over quickly so that you can take care of the more important Middle East was the Senatorial consensus. Upon leaving the session, Rusk was already "pressed for comment on Symington's statement that the United States might have to 'make a choice' between the Middle East and the Far East." He insisted that the question had not "arisen." Furious Johnson wanted the Senators to know that "this kind of music in the Senate was just what Kosygin" wanted to hear.[25]

Johnson asked "whether or not the Soviets had staged this Middle Eastern Crisis, the trouble in Hong Kong, and other diversions simultaneously to force" the US to turn its "attention from Vietnam?" CIA director Richard Helms joined Wheeler in denying "Soviet calculation," though the Soviets were sure to regard the new regional crisis "as godsend." But NEA director and former ambassador to Egypt Luke Battle doubted that Nasser would have acted that provocatively without substantial Soviet support.

Of course, an admission of Soviet culpability would prove the Atlanticist point that American concentration on the Pacific endangered its European, i.e. Middle Eastern, interests. Insistence that Israel could take care of herself eliminated the need to reorient American Pacificist policy. But Goldberg and McNamara doubted Israeli ability to take care of herself. McNamara feared that she might need to be resupplied during the war, and that Egypt would be supplied with Soviet-piloted aircraft. On May 24, the organization of an international flotilla to open the Straits was the only operative idea, but no one had much faith in it. Rusk tried to maintain calm by saying that the situation was "serious but not . . . desperate."[26]

Perhaps not, but there was no way to separate the two crises. When the Security Council met the following day, Fedorenko accused the West of trying to create a crisis where none existed so that it could become an "international policeman" and pursue policies in "many areas of the world fittingly described as an expression of 'arrogance of power.'" He refused to participate in private UN consultations, though Moscow had yet to turn down French proposals for a four power conference on the Middle East.[27]

Pacificists accused the Soviets of stirring up "trouble not only in Vietnam, but elsewhere close to the Communist frontiers, but far from the US." Atlanticists expressed the "grim hope" that the new emergency would deescalate the bombing of North Vietnam. After all, "a debate" on the Middle East" was preferable to "a showdown" in Vietnam.[28] When Johnson flew to Canada, Prime Minister Lester Pearson insisted on "peace talks with Hanoi as well as on ways to settle the current Middle East problem."[29] Reports were also reaching Rusk that Soviet officials had told British Foreign Secretary George Brown that Moscow would participate in four-power talks on the Middle East only if the Vietnam war was "tackled with similar urgency." Rusk hurriedly cabled his willingness to join talks on how tensions could "be lessened in both the Middle East and Vietnam" but "on a bilateral repeat bilateral basis."[30]

Bilateral was the key word because, as Johnson lamented, Canadians and Europeans would "not accept responsibility . . . they say it's not their trouble, and why should they get in the middle east now, too." Washington had acted alone in Vietnam and might be forced to do so again in the Middle East; or would it? Johnson asked Walt Rostow to "compile a collection of every statement" he had ever made on Israel.[31] The US, Rostow concluded, was committed: "a) to prevent Israel from being destroyed and (b) to stop aggression – either through the UN or on our own." The June 3, 1964 presidential promise that "just as the U.S. was in Southeast Asia, they would be wherever they were needed . . . it was important that there should be a feeling of security on Israel's part" was included amongst the "private face-to-face assurances."[32]

When Rusk told the Senators that the US "had no treaty obligation" towards Israel, although it might have a "moral or national interest obligations," he got an earful. Joseph Clark stated that "the blunt fact" was that the American people would "not stand for the destruction of Israel." Albert Gore added that such destruction was not in the American interest. Mike Mansfield and Frank Lausche pointedly asked "about the relevance of the Senate's 1957 Middle East Resolution."[33]

The 1957 Middle East Senate Resolution, better known as the Eisenhower Doctrine, authorized the president "to use force to assist any nation" in the Middle East "against aggression from any country controlled by international communism." During the 1964 debate over the Gulf of Tonkin Resolution, George McGovern expressed concern over the broad and open ended authority the resolution gave the president. Richard Russell noted that the resolution had "precedents in those adopted at the time of the crisis in Formosa, at the time of Crisis in the Middle East, and also in connection with Cuba." The "power" of those resolutions, he added, remained "in existence" since Congress had never "annulled" them. Humphrey agreed, and the three resolutions were printed in parallel column form in the *Congressional Record*.[34]

In 1964, Wayne Morse opposed both resolutions as unconstitutional "undated declarations of war." However, on May 23, 1967, Morse demanded that the US act according to the spirit of the Middle Eastern one because "a reading of the entire resolution" would make "perfectly clear" that it meant "opposition to all aggression." Therefore, the president had "an obligation to announce our support for Israel by our air power, Marines and Navy if called on."[35] Morse was a prime example of the "interesting reversal of roles." Rusk observed: "Doves have become hawks and vice versa." That did not make him wrong. Indeed, Luke Battle thought it "odd" that the Eisenhower Doctrine was "almost never mentioned during the Arab–Israeli War."[36]

If so, it was because Johnson planned to use the Congress as an excuse to back out of American commitments to Israel. The US had insisted that Israel consult with her before acting and Eban was coming to consult. Unknown to Johnson, Eban had a 1957 draft of a statement Golda Meir had made in the UN prior to the Israeli withdrawal from the Sinai. It stated that "interference, by armed force, with ships of Israel flag . . . through the Straits of Tiran" would "be regarded by Israel as an attack entitling it to exercise its inherent right of self defense . . . by armed force." The last three words were in John Foster Dulles's handwriting, and the document indicated that "if there was a violation (of the freedom of passage in the Straits) the United States could be counted upon to help out."[37]

Johnson sent a messenger to Gettysburg to see if Eisenhower would sanction some backtracking. Eisenhower not only refused but held a press conference affirming "that the Israelis' right of access to the Gulf of Aqaba was definitely part of the 'commitment' we had made to them." This meant that if Israel used force to open the Straits, the US not only could not regard her as an aggressor but was under a strong moral obligation to assist her.[38]

Since Johnson had asked Israel to stay her hand, He would have to tell Eban: 1. What he could offer that would be "better than a preemptive strike?" 2. How would the U.S. "guarantee Israeli security" in case Israel agreed to "exhaust diplomatic possibilities?" Already Israel had information that the UAR was about to initiate hostilities. The US sent urgent cables to Moscow, Cairo and Damascus but their effectiveness was uncertain.[39] On May 26, Rusk revised the American commitment: "Israel will not be alone unless it decides to go alone," to which Johnson added that he could not imagine that she would so decide. International action under the auspices of the UN or the maritime nations would provide the answer to the first question. The second, Johnson would argue, did not depend on him alone but also on Congress.[40]

At his meeting with Eban, Johnson declared the Dulles check, along with all others written by US Presidents, "not worth five cents" without public and Congressional support. Without the Congress, Johnson said, he was "just a six-foot-four Texan." He was "not a feeble mouse or a coward:" he would do what was "right" and secure Congressional support despite "the Vietnam trauma." There was no hurry because Israel would "whip the hell out of them." Ignoring Dulles' commitment, he emphasized "the necessity for Israel not to make itself responsible for the initiation of hostilities."[41]

He did not expect Eban to buy into the performance. "Israel is going to hit," Johnson told his advisors. But that did not displease them. At dinner that night, Johnson boasted:

> They came loaded for bear, but so was I. I let them talk for the first hour, and I just listened, and then I finished it up the last 15 minutes. Scy McNamara said he just wanted to throw his cap up in the air, and George Christian said it was the best meeting of the kind he had ever sat on.[42]

They were right. Just hours prior to that meeting, Soviet spokesman Leonid M. Zamyatin held a rare press conference at which he complained that the West sought UN guarantees for Israel just as Washington demanded guarantees from Hanoi before agreeing to stop the bombing. This Soviet bravado was based in part on the expectation that "Eban's mission to Washington would succeed." News of its failure alarmed Moscow. Ambassador Chuvakhin received immediate instructions to present Eshkol with a letter from Kosygin urging Israel "not to create a *new area of war* that could bring indescribable suffering to all nations." He woke Eshkol up at 2:30 in the morning demanding to know if Israel would fire the first shot. Eshkol answered that the first shots had already been fired by Nasser.[43]

It was the Soviet charge's turn to ask for an "extremely urgent" meeting with Rusk. Rusk delayed him until the afternoon. The charge then handed him a letter from Kosygin. Kosygin claimed "to know" that the Arabs did not "wish a military conflict," indicated that a solution to the Straits problem could be found and threatened "to give aid to the countries attacked." The meeting, Rusk wrote, led the superpowers to exchange assurances to restrain their clients.[44]

Johnson, immediately, informed Eshkol of the content of the Soviet message and threatened to label Israel "the aggressor" if it "went alone." Barbour was authorized to add that preparations for "the military aspect of the international naval escort plan" were "proceeding urgently repeat urgently," and that other nations were "responding vigorously to the idea." Therefore, "unilateral action on the part of Israel would be irresponsible and catastrophic." To convince Israel, the USSR and the Arabs of American sincerity, the Sixth Fleet was ordered to sail westward.[45]

Johnson wrote Kosygin of his restraining efforts, hinted that some moderation in Arab rhetoric might be useful, and added that it was "of vital importance" to the US "that a prompt solution be found to the issue of Strait of Tiran."[46] The Soviet–American exchange reduced American interest in direct action to open the Straits. Thereafter, in his meetings with the Senate Foreign Relations Committee, Rusk emphasized not only the importance of action through the UN but also of contacts with the USSR. Eugene Rostow was no longer permitted to use the president's name in soliciting support for the Red Sea regatta. The British understood as much, and withdrew their backing from the project.[47]

Amazingly, Rusk and McNamara spent Memorial Day supervising an elaborate "Middle East Scenario" which called for a declaration by the maritime nations, and "contingency planning for testing UAR interference" and "contingency planning for the use of force, as necessary." "Implementing action" would await the exhaustion of "measures" in the UN and Congressional passage of a special resolution which they deemed necessary on *political* grounds. In their "judgment," the two secretaries concluded, this scenario represented "the only alternative to an almost certain war."[48]

If, as McNamara insists, he knew that an Arab attack was imminent, then the plan was designed to avert an Israeli preemption.[49] It ignored the British withdrawal, the Israeli timetable, and even the American mood. There was no political need for special legislation, nor any difficulty in obtaining it. After all, Congress had never demanded legislation. On May 23, 96 House members issued a statement pledging support for "whatever action" was needed "to resist aggression against Israel and preserve peace." The following day, their number reached 108. Two days later, Seymour Halpern demanded on the House floor that Johnson request "a Gulf of Aqaba resolution," just as he had requested "a Gulf of Tonkin resolution." Congressman Emmanuel Celler went to Walt Rostow to inquire whether Johnson would welcome "a strong statement of support for his position on Aqaba" since he was sure that a "clear majority" would support one. Evron reported that sentiment for a strong US stand was no longer "confined to former doves." Johnson turned them down.[50] A Jewish lobbyist observed: "The President, who would not act without the support of Congress, was pushing Congress not to push him."[51]

A public opinion poll found growing support for escalation in Vietnam, in order to take care of the Middle East. It led to a *NYT* editorial entitled "What Price Vietnam?" which bemoaned its "baneful effects" on "conflicts from Suez to Hong Kong" and pointed out that a demand for "'total victory' . . . could lead to 'total' world war."[52] The editors preferred the implications of a question they posed a week later: "Middle East and/or Vietnam?" They argued that American commitments to Israel were stronger than to South Vietnam, that Israel did not ask the US to do its fighting, that American strategic and economic interests in the Middle East far exceeded those in Southeast Asia, and that the US had taken the place of the French and British in the region. Moreover, the crisis "reached the ironical stage where virtually every argument advanced for the Vietnam war – commitments, honor, security, interests, consistency, the self-determination of small nations – could be used in favor of helping Israel." If Washington could not fight two wars simultaneously, it should leave Vietnam. The editorial was widely quoted as an Atlanticist answer to Pacificist suggestions that "the silver lining hanging over Vietnam would be the conversion of the doves into hawks." But, if there was a conversion, it was not in the attitudes of doves towards Vietnam but towards the USSR and détente.[53]

Even isolationists like Joseph Kraft, who insisted that America would "get on nicely no matter what happened in the Middle East or Southeast Asia," believed that the Soviets used the Middle East as "a second front" and warned the administration that it was "fatal to hand the opposition the charge of a 'sell out.'" A Houston broadcaster retorted that the US could not "live completely confined" to its shores; the two conflicts were interrelated and posed a threat to the country's "very own freedom." He urged his listeners to tell their Congressmen, Senators and President to resist "aggression." Such resistance, warned *The Charleston West Virginia Gazette* would turn the superpowers into "two armed camps, moving progressively close from cold to hot war."[54] Not necessarily, argued William Randolph Hearst, Jr. Washington did not have to fall into the Soviet trap and choose between war and peace, or between the Middle East and Vietnam because "left alone, the Israelis would win." Moreover, to choose would mean to betray the dead:

> If the two fires had ignited at the same time, the U.S. would, I am sure, at first have gone all-out to aid Israel. But history has not permitted us this choice.... We have a present commitment which far surpasses all others. That is our obligation not to retreat and thus betray the more than 10,000 Americans killed thus far in the conflict with the communists in Vietnam.

Evans and Novak blamed the American predicament on a "State Department, preoccupied with Vietnam ... frozen in the posture of an ostrich" and ignoring friendly warnings of an imminent disaster in the Middle East. James Reston reported that the conversion of doves into hawks was also a European phenomenon:

> The vicious Middle East controversy has startled our old friends and allies in Western Europe. They have been saying the cold war was over in this part of the world ... but now they are not so sure. The Arab Israeli conflict is a little nearer Europe than Vietnam ... and the paradox of it is that many of the Europeans who have been most critical of his use of force in Southeast Asia are now afraid he might not follow this line in the Middle East.[55]

The Economist wrote that Russian success at vaulting "into the Middle East over the ring of alliances by which they were contained in the 1950s" gave them "bargaining power of a sort" they never had before. It had already led Johnson to "call his bombers off Hanoi" and it might tempt him to reach "a crude Israel for

Vietnam bargain." Johnson should realize that such a bargain would undermine "the more cautious men in Moscow" and provide only a temporary respite. For "the Israelis, rather than submit to being permanent hostages, would one day almost certainly decide to have it out with the Egyptians in a test of arms that the great powers might easily get drawn into."[56] Clearly, Europe was watching.

A CHANGE OF SIGNALS

American hopes for greater Arab or Soviet restraint were quickly dashed. On May 28, the Soviet defense minister told his Egyptian counterpart: "We received today information that the Sixth fleet in the Mediterranean returned to Crete the marines it had been carrying on landing vessels. Our fleet is in the Mediterranean near your shores. . . . I want to confirm to you that if something happens and you need us, just send us a signal." Nasser promptly ruled out any compromise on the Straits, stated that the problem was the aggression involved in Israel's very existence, and pledged to act without considering the possibility of an American intervention.[57]

Soviet rhetoric was just as uncompromising. Fedorenko contrasted Arab moderation with Israeli aggressiveness, emphasized that whether "Tel Aviv will risk overstepping the danger line will depend largely on those who stand behind Israel," and charged the US with barbarism and racism in Vietnam.[58] Reports of Soviet–American talks led China, which had created another crisis center in Hong Kong, to accuse Moscow of acting as the "chief accomplice in US activities to intimidate the Arab countries by force and exert political pressure on them." It urged the Arabs on:

> The great victories of the Vietnamese people's war to resist US aggression and save their country serves as a powerful support for the Arab people's struggle against US imperialism and, in its turn, the anti-US imperialist struggle of the Arab people constitutes a powerful support for the revolutionary cause of the peoples of the world against imperialism.[59]

Thompson suggested constricting further the bombing of North Vietnam as a "signal for de-escalation," and "for effect it might have on our efforts to obtain Soviet cooperation in Middle East crisis."[60] Rusk added a stick to the carrot. In a speech to the lawyers' association, he expressed willingness to enter negotiations on

Vietnam "literally without any conditions," but he also held out the possibility of mining Haiphong harbor. Privately, the Soviets warned that it "would have to send soldiers to help North Vietnam" if the US continued its escalation there. Publicly, they remarked that Rusk should not have taken time out from his Middle Eastern preoccupation just "to reaffirm" his intent to continue his "dangerous playing with fire."[61]

This Soviet/Egyptian bravado exerted enormous pressure on pro-Western regimes. On May 26, the Iranian ambassador told Johnson that "Iran felt that it was necessary to resist aggressive forces." The President answered that "the United States was trying very hard to find a 'middle way' to solve the present crisis."[62] But, Nasser's propaganda was telling the Arab world that Riyadh and Amman were "false friends" and their monarchs could no longer wait for the promised "middle way" especially after the US diverted to Ethiopia a freighter en route to the Jordanian port of Aqaba.[63] So, The kings proclaimed their support for the "liberation of Palestine," mobilized their forces, and planned a foreign ministers' conference to organize an oil embargo of Western countries supportive of Israel. On May 30, King Hussein flew to Cairo, placed his army under Egyptian command, and agreed to let Saudi and Iraqi forces enter Jordan.[64]

Suddenly, everything changed. Washington believed that such Nasserfication of the region presented it "with security crisis of major, and potentially catastrophic, proportions: NATO military positions were being outflanked. Communications between Europe, Africa and Asia were threatened. . . . Oil essential to the European (and Japanese) economies could be used as lever of political coercion." Even oil company executives demanded that the administration not "let them start eating" the US up because it was "tied down in Vietnam."[65]

Johnson decided once again to gamble on an Israeli victory. He used a letter from Eshkol which stated that Israel had postponed military action because of Johnson's personal commitment to pursue "all means" to open the Straits. To cover his political tracks, Johnson asked Goldberg: Did you understand that "I made a commitment to go to war with Egypt with the Israelis if Nasser" did not "get out of the Sinai?" Goldberg retorted that since Johnson had used the words "subject to our constitutional provisions," he had made no such commitment. Later, Goldberg explained: "I wanted to protect the President and our country and also be accurate. So the Israelis could determine what was required for their own security. I didn't want them fooled." He thought it best to provide Johnson with an alibi.[66]

Johnson instructed Walt Rostow to inform Evron that the US was no longer committed to opening the Straits. If Israel wanted them open, she would have to open them herself.[67] The meaning of this information was clear to friend and foe alike. As presidential envoy Robert Anderson told Nasser: "If Israel felt she was virtually alone she might be motivated to strike first to secure strategic advantage." Nasser replied that it "was a risk" he was willing to accept since "he was confident of the outcome of a conflict between Arabs and Israelis."[68] Amer issued his War Command No. 2 predicting that war would commence within days, in part because it was clear that the US would "under no circumstances embark on the adventure of direct action on Israel's side because of the Soviet Union's firm stand and its willingness to intervene in the event of aggression on the part of a Great Power against the United Arab Republic."[69]

Did the President give Israel the green light to strike first? Not exactly. He had given the Soviets his word and did not wish to seem incapable of controlling his client. An Arab attack was imminent, and it was important, Rusk later argued, that Israel "would take the American advice on such an important matter" and agree to absorb the first strike.[70] Could Israel count on US help if things went wrong? With the possible exception of Lyndon Johnson, no one knew the answer or was aware of any contingency plans.

On May 29, U.S. carrier *Intrepid* transited the Suez Canal because, as Rostow wrote Johnson, "Bob McNamara would feel more comfortable if it were on the other side of the canal if needed in connection with a crisis at the Gulf of Aqaba."[71] But at a meeting in Wheeler's office, General Harold Johnson asked the fleet commander whether he could promise that planes taking off from the *Intrepid* could reach within ten minutes any possible point of conflagration. The commander said they could. Johnson then asked whether the planes could discover and destroy *all* the Egyptian artillery positions along the Straits. The commander answered in the affirmative, though he would not guarantee the destruction of each and every position. Johnson argued that without such a guarantee, the carrier would be useless. The *Intrepid* continued to Vietnam.[72]

On June 2, the JCS confirmed again that "under present force ceiling" the US army lacked forces for contingencies beyond Vietnam nor could they get them into the area within the relevant time frame. There were limited forces east of Suez, but "the capability of these forces to prevail, if attacked by major UAR forces, is doubtful."[73] Post war bravado aside, Rusk fretted about the problem Washington would have "if the Israelis were defeated and were about to be driven into the sea" or if, as he expected, the Soviets did "something" to save the Arabs. After all, as McNamara noted, the US "would have a real problem if the Soviets came in to save Egypt." To improve the odds, Army Secretary Cyrus Vance organized an emergency supply pipeline to Israel and Helms shared intelligence with his Israeli counterparts.[74]

On June 2, US aircraft bombed a Soviet vessel anchored fifty miles north of Haiphong. Moscow thought it was an attempt to demonstrate that despite the Mideast crisis, the US would continue to escalate in Vietnam.[75] With this attack, Fedorenko declared, Washington lost her "moral authority to assume . . . the role of guardian of free international navigation." He described how American "ravaging hordes" made "desperate attempts to crush" and "to drown the nation (of Vietnam) in blood." Then he asked: "Does the United States not know that it is the criminal aggression of the United States in Vietnam that is posing a direct threat to peace, and *not only in South-East Asia*?" Goldberg chided him for engaging in "a cold-war exercise."[76]

War was imminent, and everybody knew it. Nor could the US force Israel to forgo preemption. Eisenhower explained: "Supposing I had been president and some combination of enemies, much bigger than us, had been gathered on the seas and in Canada and Mexico promising our extinction. If I hadn't attacked first while I had the chance I would have been tried for treason."[77] Johnson was notified, as were Soviet officers stationed in Alexandria. To cover his historic tracks, Johnson hurried to answer Eshkol's letter. He included the talking paper given Eban, but this time he expressed doubts about the international effort and made clear American refusal to "move in isolation."[78]

American diplomats even informed the Arabs. Thompson used an invitation to a future Egyptian embassy function in Moscow to tell his potential host that "things might happen in the next few days which could make my presence embarrassing." Nasser got the message. Thompson should not have worried, he spent that day in Washington interpreting Soviet hot line messages.[79] The job of preventing an Israeli surprise attack fell on the CIA station chief in

Amman who, on the evening of June 4, personally told Hussein that Israel would attack the following morning. Hussein called Nasser who had already informed his commanders two days earlier that "the Israeli attack would be launched on 5 June" and would be directed against the air force.[80]

THE CREDIBILITY GAP

On June 5, at 4:30 a.m. Walt Rostow woke up Lyndon Johnson and told him that the turkey shoot had begun; he was stating facts. The Arab air fields had been destroyed. There were celebrations in the White House and Foggy Bottom. Eugene Rostow mischievously quipped: "Remember we are neutral in word, thought and deed." So, when State Department spokesman Robert McClosky was asked whether he would reaffirm American neutrality in light of news of Arab anti-American rioting, he confirmed that the US was "neutral in thought, word and deed." Since the only news items available to the public were pre-prepared Arab victory boasts, his answer seemed more than callous. When Roche saw the exchange on television, he called Johnson and told him to turn on his set. Furious, Johnson called Rusk and ordered him and McClosky to explain.[81]

But explain what? Rusk had spent the day telling the Soviets that the fighting had taken Washington by surprise. Pleased with the Soviet hot line suggestion that the superpowers stay out of the conflict, he had no wish to make provocative statements. So he explained that "neutrality" did not mean indifference, only "non belligerence." The US was committed to "the integrity and independence of the nations in the Middle East," though "obtaining a cease fire" was her first priority.[82]

This verbal hairsplitting only confirmed the widely held notion that McClosky's statement was an accurate reflection of a policy that "slipped out." The Media reported that when the war began, the Sixth Fleet vessels were off Crete three days away from the Israeli and Egyptian coasts and their 2000 marines were enjoying a shore leave in Malta. At the same time, four additional Soviet destroyers and a frigate had sailed through the Dardanelles. The message was clear: There were no plans to save Israel had she gotten into trouble. John Stennis and Mike Mansfield explained that Vietnam had undermined American military capabilities.[83]

The public relations fiasco led Johnson to summon McGeorge Bundy to coordinate the American response to the War. But the facts on the ground were the real agents of change. On the morning of June 5, Goldberg wanted an immediate ceasefire and "informally suggested" that it be coupled with "a return of Israeli and Arab forces to their positions on May 18, before Egypt moved troops into Sinai and Aqaba." The Arabs refused and Moscow, unsure of the effect the air war would have on the ground war, made Soviet officials difficult to find.

By the following morning, the magnitude of the Arab defeat was clear and the desperate Nasser and Hussein had accused the US of fighting alongside Israel in hope of spurring a superpower confrontation. The accusation infuriated Washington and convinced Moscow to opt for an immediate ceasefire. A Soviet diplomat recalls:

> Around midmorning on June 6, we received a telephone call on an *open line* from Moscow – an extraordinary occurrence – from the Deputy Foreign Minister, Vladimir Semyonov. He said that there would soon be new instructions and that we should arrange a meeting with Goldberg immediately upon receiving them. Our new orders were to accept Goldberg's idea, but if it proved impossible to get a decision on that basis, we were to agree to the Security Council's proposed resolution on a cease-fire as the first step. The instructions, signed by Gromyko, stressed: "You must do that, even if the Arab countries do not agree – repeat, do not agree."[84]

But Washington was no longer in a hurry. Goldberg disappeared, and the White House suggested an unconditional ceasefire. To Washington's surprise, Kosygin agreed. Washington informed Goldberg who told the unhappy Fedorenko that his former "unofficial" proposal was no longer on the table. Fedorenko had no choice but to agree.[85] The ceasefire in place left Israel with useful Arab territories. During the June 7 NSC Meeting, Dean Rusk articulated the new American Middle Eastern role: "If we do not make ourselves '*attorneys for Israel*,' we cannot recoup our losses in the Arab world." The US had to turn the Israeli-held Arab territories into bargaining chips. Arab countries wishing to regain territory would have to pay a price to Washington as well as to Jerusalem.[86]

The American price could be extracted from both the Arabs and the Soviet Union. The Israeli price was simple: "NO DRAW-BACK

WITHOUT DEFINITIVE PEACE." Washington assumed that this meant making the "general acceptance of the state of Israel" a "major" American "policy point." Hence, the issue of the permanence of the Jewish state would no longer be negotiable. There might also be a difference between the armistice and peace borders.[87] Unwilling to pay the Israeli price, and doubting the willingness of others to do so, Washington had to persuade Israel to lower it. Rusk argued that he had "something to bargain with in that Israel must be grateful to the US" and it required "continuing US support." Others were not so sure. Rusk "reviewed the question of 'who did what.'" He insisted that the US "had a primary obligation" to itself to maintain peace, and what the US would have done if it were in Eshkol's shoes was "another question." In any case, the situation appeared "more manageable than five days or three days" earlier.

Rusk's comments included a grudging admission that the US had failed Israel, that the war improved the US strategic position and that a new American Mideast policy was in order. Lyndon Johnson would admit nothing of the sort. Watching a CBS special, he commented that "it was easy to tell there was some Jewish background in the commentator by the slanted method in which he was reporting." His behavior at the NSC meeting reflected his foul mood. "The President was pretty worked up," recalls Eugene Rostow. "He went around the table asking us: 'Do you agree that the message from Eshkol gave us two weeks?' Everyone agreed." He then said that he could not visualize the USSR saying it had miscalculated, and "walking away," that Washington's objective should be to "develop as few heroes and as few heels" as possible. The US might be "in as good a position" as it "could be given the complexities of the situation," but, before long, they all would "wish the war had not happened."[88]

Clearly he tried to vindicate himself by insisting that had Israel not lost its patience, he would have honored Eisenhower's pledge. For as columnist Tom Wicker remarked, it was going to be difficult for Washington to present the "war in Vietnam as necessary to honor its commitment and as one for the protection of small nations" after "finding itself unable or unwilling to assist the Israelis." It was also going to be difficult to convince the American people that the Cold War with the USSR was over or that gradual force application was the right way to fight a war. Then there was jealousy.[89]

The June 8th Israeli attack on the American spy ship the *Liberty* handed Johnson a weapon with which to tarnish the Israeli halo. Israel immediately acknowledged the mistake, apologized and offered to pay compensation to the families. But Eshkol limited the American ability to take advantage of the incident by reminding the world that "President Johnson promised great things," but was unable to deliver them. Johnson was livid. Bundy, who "had a feeling Monday (June 5) that we would not in the end have put troops in," tried to help. The strongest American card, he thought, was the attack on the *Liberty*, though it was of "more use in the Middle East than in the United States." The appropriate argument in the US was that Israel did not need help to fight Arabs; it needed and got help in keeping the Soviets out:.

> The real danger to Israel was that some other power might give active support to the Arabs. Without any threat or warning, or(sic) any kind, but simply because of here(sic) presence as a world power and here(sic) whole policy towards Israel, the US stood between Israel and such action by any other power.[90]

Perhaps Israel did not need American help, but that did not change the fact that help would not have been there had it been needed, retorted columnist Drew Pearson. Cy Sulzberger added that while the US role had been "confined to waffling," American "prestige" had risen. But the unkindest cut of all was administered by James Reston: "The Israelis are now very popular in Washington. They had the courage of our conviction, and they won a war we opposed." Bundy's special committee discussed the Reston column. An angry Johnson instructed his aides to "summarize as black a picture as we can of Soviet (weapon) shipments" and tell the Israelis that "It wasn't Dayan that kept Kosygin out."[91]

Three days later, Reston imparted a very different message in a column entitled, "Washington: 'And God Spake Unto Israel.'" It informed his readers that Israel "had an ally after all" because "the best inside story on the Middle East so far is in the 46th chapter of the Book of Genesis . . . Fear not to go down into Egypt; for I will there make thee a great nation: I will go down with thee into Egypt; and I will surely bring thee up again." Reston added that the US would seek "a genuine peace settlement" in the Middle East.[92]

What happened? The shooting war was over and with it the possibility of a superpower confrontation. There was no longer a need to appease the Soviets, or even present them as moderates.

The evidence to the contrary was too strong, and the political price too high. At first, administration analysts differed in their interpretations of Soviet intentions. On June 6, one analyst dismissed Soviet assertions of connections between the Middle East and Vietnam as mere propaganda and expressed skepticism about "the notion that the Soviet Union wanted a major crisis in the Middle East in order to throw the US off balance in Vietnam." Another argued that "Gromyko's visit to Cairo and Vinogradov's assignment as ambassador to the UAR should be regarded as early developments in a new and more active plan of a Soviet Middle East operation increasingly related to Moscow's European policy and a point of pressure to offset the US position in S.E. Asia."[93]

Additional evidence soon poured in: A Soviet CIA source confirmed that Moscow wanted "to create another trouble spot" for the US in addition to Vietnam. Its "grand design" envisaged a long war in which the US would become seriously involved, economically, politically, and possibly even militarily. The plan "misfired because the Arabs failed completely and Israeli blitzkrieg was so decisive."[94] An oil company official reported being asked by a Soviet diplomat whether the crisis had not "increased domestic pressure on the US administration to de-escalate its activity in Vietnam," whether an American military involvement in the Middle East would not diminish its willingness and ability "to continue its scale of activity in Vietnam?," and "Whether the possibility of additional crises arising besides those in the Middle East and Vietnam might not persuade the US that it is overextended?"[95]

Another oil executive reported that a Soviet official came to him "fishing for information about the impact of the crisis on US fuel supplies," and on American operations in Vietnam. The Arab states had reduced oil production. *Izvestia* happily reported West European fears of oil shortages and that "half of the total petroleum used by American troops in Vietnam" came from "the Persian Gulf, mainly from Kuwait and Saudi Arabia." The Defense Department quickly announced that US forces in Southeast Asia had "adequate reserve stocks on hand."[96]

In any case, though Reston was wrong to ascribe to Washington the role of God in Egypt, he would have been accurate to ascribe it such a role in Syria. For the first ceasefire left Egypt without the Sinai, Jordan without the West Bank and Syria intact. McGeorge Bundy told Eban "it would seem strange that – Syria – which had originated the war – might be the only one that seemed to be getting off without injury." An Israeli attack on Syria would demonstrate that Moscow was no better at protecting its client than Washington. It would further undermine Israeli relations with France and the USSR, and increase Israeli dependence on the US. When Israel obliged, Washington responded to Soviet threats of military intervention not only by ordering the Sixth Fleet eastward but also by bombing Hanoi.[97]

The vast improvement in the American bargaining power reawakened interest in a package deal to settle both Asian conflicts. Brzezinski wrote Johnson that while the USSR might not "wish to link one crisis, in which it suffered a major political setback, with another crisis, which continues to be a source of embarrassment to the United States," such a public initiative would serve Johnson well:

> If the offer is rebuffed either by Hanoi or by Moscow, Johnson will not have lost any prestige; on the contrary, the position of the US will have been strengthened. At the same time, the so-called "peace movement" within the United States will have been badly hurt, both because great many of its supporters hold an entirely different attitude towards the Middle Eastern crisis and, secondly, because Johnson's peace offer would exploit their present mood of psychological ambivalence.[98]

There were similar calls in Congress and the media. Reston reported an administration inclination to reach "a general settlement of all the problems of the last war and the postwar period." However, such daring was not in the cards, procrastination was. Israel's supporters were split between those who feared that she would have to pay the price for such a deal and those who believed that only the prospect of a Vietnamese settlement would entice Washington to pursue peace in the Middle East.[99]

Rusk "did not see how either side could make concessions in one place to obtain concessions in the other." On June 19, 1967 Johnson issued a policy statement officially linking withdrawal to peace. His advisers, who as early as June 7 had rebuffed a joint Moroccan–Iranian peace initiative, decided to postpone action on the Middle East for at least two to four months in the hope of bringing a post-Nasser Egypt back to the fold. The announcement that Kosygin was coming to New York reshuffled the cards once more.[100]

NOTES

1. George C. Herring, *The Secret Diplomacy of the Vietnam War* (Austin: 1983), 505–7; and Dobrynin, *In Confidence*, 136.
2. *Pravda*, April 25, 1967.
3. Vassiliev, *Soviet Policy in the Middle East*, 111.
4. Gilboa, *Shesh Shanim*, 86; *Pravda* and *Radio Moscow*, April 2, 1967; and interview with E. Rostow.
5. Ben Tsur, *Gormin Sovietiim*, 155; Parker, *The Six Day War*, 54, 56; Vassiliev, 111; and Weit, *Eyewitness* (London: 1973) 139–40.
6. *Pentagon Papers*, IV, 476, Memorandum from Brzezinski, April 14, 1967, NSF, CF, USSR, box 223, 229, 132a, LBJL.
7. Gaiduk, *The Soviet Union and the Vietnam War*, 118–19; *Washington Post*, May 21, 1967; Janos Radvanyi, *Delusion and Reality* (South Bend: 1978), 234–8.
8. Interview with Rusk, NSC Meeting, May 3, 1967, box 2, Vol. 4, Tab 5, LBJL; and *Congressional Record – Senate*, April 27, 1966, 10996–8.
9. *Washington Post*, May 17, 1966; and interview with E. Rostow.
10. Interview with Walt Rostow, Dept. of State to Amembassy Moscow, May 19, 1967, NSF, M.E. Crisis, box 17, 27; and Walt Rostow to the President, May 24, 1967, President's Appointment File, box 69, LBJL.
11. *Congressional Record – Senate*, May 19, 1967; *The Pentagon Papers*, IV, 169–83; and McNamara, *In Retrospect*, 271.
12. Memorandum for WWR, May 16, 1967, NSF, Memos to the Pres., box 7, 46a, LBJL.
13. *American Jewish Yearbook: 1967*, 154–5; For the President from W. W. Rostow, May 19, 1967, box 17, 21a; Circular, May 19, 1967, NSF, M.E. Crisis, box 17, Tab 10, 30, LBJL; and Parker, *The Six Day War*, 54.
14. Harold H. Saunders, "The Middle East Crisis, Preface," NSF, M.E. Crisis, box 17, 2, LBJL.
15. Radio Cairo, May 21, 1967, DCSS; and an intelligence field report, May 1967, NSF, M.E. Crisis, box 17, LBJL.
16. *Pravda*, May 22, 1967; and Parker, *Politics of Miscalculation*, 30–3.
17. Urquhart, *Ralph Bunche*, 400–16.
18. Memorandum to the President, May 19, 1967, NSF, M.E. Crisis, box 17, 21a, JCSM-287-67, M.E. Crisis, box. 18, 36, LBJL.
19. NSC Meeting, May 24, 1967, box 2, 2, LBJL.
20. *NYT*, May 25, 1967.
21. Johnson, *Vantage Point*, 587; and *The Pentagon Papers*, IV, 187. Benjamin Read, the Executive Secretary of the Department of State, pointed out the relevance of the pause dates to the Mideast crisis (July 30, 1991).
22. Bick, "Ethnic Linkages," 163; and WWR from Hal Saunders, May 22, 1967; and from HHS, May 23, 1967, NSF, M.E. Crisis, box 17, 41 and 75, LBJL.
23. Roche, LBJ-OH, 63–6; To the President from John Roche, May 22, 1967, NSF, M.E. Crisis, Box 17, 64, LBJL; interview with Roche; and *NYT*, May 24, 1967. Roche checked the teleprompter to know which version Johnson would use.

24. *Pravda*, May 24, 1967.
25. "Summary, Secretary Appearance before the SFRC," May 23, 1967, M.E. Crisis, box 17, 99, LBJL; interview with Lucius Battle (Aug. 28, 1991); and *NYT*, May 24, 1967.
26. NSC Meeting, May 24, 1967, NSF, box 2, 2, LBJL.
27. *Security Council Official Records*, 1341st Meeting, 24 May 1967, 5–6.
28. *NYT* and *Christian Science Monitor*, May 25, 1967.
29. Talking Points and Memorandum of Conversation, May 26, 1967, NSF, President's appointment File, May–June, 1967, box 66, Ic, 1f, 22, LBJL.
30. Dept. of State to Amembassy Moscow, May 25, 1967, NSF, USSR, box 223, 229, 31, LBJL.
31. *Daily Diary*, May 25, 1967, LBJL.
32. For the President from W. W. Rostow, May 19, 1967, M.E. Crisis, box 17, 21b, LBJL.
33. Secretary appearance before the SFRC, May 23, 1967, NSF, M.E. Crisis, box 19, 64a, LBJL.
34. *Congressional Record – Senate*, Aug. 6, 1964, 11410–30.
35. *Congressional Record – Senate*, May 23, 1957, 13482–3.
36. NSC Meeting, May 24, 1967, NSF, Box 2, 2; and Lucius Battle, LBJ-OH, tape 2, 16, LBJL.
37. Summary of Conversation, Feb. 24, 1957, Handwriting File, box 22, LBJL; and Jonathan Trumbull Howe, *Multicrises* (Cambridge: 1971), 362.
38. Louis Heren, *No Hail, No Farewell* (New York: 1970), 162–3; *NYT*, May 26, 1967; and interview with an Israeli diplomat.
39. Meeting on the Middle East, May 26, 1967, Appointment File, May–June 67, box 66, 1f, LBJL; Parker, *Politics of Miscalculation*, 50–1.
40. Draft, May 26, 1967, NSF, M.E. Crisis, box 17, 33, LBJL.
41. Eban, *Personal Witness*, 386–90; Johnson, *The Vantage Point*, 293–4; and Memorandum of Conversation, Appointment book, May–June 67, box 66, 1d, LBJL.
42. John Roche, LBJ–OH, 68; and *Daily Diary*, May 26, 1967, LBJL.
43. Talking Paper, June 6, 1967, NSF, M.E. Crisis, box 19, 317a, LBJL; Michael Bar Zohar, *Embassies in Crisis* (Engelwood Cliffs: 1968), 128.
44. Memorandum of Conversation, May 27, 1967, NSF, M.E. Crisis, Box 17, 61, LBJL; and Dean Rusk, *As I Saw It* (New York; 1990), 385–6.
45. Outgoing Telegram, Department of State, May 27, 1967, NSF, M.E. Crisis, box 17, 70, LBJL.
46. Department of State to Amembassy Moscow, May 28, 1967, NSF, M.E. Crisis, box 17, 75; interview with Rusk; and Memorandum of Conversation at Luncheon, June 25, 1967, NSF, CF, USSR (Glassboro Memcon) 6/67, 10, LBJL.
47. Benjamin Geist, "The Six Day War," Ph.D. dissertation, Hebrew University: 1974, 352; and interviews with Katzenbach and Roche.
48. For the President from W. W. Rostow, May 30, 1967, Agenda, May 31, 1967; For the President from Dean Rusk and Robert McNamara (with enclosures), May 30, 1967, NSF, M.E. Crisis, box 18, 4, 4a, 4b, LBJL.

49. Interview with McNamara.
50. *Congressional Record – House*, May 24, May 25, 1967; and for the President from W. W. Rostow, May 31, 1967, Appointment File, May–June 67, box 66, 1k, LBJL.
51. Kenen, *Israel's Defense Line*, 200.
52. *NYT*, May 24, 1967, For the President from Fred Pazner, Oct. 6, 1967, box 194, LBJL.
53. *The Congressional Record*, May 23, 1967. 1352, May 31, 1967, 14292 and 14389, and June 1, 1967, 14483.
54. *Washington Post*, May 29, 1967; *Congressional Record – Appendix*, June 6, 1967; *West Virginia Gazette*, May 24, 1967; and *Congressional Record – Senate*, May 31, 1967, 14378.
55. William R. Hearst, *The Case for Israel* (Hearst Papers: 1969), May 28 and June 4, 1967; *The Washington Post*, June 5, 1967; and *NYT*, May 31, 1967.
56. *The Economist*, June 3, 1966.
57. Parker, *Politics of Miscalculation*, 32; and Theodore Draper, *Israel and World Politics* (New York: 1968), 224–31.
58. *Security Council Official Record*, 1343rd Meeting, May 29, 1967, 20.
59. *Peking Review*, June 2, 1967, 34–5.
60. Department of State from Amembassy Moscow, May 29, 1967, NSF, CF, USSR, box 223, 229, 10, LBJL.
61. Incoming Telegram Department of State, May 31, 1967, NSF, U.K., box 211, 2, 10, LBJL; and *Pravda*, May 30, 1967.
62. Memorandum of Conversation, May 26, 1967, NSF, Iran, box 136, 290, LBJL.
63. W. W. Rostow to the President, May 26, 1967, NSF, M.E. Crisis, box 17, 45, LBJL; and *NYT*, May 27, 1967.
64. *Davar*, May 29; and Geist, "The Six Day War," 296.
65. Interview with Walt Rostow, Eugene Rostow, "The Middle Eastern Crisis in the Perspective of World Politics," *International Affairs* (April 1971), 280–1; and Horace Busby to the President, May 31, 1967, Appointment File, box 67, LBJL.
66. Helms, LBJ-OH, tape I, 36; and Goldberg, LBJ–OH, 21–5.
67. W. W. Rostow to the President, May 31, 1967, Appointment File, 1k, LBJL.
68. Parker, *Politics of Miscalculation*, 235.
69. "War Command no. 2," *International Problems* (Nov.–Dec. 1967), 17.
70. Interviews with McNamara, Rusk and Yariv (the quote is Rusk's).
71. Battle, LBJ-OH, 45; Katzenbach, LBJ-OH, 9; From Walt Rostow to the President, May 29, 1966, NSF, M.E. Crisis, box 17, 102, LBJL.
72. For the President from W. W. Rostow, May 31, 1967, NSF, M.E. Crisis, box 17, LBJL; and Dan Patir, "Miyomano Shel Dover," *Dvar Hashavua* (June/July, 1970), 36.
73. Memorandum for the Secretary of Defense, June 2, 1967, JCSM-310-67, NSF, M.E. Crisis, box 18, 36, LBJL.
74. Interview with E. Rostow and McNamara; and Memorandum of Conversation, June 2, 1967, NSF, UK, box 211, 100, LBJL.
75. Memorandum of Conversation with Mr. Gely Skritsky of the Soviet

Embassy," June 6, 1967, NSF, USSR, box 223, 229, 140a, LBJL.

76. *Security Council Official Records*, June 3, 1967, 15–23. Chuvahkin told an Israeli official that when Johnson declares his support for the rule of law in Tiran, he should remember that he is undermining that rule in Vietnam. June 4, 1967, Six Day War, diplomatic cables, Yad Eshkol.
77. C. L. Sulzberger, *Seven Continents and Forty Years* (New York: 1977), 472.
78. Bick, 163; *Maariv*, June 5, 1992; and "Dear Mr. Prime Minister," June 3, 1967, NSF, M.E. Crisis, box 18, 58, 58a, LBJL.
79. Mohamed Heikal, *The Sphinx and the Commissar* (New York: 1978), 180.
80. Andrew and Leslie Cockburn, *Dangerous Liaison* (New York: 1991), 149; Anwar El Sadat, *Those I Have Known*, 134; and Mahmoud Riad, *The Struggle for Peace in the Middle East* (London: 1981), 24.
81. Interviews with E. Rostow and Roche.
82. Interview with Rusk; and Joe Califano to the President, June 5, 1967, NSF, M.E. Crisis, box 18, 112, LBJL.
83. *NYT*, June 5, 6, and 7, 1967.
84. Arkady Shevchenko, *Breaking with Moscow* (New York: 1985), 177–8.
85. Rafael, *Destination Peace*, 159–62.
86. NSC Meeting, June 7, 1967, M.E. Crisis, box 18, LBJL.
87. Handwritten memo to the President from Walt, June 7, 1967, NSF, President's Appointment File, box 67, LBJL.
88. NSC Meeting, June 7, 1967, M.E. Crisis, box 18, LBJL; Daily Diary, June 5, 1967.
89. *The Atlanta Constitution*, June 8, 1967.
90. For the President from McG. B., June 9, 1967, NSF, M.E. Crisis, box 18, 99, 99a, LBJL.
91. *The Washington Post*, June 10, 1967; *NYT*, June 11, 1967; Informal Session of the special Middle East committee, June 13, 1967. NSF, M.E. Crisis, Appendix I, box 19, 102, LBJL.
92. *NYT*, June 14, 1967.
93. International reaction to the Middle East hostilities and "Israeli Objectives in the Current Crisis – Soviet Policy and Miscalculation," June 6, 1967, NSF, M.E. Crisis, box 18, 317a, LBJL.
94. CIA Report, June 8, 1967, NSF, M.E. Crisis, box 18, 185, LBJL.
95. "Conversation with Mr. Gely Skirtsky, 6 June 1967," June 7, 1967, NSF, U.S.S.R., box 223, 224, 140, LBJL.
96. *Izvestia*, June 9, 1967; For W. W. Rostow from Nathaniel Davis, June 6, 1967, NSF, M.E. Crisis, Box 18, 318; and *NYT*, June 8, 1967. In fact, a CIA study revealed that "the closure of the Suez Canal" would "affect about 45 percent of North Vietnam's seaborne imports" by increasing their average voyage from Black Sea ports from 20 to 36 days and from Polish ports from 27 to 36 days. Intelligence Memorandum, CIA, June 7, 1967, NSF, M.E. Crisis, box 18, 324, LBJL.
97. Eban, *Personal Witness*, 423; and interviews with Katzenbach and E. Rostow. The partial pause was lifted for June 9 and 10.
98. Memorandum from Z. Brzezinski, June 7, 1967, NSF, M.E. Crisis, box 17, 304a, LBJL.

99. *Christian Science Monitor*, June 8, 1967; and *Congressional Record*, June 7, 15215–67, June 8, 15226, June 12, 15372, 15396.
100. *NYT*, June 11, 1967; "US Policy and Diplomacy in the Middle East Crisis," May 15–June 10, box 20, 2a 151–5; and NSC Special Committee meeting, June 12, 13, NSF, M.E. Crisis, App.I, box 19, 101, 102, LBJL.

8 Israel Survives

UNPREPARED

When Israel realized that it had become a pawn in a global chess game, it could do little to prevent a war no one saw coming. Diplomat and historian Richard Parker wrote: "What cries out for explanation now, a quarter century later, is that a scant three weeks before June 5 no one – statesman, scholar, soldier, Eastern or Western, Israeli or Arab – has predicted a general Arab–Israeli war in June or even in 1967." Indeed, on May 5, 1967 the military intelligence service predicted that Israel faced no existential treat as her "security preoccupation" would revolve around Palestinian infiltration.[1] This consensus is startling considering the effect Syrian support for FATAH infiltration had on Israeli–Soviet relations.

On April 7, there was a major air battle over Syria in which 130 planes participated, 6 Syrian MIGs were downed, and Israeli planes flew over Damascus. On April 21, the Soviet foreign ministry presented the Israeli ambassador with an oral document. Its first paragraph decried the collusion of imperialist forces with Israeli militarists against the decolonizing Afro-Asian world. The second paragraph was devoted to colonialist aggression in Vietnam, and the third again asserted that the forces responsible for the Vietnam war were "pushing the Middle East to the edge of war in order to secure larger oil revenues and are not taking into account its destructive effect on these countries and on Israeli territory." Moscow had to "pay attention" to events in "the vicinity of her borders," and Israel should not follow the advice of impatient political forces who were willing to become "playthings of hostile outside forces."[2] When this was followed by an April 26 letter accusing Israel of "jeopardizing the vital interests of the people and the fate of the country," the director of the foreign ministry, Gideon Rafael, flew to Moscow to try to convince the Soviets that Israel was not part of any anti-Syrian conspiracy. He failed. Moscow made clear that it would consider any anti-Syrian action, a CIA "assignment."[3]

On May 11 Israel wrote to the President of the Security Council warning that it considered Syrian support for "people's war" a flagrant violation of the General Armistice Agreement and regarded "itself as fully entitled to act in self-defense as circumstances warrant." U Thant agreed:

> I must say that, in the last few days, the El Fatah type of incidents have increased, unfortunately. Those incidents have occurred in the vicinity of the Lebanese and Syrian lines and are very deplorable, especially because, by their nature, they seem to indicate that the individuals who committed them have had more specialized training than has usually been evidenced in El Fatah incidents in the past. That type of activity is insidious, is contrary to the letter and spirit of the armistice agreements and menaces the peace in the area.[4]

Chief of Staff Rabin explained that since Syria itself activated the terrorists, the aim of Israeli reprisals had to be "different from those undertaken in Jordan and Lebanon." The Soviets interpreted Rabin's words as a threat to the Damascus regime. The Egyptians assumed that Israel intended to force a change in Syrian policy as it did in Egyptian policy. They told U Thant:

> We understand that Israel does not intend to annex Syria, and Damascus is not part of their plan. Their plans are confined, however to south of Syria where the bulk of the Syrian Army is deployed . . . Israel could . . . invade south Syria. . . . Israel then, supported by its friends, would agree to having a new UNEF on the Israel–Syrian frontier.[5]

Israeli officials do not deny that they contemplated a major retaliatory operation against Syria, but argue that it would have been carefully designed not to trigger the Egyptian–Syrian mutual defense pact. In fact, on May 5, Nasser sent his prime minister to Damascus to warn that their mutual defense pact applied "only in the event of a general attack on Syria," and not "to merely local incidents."[6]

Nasser himself acknowledged that he had no intention prior to May 13 of getting involved in the ongoing Syrian–Israeli–FATAH fight; he then received a series of Soviet warnings of an "immense concentration of Israeli troops on the Syrian border." The veracity of the reports were of little interest either to the Egyptians or the Soviets. Amer was not surprised when his chief of staff denied the Soviet reports and ambassador Chuvakhin insisted that his job was not "to observe facts in Israel" but "to present the views of Moscow."[7]

In his May 14 battle command, Amer explained that the decision to march into the Sinai "was made with a complete awareness of all the global conditions and the international circumstances related to the situation and to the position of the imperialist forces helping Israel." Those conditions convinced Egyptians of the imminence of another round of conservative coups. The 1965 escalation in Vietnam was followed by the removals of Sukarno, Ben Bella and Nkrumah; the 1967 escalation had already produced a coup in Greece. Soviet intelligence gave Nasser a recording of an American agent discussing plans for Greek-like coups in Arab countries.[8]

A raid on the AID offices in Yemen had produced proof of CIA mischief there, and the mysterious publication of an anti-religious tract in Damascus caused a general strike which severely weakened Syria's rulers. Since revolutionary regimes "constituted Egypt's first line of defense," Amer argued, their demise would isolate the Egyptian regime which the US was "actively working to unseat."[9] However, "the Vietnam war totally exhausted the military potential of the United States," while the Soviets built up their Mediterranean navy. Acting publicly on Syrian behalf, at Soviet prompting, would force Moscow to protect Nasser and his regime from the US.[10]

Had Nasser wanted to deter Israel, he could have repeated his successful 1960 exercise of moving troops into the Sinai in secret and dispersing them after an agreement had been reached. But, in 1967, he publicized his every move and emphasized the role of Soviet warnings as if to caution Moscow not to leave itself open to Chinese charges of betrayal. Indeed, Nasser responded to the initial Soviet silence by getting Shukayri to tour Gaza with the Chinese ambassador and the NLF representative.[11]

Israelis did not miss the ascendence of the "hawkish" Brezhnev-Grechko forces, advocates of what the head of the Israeli Communist Party called a Chinese-style foreign policy concerning the Arab-Israeli dispute. However, they doubted Soviet willingness to protect Syria directly and did not foresee that Nasser would buy Soviet assurances that the Arabs could beat Israel on an "isolated" battlefield.[12] Eban's misreading of the effect of the Vietnam War on the Middle East was just as tragic:

> Since the Vietnam crisis, I have felt that Israel's position in the United States has, if anything, become more secure. Vietnam taught American Presidents that any true definition of the national interest must include a capacity for reconciling the domestic consensus with foreign policy. . . . There is also the feeling that a humiliating defeat for Israel in the Middle East would be a Soviet

> victory of such strength and resonance that it would leave the United States enfeebled.... To honor the commitment to Israel, it is not necessary for Americans to be pro-Israeli. It is enough to be pro-American.[13]

The trouble was that the very strategic, political and emotional attachment Americans exhibited towards Israel made her such an attractive target for both Moscow and Cairo. A correct reading of the global situation might not have prevented war, but it would have enabled Jerusalem to undertake the necessary military and diplomatic preparations for it. Instead, on May 21, when Eban asked Rabin "what the diplomatic establishment could do to help the army," Rabin said, "time, time, time!" With UNEF on the Egyptian border, the army had been deployed on the Jordanian and Syrian fronts and needed time to redeploy. The assumption that Israel would not have to fight before 1970, and the corollary decision to opt for American weapons had slowed military modernization. Few new American tanks had reached Israel, and the army needed time to return to service equipment it had thought obsolete.[14]

Even more critical was the aircraft shortage. In 1956 Israel had 236 bombers and fighter planes, and the Arabs had 277. In 1967 Israel had 247 planes, including 44 training aircraft, and the Arabs had 571. This shortage led foreign experts to take a somber view of Israel's war prospects and enhanced Nasser's confidence that Israel would either not fight or that his superior Soviet aircraft would render him victorious. A wary Israeli cabinet member exclaimed: "I am ready to fight but not to commit suicide."[15]

These shortages influenced policy. France, the major source of aircraft, was the first to embargo military supplies. It relented, only to reinstate the embargo a couple of days before the war. The US, too, used economic and military aid as a lever. Paradoxically, the aircraft shortage increased air force pressure for prompt action. Eshkol summed up the Israeli war prognosis: "The first five minutes would be critical" and victory would belong to the air force which would "hit first the airports of the other." Fear of Egyptian preemption led Weizman to suggest that the air force act alone until the ground forces were ready. Egyptian penetration of Israeli air space, and Israeli failure at interception, was just as troubling. When Eshkol suggested that air patrols be instituted to protect security objectives, such as the Dimona nuclear research facility, Weizman countered that such patrols would "finish our air force."

Air patrols might force the cancellation of the plan on which victory depended.[16]

In 1956, the British and French protected Israeli skies; in 1967, they would be wide open. The change reflected Israel's essential loneliness at a time when "Soviet fingerprints could be found everywhere." U Thant ignored Israeli advice to show flexibility and then succumbed to Nasser's request at a speed that left Jerusalem breathless. Israeli pleas for help in convincing Nasser not to take steps which would make war inevitable fell on deaf ears. Eban observes, "If any of the major powers addressed strong admonitions to Cairo between May 14 and May 22, their efforts are still unknown."[17] Washington demanded consultations, but refused to reiterate her commitment to Israel. Eshkol told his Cabinet that he was "afraid that the Western countries would refuse to intercede in Moscow on Israel's behalf."[18]

Israel demonstrated moderation: When asked: "Can Israel let it appear that his show of force has kept Israel from attacking Syria?," Evron answered that it could "provided" there were no "serious terrorist attack" and/or "interference with Israeli shipping through Aqaba." She appealed to American self interest: Her ambassador to Moscow told his American counterpart that there was a Soviet plan to evict the West from the Middle East and that Nasser's moves were intended to test Western obligations towards the area.[19] She used her political clout: Letters and telegrams poured into presidential and Congressional mailboxes.

It was all for nought. Egyptian forces poured into the Sinai. Eugene Rostow informed Israel that "the Egyptian forces had the right to be anywhere on Egyptian territory that the Egyptian government desired." On May 20, the MOSSAD used an emergency communications channel to transmit a message from Eshkol to Nasser: "We don't want war. We will withdraw all our units now stationed on our frontiers if you withdraw your armies from Sinai to previous positions." The Israeli cabinet had already decided that "this was not the time to solve the terrorist problem." Cairo replied: "You will get our answer in time."[20]

On the eve of Nasser's closure of the Straits, Eban met with Rabin. Rabin wanted to know the length of time a military campaign could last. Eban retorted: Israel was alone. No superpower would come to its aid. The IDF would probably have 24 to 72 hours before international pressure would curtail action. Rabin was taken aback. To go to war under such circumstances seemed absurd.[21]

It was a long-held premise of David Ben Gurion that Israel should never go to war without the backing of a superpower. The Eshkol coalition placed its trust in the conventional Israeli army, international good will and American guarantees. Dayan's sojourn to Vietnam further decreased his confidence in American commitments. In a crisis, he concluded, the "superpowers would dictate events in the Middle East" according to their global interests unless Israel forces them to take her well-being into account by potentially targeting nuclear warheads at Moscow.[22] Israel not only had no such delivery system but the Eshkol government had even delayed the development of the Jericho missile.

Sharing De Gaulle's analysis that Moscow initiated the crisis as a response to events in Vietnam, and aware of the country's isolation, Ben Gurion and Peres argued that Israel should "dig in for six months or a year without taking any military initiative." But Dayan concluded that, desirable or not, Israel could not escape a war and he proceeded to reacquaint himself with the IDF. He told the commander of the Southern forces: "You will win this war. We will screw the Arabs, but you will have 20,000 to 30,000 fatalities. Everyone. The best of our youth." For a nation of two and a half million, that would indeed have been a pyrrhic victory. Yet, the commander recalled that Dayan was the first person he heard express his belief in victory.[23]

An anxiety filled Rabin sought advice from Ben Gurion and Dayan. Ben Gurion opposed the precautionary mobilization of reserves because it constricted the time for diplomatic maneuvering. He told Rabin: "You, or whoever gave you permission to mobilize so many reservists, made a mistake. You have led the state into a grave situation. We must not go to war. We are isolated. You bear the responsibility." Clearly, he wanted Rabin to rectify his mistake. Dayan held his fire. The proper thing to do on the eve of the battle was to imbue confidence in the force commander. Rabin writes: "He spoke of the IDF with admiration, and I was grateful to him for that. If I was to be blamed for recommending mobilization of the reserves, thereby causing the situation to deteriorate and placing the country in danger, at least no one could accuse me of failing to prepare the IDF for the grave test in store for it."[24]

Rabin was clearly out of his depth. Since Ben Gurion's departure, Rabin had functioned as the country's chief security officer. But the young chief of staff, who had relished his uncommon power, was unnerved by the unexpected developments. Eshkol understood the gravity of the situation, but repeatedly asked Rabin, "What should we do next?" or "What do I want from the cabinet?" Rabin complained more and more loudly that he was not receiving clear instructions.[25] In Israel of 1967, such leadership weakness could not be kept secret. Israelis from all walks of life instinctively turned to their founding father as demands that Eshkol step aside in favor of Ben Gurion grew louder. They came from members of the leftist MAPAM and the rightist GAHAL. Nasser had concluded that Israel would not fight even if he closed the Straits, in part because its leadership was divided.[26]

When Johnson's long delayed letter to Nasser was shown to Harman, he exclaimed that Nasser would regard the letter "as an invitation to interfere with shipping in the Straits." The letter was delivered after the closure of the Straits, along with the "more explicit" note-verbale. Foreign Minister Riad described Nasser's incredulity:

> For the previous ten days Nasser had been questioning me closely over US intentions and so I promptly delivered the two communications to him.... Nasser asked if I was confident that this reflected a sincere and genuine position by Johnson. I said that I did not think the President of the United States of America would put his seal to an official document to beguile and deceive us. Yet Nasser was not reassured. After a moment's silence he said: "I doubt gravely the sincerity of Johnson. For a man who has always sided with Israel it is inconceivable that, all of a sudden, he would become even-handed."[27]

The Egyptian media reported that Eastern Europe, the Soviet Union and China would back the UAR if the US would be foolish enough "to make the same mistake she did in Southeast Asia." Israel was clearly in a bind.[28]

EBAN TO THE RESCUE

When the Israeli Cabinet met on May 23, it seemed to have two choices: go to war despite the lack of army readiness and the diplomatic isolation, or swallow hard and hunker down. The second option meant turning the government over to RAFI. Interior Minister Haim Shapira insisted:

> Because the situation is so severe, and we should not go to war under such circumstances. Only a personality known as an activist could tell the nation the unpopular truth without endangering the country with internal collapse. Only David Ben Gurion could tell this to the nation. But if his addition is impossible, Dayan could also do this."[29]

But there was the third option. Johnson asked Israel to delay action for 48 hours, and Eshkol was reluctant to turn him down. His memories of Samu and of the 1956 Soviet–American cooperation were too vivid. Some argued that, in the Vietnam era, Soviet–American relations were too strained to permit such collaboration. But others emphasized the American desire to avoid war at all costs. The French told Israel that the crisis had been instigated by the USSR because of Vietnam. If so, argued Eban, perhaps Moscow would not "agree to lose it." Eban thought he had a way to draw Washington into "the Middle Eastern whirlpool." Moreover, Rabin was unwilling to say that a 48-hour delay would jeopardize the outcome. The Cabinet decided to give Johnson time by authorizing Eshkol to send Eban to America.[30]

Eshkol preferred to send Golda Meir, a tougher negotiator, but she declined and Eban insisted. Rabin had collapsed, and Eshkol was under enormous political pressure. No one considered the probability that an official meeting between Eban and Johnson was bound to result in an American demand for a significant delay in military action. But then, the Israeli army was not even fully mobilized yet.[31]

Eban's trip was an attempt to justify the Eshkol/Eban foreign policy. The two believed that, by closing the Straits, Nasser had handed Israel a secret weapon in the form of a written American guarantee. If Washington did not want Israel to open the Straits, she would have to open them herself. Such an American undertaking would vindicate their trust in presidential commitments, eliminate the need to turn over the government to Ben Gurion or Dayan, and save Israel from war.

Already Washington had promised to notify Moscow that "interference with the freedom of navigation would be considered an act of aggression which entitled Israel to defend itself." The US had also floated the idea of an international task force to open the Straits, had ordered units of the Sixth Fleet towards the Eastern Mediterranean, and had agreed to provide Israel with 100 troop carriers, spare parts for tanks and even information on improving the capabilities of the Hawk anti-aircraft missiles.[32] Opening the Straits, Eban could argue, would rescue the Johnsonian principle of "commitment" from drowning in the marshes of Vietnam:

> Here, the American risk was minimal. Israel was strong, resolute and united. . . . The likelihood of Soviet or Chinese intervention was less than in Vietnam. The tactical objective, the cancellation of the Eilat blockade was limited in scope and entirely feasible. It was everything that the Vietnam War was not.[33]

As Eban and Eshkol saw it, a public meeting with Johnson was a no lose proposition as it would put the Americans "on the spot" and assure that at least they "would not act against" Israel once a war began. News that De Gaulle, who had remained ominously silent, was willing to see him led Eban to stop in Paris on his way to Washington. De Gaulle was threatening to cut the massive military airlift which poured in from France. Also, State had already tried to engage the British and the French in daily consultations about the crisis. The French ambassador soon called it quits with a pointed reference to 1956. If Israel could persuade the French to join the Red Sea regatta, Washington would be thrilled.[34] But De Gaulle told Eban that Western solutions were passé. The more Israel looked to the West, the less would be Soviet readiness to cooperate. Israel had "a case," De Gaulle said, but acting on it would put her own existence in jeopardy. The French military concluded that Israel would either lose or be terribly damaged. Eban continued to London and was delighted to find Wilson enthusiastic about the regatta and raring to discuss its "nuts and bolts" with the Americans.[35]

In New York reporters inquired whether Eban "was asking that American soldiers risk their lives for Israel?" He said that he was not; he merely came "to seek US respect for Israel's right of self defense." They remained skeptical. In the meantime, urgent cables from home indicated that Israeli intelligence had gotten wind of an Egyptian plan to launch a preemptive air attack on the night of May 27. The only way Israel could continue to refrain from action, argued Rabin, was if Johnson agreed to issue a statement declaring that "any attack on Israel would be considered an attack on the United States." When confronted with the unlikelihood of such an American declaration, he retorted: "For the sake of history, I want it written down that before we acted, we fully exploited all the diplomatic avenues available to us."[36] Eban showed Rusk the ominous cables. Since US intelligence did not know of the Egyptian plans, his hosts dismissed the Israeli alarm, but informed the Soviets and the Egyptians of the Israeli suspicions and warned them not to initiate hostilities. Johnson and his men who believed their own intelligence resented what they viewed as undue Israeli pressure.[37]

To strengthen his hand, Eban wanted to focus attention on the Eisenhower/Dulles guarantees. He asked Harman to "call Scotty Reston and remind him that in March 1957 he published an article summarizing the understandings between Golda and Dulles." A few minutes later, Reston called back to say that he found the article and got the point. Reston published a column on Johnson's failure to honor Eisenhower's pledge "to act unilaterally, if necessary" and recognize Israel's right to do the same.[38]

Eban's encounters with policy makers continued to be disastrous. McNamara and Wheeler doubted the utility of the international naval force, but assured the unhappy foreign minister that there was nothing to worry about. Israel would win the war in one week if she struck first, and in two if the Egyptians attacked first. The difference was "minor." Israel should sit fully mobilized and await the outcome of dubious American diplomatic initiatives.[39]

Finally, after a series of unnerving delays, indignities and mishaps, Eban found himself in the President's private White House apartment being told that the fulfillment of past guarantees depended on public and Congressional support which were difficult to come by in the Vietnam era. If Israel wanted American help, it had to risk an air attack on itself. The US would try in the meantime to organize an international regatta, and Israel should help her do so. Twice Eban suggested that the Israeli and American military get together to plan their response if Israeli rather than the American intelligence proved to be accurate, but was adroitly deflected.

Finally, Ambassador Harman lost his patience. Disregarding protocol, he said that he hoped the Israeli military experts were wrong, "but nevertheless if Israel was attacked, it would not have any telephone number to call, no military group to plan with." Eugene Rostow reminded him of American warnings to the UAR, but Johnson demurred. He said that while he did "not wish to establish any joint staff which would become known all over the Middle East and the world," McNamara should get together with the Israelis and look into the problem. McNamara remarked that he would be thrilled to be better informed about Israeli plans. "It was agreed some liaison arrangement would be made." The following day, Eugene Rostow suggested starting "the military liaison" with intelligence coordination. To Harman, "it was 100% clear," that no serious emergency planning was going to take place.[40]

Johnson insisted that his meeting with Eban would receive no media coverage, and he made Eban leave the White House through the back door. But NBC's Joseph Hersh found him at the airport. Eban took only one question: "Are you leaving as an optimist or a pessimist?" "I am a realist," was the retort broadcast around the world along with the evaluation that Eban had left the US empty handed.[41]

Especially rattled by the news were the Soviets whose strong opposition had convinced Nasser to call off the Egyptian preemptive attack earlier that day, May 26. Consequently, while Eban was flying home, Eshkol and his wife were "entertaining" Chuvakhin in their bathrobes. He came knocking on their door at 2:30 a.m. with a note from Kosygin urging Eshkol not to permit "war-loving circles" to gain the "upper hand." Eshkol made no promises, but suggested reapplying Tashkent formula to the Middle Eastern dispute and expressed willingness to go to Moscow. Chuvakhin promised to transmit the offer to his superiors.[42]

A two day Cabinet battle commenced on May 27. Eban led the pro-delay forces, and explained the obstacles that Vietnam placed on Johnson. If "misguidedly" or not, Johnson believed that given time he could overcome those obstacles, Israel "had an interest in granting him the time." The Americans believed the Israeli military was strong enough to wait. Politically, as long as there was a chance that Washington would come through, there was no need to hand over the leadership to Ben Gurion or Dayan. But Rabin despaired of the possibility that the US could ever be prevailed upon to permit Israel to preempt. He saw no reason to wait and make the war costlier. Others argued that "the past two weeks represented an impressive diplomatic achievement," but it was time to act. The manifest international impotence in the face of Nasser's admission that "his basic objective" was "to destroy Israel," and that all his moves were carefully planned towards that end, produced a major shift in world opinion from one of trepidation to open identification with the Jewish state. Western governments would be thus hard pressed to condemn a preemptive move, or rob Israel of the fruits of victory. Eshkol pleaded with the Cabinet not to make fateful decisions at 5 a.m.

By the time it reconvened, Eshkol had received strong messages from Washington, Paris and London urging restraint. "A top American official" had even gone to Amit's home and told him that, if Israel preempted, the US would "land" forces in Egypt "to protect her." Moreover, Nasser's mouthpiece Heikal reported that the Egyptians, to their ultimate peril, had acceded to Soviet demands and decided to ditch the first strike strategy in favor of "a second blow." He also stated that war was inevitable, which meant that Nasser had rejected a Middle East Tashkent. Johnson limited the political usefulness of his promises by prohibiting Eshkol from making them public. Eban and the religious ministers had to threaten resignation before the Cabinet agreed to turn down the IDF's recommendation for immediate action.[43]

Eshkol decided to explain the Cabinet decision to the country. His own job was on the line. The demand for the creation of a national unity government, which would mean turning over decision making powers to Ben Gurion or Dayan, seemed almost unstoppable. The papers printed calls for a such a change from leading industrialists, former chiefs of staff, police, university professors and other public figures. "We need men with international reputations who can surprise and not only be surprised," wrote an eminent physician. "Only a national unity government can guarantee all of us that the policy of cool restraint which is supposed to be the acknowledged policy of the government is not the result of hesitancy, lack of initiative or unfounded expectations," wrote Amos Kenan, a radical leftist columnist. Golda Meir retorted that such "talk" was undermining the government's negotiating position. Israel's friends were "being tested." "If they would not be able to prevent the wounding of the State of Israel, it would signal the general decline of civilization and the moral standing of humanity."

Her argument was not aided by reports from abroad: "The word Vietnam is heard here like a magic spell designed to deflect any suggestion that the US use force to open the Straits," wrote one correspondent. Another viewed Johnson's inaction as revenge for Israeli and American Jewish failure to support his Vietnam policy. Analysts also explained Soviet interest in using the Middle Eastern arena to get back at the Americans for Vietnam, to exploit Western disunity caused by its preoccupation with Vietnam, and to work out "a package deal" with the US. They also got hold of a French note of caution delivered to the Egyptian and Israeli ambassadors: "You will fight and in so doing you will become playing pieces in the global contest between the United States and the Soviet Union. Think before you turn your countries into a 'second Vietnam.'"[44]

Eshkol's May 28 radio address failed miserably. The attempt of the hurried prime minister to read a text full of erasures and corrections on live radio ended up convincing the nation that he shared their fear and confusion. Eshkol, refusing to admit defeat, told his outraged generals that, because of his personal acquaintance with Johnson, he believed the American president would "fulfill his promise." His speech to the Knesset the following day was just as defiant: The army was "at the zenith of its strength in manpower, fighting spirit and military equipment" and the ties Israel had forged with other nations had helped, and would continue to help. He also reported that Nasser had upped the ante once more: "The Egyptian President has proclaimed his intention and readiness to attack Israel for the purpose of destroying her. Yesterday, he went further and threatened to begin at once with extensive sabotage operations against Israel, her towns and villages, and her citizens. This very day attacks have been carried out against us from the Gaza strip." Nasser was clearly getting restless.[45]

THE LOT IS CAST

The UNEF removal from Gaza immediately raised the question of Palestinian infiltration. UNEF had provided Nasser with an excuse for prohibiting it. To give substance to the policy of PLO "preparedness," as opposed to FATAH's immediate action, Nasser, with UNEF acquiescence, had gradually moved PLA soldiers into Gaza where they manned a series of posts parallel to UNEF positions. On May 14, Nasser asked UNEF to withdraw from their posts in territorial Egypt and concentrate their forces in Gaza. That would have precluded PLO infiltration into Israel and prevented Gaza from becoming an early Israeli target. Shukayri tried to change Nasser's mind by revealing the existence or PLA units there. But when given a choice between no withdrawal or full withdrawal, Nasser chose the latter. The 72 UNEF posts in Gaza were turned over to the PLA.[46]

"Nasser permitted Shukayri to get organized," but would "he permit him to act?" That was the question asked in trepidation in Israel and, provocatively, in the Jordanian press. The Egyptians wrote that he would:

> The Fedayeen are the owners of Palestine and Israel does not have the right to challenge their rights. Had the United States with all her power succeeded in blocking what she calls infiltration into South Vietnam? . . . *THE ACTIONS WITHIN THE CONQUERED TERRITORY OF PALESTINE ARE LEGITIMATE.* These actions will not end and there is no force in the world that could end them.[47]

Israel let it be known that a major terrorist incident would produce a strong response. But Israeli intelligence worried. Failure to act, it cautioned Eshkol, would lead to "terrorist activities" against which "Israel would be helpless." Nasser might embark on imaginative scenarios such as a massive crossing of the border by Palestinian refugees. The existence or absence of PLO insurgency emerged as a barometer of Egyptian intentions and, for the first two weeks of the crisis, peace reigned. Therefore, its termination signaled a shift in Nasser's thinking. As he told the Egyptian National Assembly, he had succeeded in restoring "conditions to what they were in 1956" and "God" would help him "to restore conditions to what they were in 1948." To cover his campaign with the aura of national liberation, he needed to be seen as leading an Arab coalition on behalf of the PLO. Permitting the PLA army to undertake mining operations, and to open fire on Israeli border settlements, was the first step in redefining the nature of the crisis; accepting Jordanian surrender was the other.[48]

On May 21, the Jordanian chief of staff came to Cairo to propose reconciliation between Hussein and Nasser. He was turned away unceremoniously. On May 29, Nasser agreed to sign a mutual defense pact with King Hussein. Strategically, Nasser had always insisted that an attack on Israel could only originate from the West Bank. Jordanian forces were weak but, within a day, Iraq joined the pact and promised to send Iraqi units to Jordan. An Egyptian general was given command over the joint forces, and Egyptian commando units were dispatched to Aqaba. Hussein flew to Cairo to sign the pact and Nasser forced him to take Shukayri (the man who declared that "to liberate Tel Aviv" the PLO had first to "free Amman") back to Jordan. The following day, Hussein and Shukayri paraded down the main street of Amman and control over the Palestinians was transferred to the PLO, which began to distribute weapons to the population at large. The stage was set for an intensified "people's war."[49]

On May 22, Johnson wrote Nasser that "the great conflicts of our time are not going to be solved by the illegal crossings of frontiers with arms and men – neither in Asia, the Middle East, Africa, or Latin America. But that kind of action has already led to war in Asia, and it threatens the peace elsewhere." In his belated June 2 reply, Nasser carefully decoupled Vietnam and the Middle East by writing that he agreed with Johnson in principle, then denied responsibility for Palestinian actions:

> If you are referring to the crossing of the demarcation lines by some individuals of the Palestinian people . . . I may ask how far any government is able to control the feelings of more that one million Palestinians who, for twenty years, the international community – whose responsibility herein is inescapable – has failed to secure their return to their homeland.[50]

Hence Rabin's observation that Israeli failure to go to war in 1967 "would have led within a short period of time to a difficult guerrilla war" followed by an Arab attack in which Israel would not have been aided by "anyone!" But Eshkol, whose political survival depended on the materialization of outside help, told his commanders: "You have to believe that the President of the United States does not lie. If time went by and nothing will be achieved I, Levi Eshkol, will tell him [Johnson] personally that I see myself free of my vow [to wait]."[51]

On May 28, the Israeli government decided to give the Americans *two to three weeks* to open the Straits; Ambassador Barbour was so notified on May 29. But news from Paris and Washington as well as Cairo, changed things. The Soviets finally notified the French that they would not participate in a four power conference because the Arabs were opposed, the Americans and British supported Israel and the US was involved in Vietnam. Joe Alsop told Evron that Washington doubted direct Soviet interference. So, on May 30, Eshkol wrote Johnson a letter welcoming his commitments and promising to defer action for *a week or two*. To begin intelligence coordination, take Washington's temperature and convince Johnson to let Israel preempt, MOSSAD chief Amit flew secretly to Washington.[52]

Amit left Israel intent on presenting the following case: Events in the Middle East were part of the global struggle. The kind of Soviet influence in the area inherent in the Egyptian–Jordanian–Iraqi pact would present the US with a serious problem, as would the victory of the militant faction in the USSR which seemed to be responsible for the activation of the Middle Eastern front. Israeli forces were fully mobilized and the Israeli economy could not afford to keep them so for any length of time. Israel therefore wanted the United States: (1) To replenish the Israeli military arsenals after the war. (2) To give it political backing in the UN. (3) To isolate the battlefront.

Amit met with Helms, who informed him that "he couldn't agree more" with his analysis, that regardless of what Israel had been told, he did not head the task force to organize the regatta, and that Amit must see the men who really counted – Johnson, McNamara and Rusk. Helms arranged for Amit to meet with McNamara. The first of Amit's discouraging reports coincided with a cable from Evron indicating that, instead of organizing a regatta, Washington was sending special envoys to cut a deal with Nasser.[53]

In a last ditch effort to spur Johnson into action, Eshkol asked Eban "to hold a press conference with maximal reverberations." Eban told reporters that Israel was "a coiled spring." The May 31 conference rattled the Russians, not the Americans. They warned that following the line of action advocated by the "warmongering circles . . . would bring irreparable harm from Israel's point of view." Following that line was, indeed, Eban's solution to the failure of American guarantees. He hoped that, if all went well, the Eshkol government (not a National Unity one) would get the credit. On June 1, without even consulting Eshkol, Eban told Rabin that he withdrew his objections to preemption. It was too late. As the demand for a government reshuffle was emanating from his own party secretariat, Eshkol had already swallowed hard and turned over the post of defense minister to Dayan, showing his mettle by staying at his post as prime minister despite the fact that the whole world knew that, in the upcoming war, his role would be mostly ceremonial. The fig leaf designed to cover up MAPAI's surrender to RAFI was the creation of a "national emergency Cabinet" which included the GAHAL party headed by Menachem Begin. This legitimization of the right emerged as one of the important unintended consequences of the crisis.[54]

Dayan's appointment was treated with enormous relief in Israel, and as a declaration of war in the rest of the world. The news reached Amit at a meeting with McNamara and Maxwell Taylor. McNamara jumped off his chair, half hugged Amit and said: "I admire that person, give him my regards and my best wishes." Amit concluded that McNamara was no longer opposed to Israeli preemption. During the rest of the meeting, McNamara talked with the President twice and told Amit that Johnson knew Amit was in his office, was expecting a full briefing and that he would read Amit's report. Amit was peppered with questions ranging from the length of time Israel needed to secure victory, to projected Israeli casualties, to his evaluation of Soviet intentions. Upon hearing McNamara's skeptical response to his comment that it would be advisable to accelerate the preparations for the Red Sea regatta, Amit told his hosts: "I am going home in the belief that you won't do anything. I will recommend that Israel go to war." McNamara retorted: "I read you clearly, it was very helpful."[55]

But his most important encounter took place with Lyndon Johnson "outside receiving hours." Amit explained that the strong Israeli preference for preemption emanated from projected casualty figures. "If we can get the first blow in, our casualties will be comparatively light. Hundreds of dead – but no more. If we have to sit and wait for them to attack, we will still win – but our dead will be closer to ten thousand." Johnson told Amit that if Israel insisted on going to war, he would not stand in her way. Unwilling to assume full responsibility for presenting the probable American response to an Israeli preemption, Amit insisted that Harman return with him to Israel to present his own assessment of the situation. Harman went to see Rusk. Rusk cautioned him not to preempt but otherwise "sent him away empty handed" and Harman thought Rusk knew it.[56]

After an overnight flight in a cargo plane filled with medical supplies and gas masks (Egypt had used poison gas in Yemen), Amit and Harman rushed directly to an ongoing Cabinet meeting. Both recommended further delay. Officially, Amit reported that the American administration was deeply divided, with various forces pulling in different directions. The Americans would not act against Israel if she waited until they suffered additional setbacks and then tied her action to the Straits. Unofficially, Amit reported that he found amongst many people a desire for a prompt Israeli action which would lead to the deflation of Nasser. He recommended testing the blockade by sending a ship through the Straits. Both Amit and Harman emphasized American opposition to preemption and the lack of American promises of support. Amit said: "If we start a war and succeed, everybody will be with us. But if we do not succeed – we would have difficulty."[57]

In his first day in office, Dayan gave Rabin orders to be ready to start operations on June 5. But the Cabinet debate continued: Should Israel send a ship through the Straits before attacking? That was the course recommended by Amit and Harman. Dayan argued that it was not possible to deceive the Americans, and it was an "idiocy to wait for them!" Between May 23 and June 3, the number of Egyptian divisions in the Sinai had increased from two to six. Dayan warned: "We will be busy in El-Arish and they will take Jerusalem. If we wait 7–9 days, there would be thousands of dead.... We will strike and then embark on diplomatic activity. We must do this regardless of political disadvantages." It was not an easy sale. The June 4 Cabinet debate, which authorized preemption, lasted seven hours.[58]

To recover a measure of tactical surprise, Dayan released a large number of Israeli reservists and told reporters that it was either too late or too early for an Israeli military response. To calm the US, he added that Israel was not another Vietnam:

> I do not know whether we got... promises or not, but... I, personally, do not *expect* and do not *want* anyone else to fight for us. Whatever can be done in the diplomatic way I would welcome and encourage, but if somehow it comes to real fighting I would not like American or British boys to get killed here, and I do not think we need them.[59]

Ben Gurion's tutelage showed in Dayan's strategic thinking. He insisted on capturing the Straits, but prohibited advancing to the Suez Canal or any serious operations against Gaza, Syria or Jordan. Originally, the plan had called for the capture of Gaza and the northern Sinai all the way to the Suez Canal. These territories would then be returned for an Egyptian agreement to open the Straits. His instructions were only partially followed.[60]

DECISIONS UNDER FIRE

Shortly after the war, Dayan told a closed parliamentary forum:

> The Six Day war was the least preplanned war. In the Sinai war we decided on the military moves ahead of time. In the Six Day War we did not. Not in the West Bank, not in Jerusalem and not in Syria.... There was operative planning by the army, but

no political planning. We did not prepare a plan to where we were going. The goals were set during the War.[61]

Hours before the war began, Harry McPherson stopped in Israel on his way back from Vietnam "to show the Israelis that we were friends and to take any messages back to him [Johnson] that they wanted." He brought an enigmatic message from Johnson: "May God give us strength to protect the right." Still, Israel went to war without an American promise to "isolate the battlefield" and with the Sixth Fleet far from her shores.[62]

Eshkol waited until he was secure in the success of his air force before answering Johnson's June 3 letter. Eshkol had considered muddying the waters on the question of the first shot, but McPherson insisted that Johnson had to know whether he was "going to be talking on behalf of a country that was literally attacked or a country that launched a preemptive attack?" Eshkol wrote that Israel was "engaged in repelling the aggression" which Nasser had built up against it, i.e. Israel had a convincing *casus belli*. He gently reminded Johnson that the US had made "impressive commitments" to "pursue vigorous measures" to open the Straits, but had found their fulfillment "difficult." A less diplomatic Israeli citizen leaned into Barbour's car and said: "Don't believe the Americans. They'll lie to you."[63]

McPherson wrote: "After the doubts, the confusions, and ambiguities of Vietnam, it was deeply moving to see people whose commitment is total and unquestioning." Eshkol's allusion to Vietnam was more subtle: "We rely on the courage and determination of our soldiers and citizens. Indeed maximum self-reliance is the central aim of our national revival. My information is that our defense is reaping success." McPherson elaborated: There was never any doubt about the outcome because "there was simply no alternative."

Eshkol did ask "that everything be done by the United States to prevent the Soviet Union from exploiting and enlarging the conflict" or as McPherson reported, "they wanted us to keep the Russians off their backs and they wanted 'two or three days to finish the job.'" Eshkol's conclusion that the war could "create conditions favorable to the promotion of peace and the strengthening of forces of freedom in the area" was translated by McPherson to mean that, since Israel got Washington "out of a difficult situation in the Middle East," the US should not repeat the 1956 scenario and force Israel "to withdraw within their boundaries with only paper guarantees that fall apart at the touch of Arab hands" but instead help it to secure "a peace treaty that recognizes the State of Israel" in lieu of the conquered territories.[64]

On the first day of the war, Eshkol publicly announced that Israel had no territorial ambitions. Indeed, that day, Israel was willing to accept a ceasefire in return for the opening of the Straits. The Egyptian air force was destroyed, Israel suffered only minimal casualties, and a settlement under a joint Soviet–American sponsorship would secure for Israel a superpower guarantee of her existence and territorial integrity. Amer read the situation correctly and begged the Soviet ambassador to secure an immediate ceasefire, but Nasser refused to believe that all was lost. Subsequent decisions under fire turned the region, just as De Gaulle had predicted, into a central Cold War battlefront.[65]

Dayan's determination to safeguard Israeli independence increased after witnessing the way the American presence had robbed the South Vietnamese of any semblance of control over their own lives. His efforts to retain some relations with Moscow were manifest in his opposition to plans to reach the Suez Canal or capture the Golan Heights. Eshkol and Eban were not only livid at Soviet willingness to sacrifice Israel on the altar of the Cold War but they no longer believed that Israeli actions or inactions impacted Soviet behavior. Intentionally or not, the Israeli success served Western interests and only the US could neutralize the inevitable Soviet retaliation. When Moscow warned that unless Israel agreed to an immediate UN mandated ceasefire (without waiting for Syrian or Egyptian responses) it would "reconsider" the future of diplomatic relations with Israel and would "examine and implement other necessary steps which emanate from the aggressive policy of Israel," Israel immediately notified Washington. She also passed along her Soviet experts' view that the threats were not a "serious ultimatum" but merely part of Moscow's "effort to retrieve" a "portion" of its "Vietnam diplomatic losses in present situation."[66]

At first Dayan called the shots, and no one argued with him. But Eban's report that "an Israeli military success on the Syrian front would not incur displeasure in Washington," caused an internal debate. The American scenario was tempting. Though the Syrian military confined itself to the shelling of border kibbutzim, it inflicted enormous damage on them. Their members did not expect the war to end with the Golan Heights still in Syrian hands. Eshkol was also interested in capturing the Jordan water sources which the Syrians were diverting. He organized kibbutz delegations and incited army commanders. However, Dayan would not be moved. He even shocked the cabinet with the heretical suggestion that the kibbutzim be moved.

The Syrian front was under the direct control of Soviet advisers. For days, Russian speaking Israelis had been monitoring commands directing Syrian artillery. An attack on Syria would offend both the Soviets and the French. Dayan also worried about the ability of the "corroded" Israeli forces (the air force had lost 30 percent of its meager fighter planes) to fight a three front war but Eshkol had the Cabinet's support. When the army intelligence intercepted a cable from Nasser to Syrian president Attassi admitting that "they had lost this battle" and advising him to save his army by agreeing to an immediate ceasefire, Dayan concluded that at least "his short term reasons" had lost their force. To preempt Eshkol, Dayan ordered an attack on the Golan Heights. Reports of the collapse of the Syrian front notwithstanding, the conquest of the Golan was long and bloody.

Moscow threatened direct intervention. Washington countered the Soviet threats, but pressured Israel to end the fighting "so that the war would not end because of a Soviet ultimatum." An irate Goldberg "ordered" UN ambassador Rafael to accept a ceasefire resolution without instruction from Israel. Rafael retorted that he received his orders from Eshkol, and not from Johnson. In the Politburo, Soviet "hawks" demanded military intervention but Gromyko convinced them that cutting diplomatic ties with Israel would suffice. Such an announcement was made on June 10. On June 18, the Soviet diplomatic staff sailed home from Haifa. They took along their own POWs, five officers including one general, captured by Israel during the battle of the Heights.[67]

A cold war between Israel and the USSR commenced. But Israelis were too intoxicated by the unexpected discovery of their spiritual roots to notice. The conquest of the West Bank and East Jerusalem followed an Israeli and American failure to convince Jordan to stay out of the war. The decision to capture the Old City of Jerusalem was taken with trepidation. It was going to cost many lives and the Cabinet was sure Israel would not be permitted to keep it. The head of the religious party said: "I guess they'll suggest turning the old city into an international city and I am personally not against it."[68]

Then, something happened. "When a person fights for his life not as an isolated individual," explained philosophy professor Eliezer Shveid, "but as a part of a community and a member of a nation – whose existence is threatened by belonging to it, the walls separating the individual and the community fall and are replaced by a sense of identification with the collective as a collective. Then the history of the nation becomes a biographical experience and cultural symbols and traditions receive a direct personal meaning."[69] The battle weary young paratrooper praying at the Western Wall crystallized that type of experience not only for Israelis but for Jews the world over, and rebonded them with their God in a manner which surprised them all. Dayan did what Jews had done for generations: He scribbled a note and placed it amongst the ancient stones. It read: "May peace descend upon the whole house of Israel."[70] It did not.

NOTES

1. Eban, *Personal Witness*, 352–3; and Parker, *Six Day War*, 3.
2. Soviet Foreign Ministry announcement, April 21, 1967, Israeli–Russian Relations, 809/00, ISA.
3. The warning was printed in *Pravda*, April 27, 1967.
4. *Security Council Official Records*, Supplement for April, May and June 1967, Doc. S/7881; and Andrew W. Cordier and Max Harrelson, *Public Papers of the Secretaries-General of the United Nations, U Thant* (New York: 1976), 414.
5. *Jerusalem Post*, May 12, 1967; and Parker, *Politics of Miscalculation*, 228.
6. Haber, *Hayom Tifroz Milchama*, 150; Interviews with Yariv and a source close to Eshkol; and Bar Zohar, *Embassies in Crisis*, 10.
7. Parker, *The Six Day War*, 42 and 59.
8. "Battle Order No. 1," *Maarchot* (June 1968), 100; and Gilboa, *Shesh Shanim*, 86.
9. Parker writes that "there had been enough US involvement with anti-Nasser elements to make such suspicions understandable." *Politics of Miscalculation*, 100.
10. Haber, 154.
11. *Maariv*, May 19, 1967.
12. Gilboa, 9 and 91, 308; *Kol Haam*, May 17, 1966; and interview with Yariv.
13. Abba Eban, *Autobiography* (New York: 1977), 599.
14. Eban, *Personal Witness*, 340, 364; Rabin, *Pinkas Sherut*, 130, 152 and 162.

15. Arie Brown, *Chotam Ishi* (Tel Aviv: 1997), 109–10; Eban, *Personal Witness*, 407 and 447; Haber, 166–8, 249, 276–7; and Nutting, *Nasser (*New York: 1972), 398.
16. Haber, 162 and 186.
17. Interview with Amit. Quandt, "Lyndon Johnson and the June 1967 War," 216; Urquhart, *Ralph Bunche*, 404; and Eban, *Personal Witness*, 361.
18. Embassy Washington, May 18 and 22, Diplomatic cables, Six Day War, Yad Eshkol; and Haber, 161.
19. Memorandum for the Record, May 19, 1967, NSF, M.E. Crisis, box 17, 25a, LBJL; and Haber, 173.
20. Eban, *Personal Witness*, 362; and Dennis Eisenberg, Uri Dan and Eli Landau, *The MOSSAD* (New York: 1979), 159.
21. Rabin, *Pinkas Sherut*, 146–7.
22. Hersh, *The Samson Option*, 176.
23. Eban, *Personal Witness*, 403; Slater, *Warrior Statesman*, 246, 250.
24. Rabin, 76.
25. Haber, 155–83.
26. Geist, "The Six Day War," 172; and CIA report, May 1967, TDCSDB–315/01755–67, NSF, M.E. Crisis, box 17, LBJL.
27. Geist, "The Six Day War," 172–3; Riad, *The Struggle for Peace*, 17–18.
28. *Al Hawadat, Al Siah*, May 19, 20, 1967.
29. Haber, 161.
30. Embassy Paris, May 23, 1967, Diplomatic cables, Six Day War, Yad Eshkol; Eban, *Personal Witness*, 368; Haber, 163–70.
31. Haber, 170–1; and interview with a source close to Eshkol.
32. Haber, 165, 173.
33. Eban, *Personal Witness*, 393.
34. "Interview with Abba Eban," *Skira Hodshit*, March 1987; *Maariv*, Oct. 4, 1967; interview with E. Rostow.
35. Eban, *Personal Witness*, 374–6; 396 and Diplomatic cables, France, 256, Six Day War, Yad Eshkol.
36. Haber, 191 and 188; Eban, *Personal Witness*, 381; Rabin, 164–5.
37. Eban, *Personal Witness*, 379–83.
38. Interview with an Israeli diplomat; and *NYT*, May 28, 1967.
39. Eban, *Personal Witness*, 385; Patir, "Miyomano shel Dorer," May 26, 1967, 14; and interview with McNamara.
40. Memorandum of Conversation, Appointment File, May–June, 1967, box 66, 1d, LBJL; American Embassy, May 27, 1967, diplomatic cables, Six Day War, Yad Eshkol; interview with an Israeli diplomat.
41. Patir, June 26, 1967, 15–16; and *NYT*, May 27–8, 1967.
42. William B. Quandt, *Peace Process* (Berkeley: 1993), 512n; Haber, 191; *Haaretz*, June 5, 1992; and interview with a source close to Eshkol.
43. Patir, May 27–8, 1967; Haber, 192–3, 197; Rabin, 177; *Maariv*, June 5, 1992; Brown, *Chotam Ishi*, 23–4; and interview with a source close to Eshkol.
44. *Haaretz*, May 22, 26, 28, 30, 1967; and *Maariv*, May 22, 24, 25, 26, 28, 29, 1967.
45. Speech of Prime Minister Levi Eshkol, May 29, 1967 as printed in

Draper, *Israel and World Politics*, 248–54; Haber, *Hayom Tifroz Milchama*, 196; and Geist, “Six Day War,” 279.
46. Indar Jit Rikye, *The Sinai Blunder* (New York: 1980), 160–1; and PLO radio, May 16, 1967
47. *Tamzit Shidurim* and Radio Cairo, May 19, 1967.
48. Haber, 152, 164 and 205; interviews with Yariv, and Amit; and Draper, *Israel and World Politics*, 232.
49. “Ashaf,” *Maarchot*, Oct. 1968, 25.
50. Parker, *Politics of Miscalculation*, 225–6 and 239–41.
51. *Maariv*, June 2, 1972; and Haber, 200.
52. French Embassy and American Embassy, May 29, 1967, diplomatic cables, Six Day War, Yad Eshkol.
53. Interview with Amit; Patir, May 30, 1967, 19.
54. Eban, *Personal Witness*, 402–6; interview with a source close to Eshkol.
55. Patir, June 1, 1967, 19; and interviews with Amit. McNamara denied meeting Amit.
56. Interviews with an Israeli diplomat and a source close to Eshkol; and Eisenberg, *The MOSSAD*, 161. Rabin’s estimate of Israeli casualties was 50,000. Aronson, *Politics and Strategy of Nuclear Weapons*, 389.
57. Interview with Amit; and Haber, 217.
58. Haber, 218
59. Geist, 379.
60. Haber, 273; and Baron, 35–9.
61. Ibid.
62. Harry McPherson, LBJ-OH, Tape 4, 22; Eban, *Personal Witness*, 409.
63. Harry McPherson, LBJ-OH, Tape 4, 25 and 35; Harry McPherson to the President, June 11, 1967; and “Message from Prime Minister to the President,” June 5, 1967, MSF, M.E. Crisis, box 18, 170 and 198, LBJL.
64. Ibid.
65. Dagan, *Moscow and Jerusalem*, 226; Rusk, *As I Saw It*, 387; and Sadat, *In Search of Identity*, 174–6.
66. From Amembassy Tel Aviv to Secstate, June 7, 1967, NSF, Israel, box 138, 50, LBJL.
67. Brown, 82–111; interview with a source close to Eshkol; Rafael, 164–5; and Vassiliev, 70.
68. Brown, 56–9; Haber, 230–1.
69. Eliezer Shveid, “The Religious Aspect of the Six Day War,” *Bead Vaneged* (May 1969), 20.
70. Yael Dayan, *My Father, His Daughter* (Jerusalem: 1976), 184.

9 Jewry Transformed

THE ATTEMPT AT INFLUENCE

When the crisis began, Jewish leaders knew that their ongoing argument with Johnson over Vietnam left them open to the following:

> The foreseeable has now eventuated. Jewish organizations . . . The American Jewish Congress and the American Jewish Committee are importuning our President to insure Israel's security in the face of poised Arab aggressor allies of the No. Vietnamese and Vietcong.
>
> The American Jewish Committee, of which I am a member, comes into "court" with half clean-hands – The American Jewish Congress – with unparalleled 'Chutzpa' with all-dirty hands. The former at least took no public position on the Vietnam crisis – The American Jewish Congress *this week* – features a fervid opponent of our policy – part of a long public campaign against Pres. Johnson's policy in S.E. Asia.[1]

Worried about quips on "Hoves and Dawks," anti-war leaders maintained a low profile and shied away from public appeals for a strong pro-Israeli stance. Thus, the steering committee of the Presidents' Conference criticized as too provocative AIPAC statements which blamed the crisis on the Soviets and appealed for an American ship to break the blockade. But these apprehensions gave way to the fear that Washington's reluctance to stand by Israel was "attributable to the ugly resentments expressed by some administration spokesmen and Congressmen" against Jewish critics of the Vietnam War. Indeed, Walt Rostow called Johnson's taunting of Jewish leaders with State's version of the May 23 Middle Eastern address "a little therapy."[2]

The President told Eban that "a bunch of rabbis" told him "to put the whole American fleet into the Gulf of Aqaba" but objected to his sending "a [expletive deleted] screwdriver to Vietnam." Of course, those rabbis would have loved to remind him that he sent half a million men to Vietnam, and not one ship to Aqaba, and "what the so-called hawks asked for, in the first place, was an American position in the Middle East which might . . . have entirely avoided the outbreak of hostilities."[3] Also, since US preoccupation with Vietnam caused Nasser and the Soviets to labor under the "misconception" that Vietnam "*drained*" American "*strength*" and "*limited*" its "*freedom of action in the Near East*," it was only fair, as Javits pointed out after a meeting with McNamara, that the US help Israel deal with the unintended consequences of that "misconception."[4]

In any case, rabbis had little access to the President. When Prinz asked for an audience with Johnson, Walt Rostow advised the president to turn the request down. Since the administration did not know "where it was going," Johnson might say too much or too little and pay a diplomatic or political price for it. Rostow told Prinz that Johnson felt "it inadvisable to receive at the White House any group of U.S. citizens concerned with the Near East crisis." Later Prinz asked about an "off the record" meeting in New York, but was again turned down.[5]

The ball was thus in the court of Johnson's personal friends and advisers who supported and even helped formulate his Vietnam policy. Senator Javits and Congressman Celler represented Jewish Congressional concerns to the White House. Abe Feinberg, Arthur and Mathilde Krim, Abe Fortas and David Ginzberg were the conduits to the leadership, and Eppy Evron represented Israel. Together they emphasized their own loyalty, trust and understanding of Johnson's predicament, made clear that it was "not realistic" to expect them to "moderate public opinion," and warned him of the negative political consequences which would ensue from his failure to help Israel.[6] Prior to the closure of the Straits, they worked to convince Johnson to rejuvenate the deterrent force of the American commitment to Israel.

Mathilde Krim, a former Israeli and a close friend of the President, decided to provide herself and Johnson with an alternative analysis of the situation. She turned to Sam Mark of the "dovish-leftist" Institute of Mediterranean Affairs. Mark recommended that Johnson issue a statement which would set forth not only the American commitment to Israeli security but also include a serious initiative for a negotiated settlement of the Arab–Israeli dispute "on the basis of dignity and respect for the United Nations Resolutions." He also warned:

> A "laissez faire" policy in the Middle East far from vindicating the American stance in Vietnam would, in the eyes of many,

> rather completely invalidate it and would arouse great suspicion as to the sincerity and purity of America's motives, both in the Far East as well as in the Middle East. Many would suspect that freedom and national independence are not the real issues at stake – but that American foreign policy is dictated at best by strictly (and perhaps erroneous) strategic considerations or at worse, by some sinister motivations both in the Far East and in the Middle East.[7]

One of the main arguments advanced by Johnson's Jewish friends was that American inaction in the Middle East would erode support for the Vietnam War. White House mail proved their point: A Democratic precinct captain wrote that the value of the American presence in Vietnam would be "deprecated" if it precluded "assisting proven friends and allies like Israel" since it would imply that Washington's commitment in Vietnam was "to be to the exclusion of all else." A group of Pennsylvania citizens asserted that it made "no sense to fight for democracy in the Far East" while letting it be "destroyed in the Near East." Then there was this telegram: "We gave a boy for freedom in Vietnam. Act Now. Support Israel's Right to Freedom."[8]

When Nasser closed the Straits, the insiders knew they had lost the first round. They shifted their attention to the wording of the Presidential statement setting forth the American response to closure. In this instance, they succeeded in convincing Johnson to amend State's draft in a way which emphasized the international character of the Straits. Afterwards, they were generous with their praise. Feinberg called to relate his and Goldberg's approval of the statement. Evron conveyed his understanding of Johnson's "terrible dilemma" along with "his deep personal gratitude" for the "wonderful" final product. He also reported that the embassy "was flooded with telephone calls from people we both would respect, who were deeply gratified by your statement."[9]

But the statement was part of a package deal which delayed Israeli action. Eugene Rostow, who blamed "the realities created by the Vietnam War" for the American timidity, argued that Washington bore "an enormous responsibility" for the consequences of preventing Israeli preemption and worked hard to advance the prospects of the "Red Sea Regatta." The forthright Goldberg found himself torn between concern for Israel and his duties as an American diplomat. He told Harman that "the Vietnamese situation forces him to tell Johnson to go to the UN before taking military action."[10]

By the third week of the crisis, cognizant of the deteriorating Middle East situation and the unlikelihood of American action, Johnson's Jewish advisers began to press Israel to go and Johnson to let it go. Goldberg led the pack. He repeatedly emphasized to Israeli officials the limits of Johnson's commitments. When Johnson seemed ready to agree, Goldberg assured him that Jews would not blame him for reneging on his past commitments.[11]

Two memos sent to the president on May 31, the day it became clear that "Israel stood alone," suggest that at this late stage even the self-described "socialist, non-Zionist" Walt Rostow joined the Jewish effort to impress upon Johnson his vulnerability on the issue of "credibility." The first was from Ben Wattenberg:

> I thought you would like to see a copy of what you said extemporaneously in Ellenville, New York, last August . . . I don't believe anyone remembered it – Roche says it was not in the State Department file, Hal Saunders had not seen it and says *it is the only public occasion where you have equated Israel and South Viet Nam.*
>
> Walt and I agree that we wish we could write speeches as well as you talk them. When the time is ripe, this statement ought to be conveniently "remembered" by the press, Jewish leaders, etc. (– unless it surfaces by itself prior to that – it is on the record.)[12]

In fact, a week earlier, a New York Congressman had already recalled the Presidential pledge in Ellenville.[13] But the reference was not picked up by the press. Of course, Wattenberg and Rostow could have made sure that it would have been. Later that day, Rostow's memo outlining his conversation with Evron let Johnson know he was disappointing his trusting friend. Evron said that his cabinet had delayed action on the basis of Evron's personal assurances that Johnson would come through. Evron then asked:

> "Am I wrong in assessing the President's personal determination as I did?" I said that, as a government servant, it would be wrong for me to communicate that kind of judgement. I said, "You have known President Johnson for a long time and have the right to make your own assessment."
>
> With tears in his eyes, he said: "So much hinges on that man."[14]

Everything possible was done to pacify that man. Krim and Feinberg organized a series of fund raising events for the June 3 weekend in New York. The dinner honoring the president was attended by 1650 Democrats, "many of them members of the city's large and influential Jewish community," who applauded loudly when Johnson said: "I know that you share my deep concern tonight about the situation in the Middle East. We are working day and night on this problem." An impressed Robert Kennedy gave Johnson "the warmest endorsement the Senator ever offered." It was while Johnson was sitting between Mary Lasker and Mathilde Krim, enjoying a glittering dinner dance, that Feinberg bent over and told him that the war would start within 24 hours.[15]

Jewish organizations also made sure that there were no major anti-war demonstrations that weekend. A non-sectarian peace organizer noted that, under normal circumstances, 5,000 protesters would have been expected to greet Johnson; he would be lucky if 2,000 showed up. He got only between 1,000 and 1,400. So, peace groups had no choice but to put off demonstrations and lobbying efforts planned for the second weekend of June until the Middle East situation got clarified. Of course, there was a limit to the best laid plans. On the day following the fundraiser there were two pictures on the front page of the *NYT*: one was of Kennedy and Johnson entitled "Fellow Democrats;" the other of a handcuffed Captain Howard Levy sentenced to three years of hard labor for refusing to train Vietnam bound Green Beret fighting medics.[16]

In any case, at the noon hour of June 5, when Robert McClosky defined American Middle Eastern policy as "neutral," all their efforts seemed in vain. To disillusioned Jews, his words reflected willingness "to purchase world peace . . . at the expense of Israel's liberty" and "see Jewish blood flow into the Mediterranean to insure the continued flow of oil." Hans Morgenthau remarked, had Israel succumbed, "the President of the United States would have invited leading rabbis to the White House to recite memorial prayers."[17]

Moreover, American neutrality, as astute reporters immediately understood and as David Ginzberg and Abe Fortas warned, would have prevented Israel from raising money in the US and would have entailed imposing on Israel the very economic sanctions Johnson helped block in 1956. Shifting neutrality to non-belligerence solved the Emergency Fund's problem but Rusk's emphasis on American support for "territorial integrity" raised fears that, once again, Israeli blood would be shed in vain because once again the US would insist on Israeli withdrawal without Arab recognition of her legitimacy.[18] On June 6, the US changed its mind, but hardly as the result of the Jewish efforts in or out of the administration. The experience transformed American Jewry.

SOMETHING HAPPENED

"As the Arabs began to close in on Israel in the second half of May, American Jews, so frequently accused of indifference and passivity, turned into a passionate, turbulent, clamorous multitude, affirming in unprecedented fashion that they were part of the Jewish people and that Israel's survival was their survival," wrote historian Lucy Dawidowicz. The Arab threats to annihilate Israel, and the international reluctance to protect her, filled Jews with dread. Heschel wrote: "The darkness of Auschwitz is still upon us, its memory is a torment forever. In the midst of that darkness there is one gleam of light: the return of our people to Zion. Will He permit this gleam to be smothered?"[19]

If so, could Judaism survive? Some Jews believed it could not. A congregant asked Rabbi Irving Greenberg: "What shall we do if Israel fights and we lose?" The rabbi answered: "You will find a sign outside our synagogue that we are closed." In short, American Jews who blamed themselves for not doing enough to prevent the first Holocaust were not only determined to prevent a second one but believed that their own survival as Jews was at stake.

Seemingly overnight, the rules of the game had changed. Students and academicians suddenly realized the meaning of their ethnic and religious heritage. Civil rights and peace activist Alan Dershowitz recalls:

> I doubt that I would have become involved in Jewish issues as intensively as I did. But I felt my second-class citizenship as a Jew quite palpably . . . If my support for Israel were perceived as too strong, too emotional, I would be seen as the kind of person who placed his parochial Jewishness before his other, more universal values. In the days just before the Six-Day War, My Jewishness *was* my most important value. . . . And I decided not to hide my feelings.[20]

Dershowitz's experience was typical. Polls showed that 99 percent of the American Jews supported Israel before, during, and after the war. Their commitment to Israel went far beyond unprecedented financial donations. Tens of thousands donated their blood or volunteered to go to Israel. At Case Western Reserve University, the 200 available applications were gone within fifteen minutes. Some wished to fight, other to fill the civilian jobs vacated by Israelis. Thousands of others engaged in local organizational activities. I. E. Kenen of AIPAC recalls:

> Washington Jews wanted a major demonstration and, in preparation, the Jewish Community Council invited 200 leaders to a planning session . . . 800 jammed the hall. . . . I mentioned our need for volunteers, which brought but one question: "What's your address?"
>
> When I arrived at the Colorado Building a short time later, the lobby and the elevators were jammed, and for days we had many bright Washingtonians in our office, clipping scrapbooks, folding letters, stuffing envelopes, and abstracting speeches.[21]

Afterwards, sociologist Marshall Sklare tried to assess the impact of the crisis on the Jewish community. He chose a location where his earlier study indicated the response would be minimal. He found that "feelings of Jewish identity – albeit on the unconscious level" – were more abiding than he had "any reason to suspect previously." When asked whether she had family in Israel, a woman answered "two and a half million."[22]

This mood was reflected in the behavior of academic Jewry. A group at Cornell University named themselves the Ad Hoc Committee of American Professors and began to solicit signatures for an advertisement calling upon the American government to "safeguard the integrity of the state of Israel." Within three days 3,742 academicians, including three Nobel laureates, from 128 universities signed the document; 1,500 additional signatures came in after the ad went to press. This response prompted them to create the American Professors for Peace in the Middle East; 8,000 professors from 170 universities joined within a month.[23]

In a letter to the editor of the *Village Voice*, Nancy Weber described her generation's epiphany:

> Us. Two weeks ago, Israel was they; now Israel is we. I will not intellectualize it. . . . I will never again be able to talk about how Judaism is only a religion, and isn't it too bad that there has to be such a thing as a Jewish state. . . . I will never again kid myself that we are only the things we choose to be. Roots count. I was walking along the street listening to a transistor radio when

> I first heard that the Israelis, the Jews, had reached the Wailing Wall and with guns slung over their shoulders were praying there. No one was watching me, but I wept anyway. Sometimes even the tear-glands know more than the mind.[24]

Nor would Jews permit their commitment to Israel to be compromised by any embarrassment over their opposition to the war in Vietnam. They urged the American government to take strong action to keep the peace in the Middle East, which at first meant strong verbal support for Israel and, later, US unilateral or multilateral action to keep the Straits open. Historian Barbara Tuchman implored Johnson to act with "the nerve and firmness of intent" and in that way "restore the prestige" the country lost in Vietnam. If the US failed to support "its stated position" on the Straits because of the war in Vietnam, she warned, its "uneasy rationale – called 'resistance to aggression'" – would collapse "hollowly and publicly" regardless of efforts to convince the public that "carnage" in Vietnam meant "freedom," and "scuttle" in the Middle East meant "peace."[25]

In the end, for Tuchman, as for Jean Daniel of the leftist *Le Nouvel Observateur*, the only relevant questions were: "Is Israel threatened with death? Yes, undoubtedly. Can we accept this? No, at no price." On the haunted European continent, where the impact of the Holocaust was most direct, silence was not an option as non-Jews Jean Paul Sartre and Simone de Beauvoir readily admitted. It was also not an option for those who, like the famous couple, spent time in the area studying the situation first hand. They were quick to sign a statement declaring that it was "impossible to understand, regardless of whatever game the Great Powers follow" how a part of public opinion could accept "as self evident the identification of Israel with the aggressive and imperialist camp," and how people could forget that Israel was the only country whose very existence was in jeopardy.

Hundreds of continental intellectuals from the right to the left appealed for international action on behalf of Israel. They included Pablo Picasso, Raymond Aron, François Mauriac, Jean-Jacques Servan Schreiber, Günter Grass, Federico Fellini and Vittorio de Sica. In France, only half of the volunteers for Israel were Jewish; many were Catholic priests. Claude Lanzmann cried: "I will yell 'Long Live Johnson,' if he will be the only one who would save Israel." At a joint Gaullist–Communist rally in France, Communists carried placards declaring that between the party line and Israel, they chose Israel. They were invaluable as legitimizers of an anti-Vietnam, but pro-Israel, stance.[26]

In Britain, where the experience of the genocidal past was less direct, there was greater adherence of non-Jewish intellectuals to ideological lines. Still, enough Vietnam doves turned into Middle East hawks for historian Robert Conquest to note that the crisis had "shaken up the thoughtless orthodoxies previously prevailing" and forced some intellectuals to start "to think – and to resent their earlier bondage." Summarizing a major Anglo-American symposium on the subject, *Encounter* remarked that intellectuals came to realize that speaking "truth to power" required some knowledge of what that truth was, "not only in the sense of a consciousness of eternal values but also in that of a more pied-a-terre familiarity with the facts of a political problem which determined the application to it of higher principles."[27]

THE ALLIES THAT FAILED

In the US, the reluctance of many peace movement leaders to engage in such an exploration drove a wedge between them and their Jewish allies. "I think it is inconsistent to favor unilateral intervention in one part of the world when I'm already opposed to unilateral intervention in another part of the world," was the reason Arthur Schlesinger Jr. gave for refusing to sign an appeal to Johnson to maintain free passage in the Straits and "not let Israel perish." John Kenneth Galbraith declined first on the ground of inconsistency, and then because the wording was "too strong." Robert Lowell said he opposed all wars. Interestingly, when a labor leader characterized the position of Democrats who conditioned their support for political candidates on an anti-war stance, as "monomania," Schlesinger retorted that the term should be applied

> to those who would have us so deeply involved in a land war on the mainland of Asia that we lose our capacity to deal with challenges in other, and more important, parts of the world – a situation dramatized vividly for us . . . by the crisis in the Middle East.[28]

Apparently, Schlesinger was amongst those cowered by the administration effort "to convert its critics, or at least soften their opposition by exploiting their seeming ambivalence in opposing

Vietnam intervention and, at the same time, favoring support of Israel." Only 54 intellectuals of all faiths signed the appeal. They included Michael Harrington, Daniel P. Moynihan, Ralph Ellison, Willie Morris, Dwight McDonald, Whitney Young and Elia Kazan. This meager number not only disappointed Jewish liberals, but also left them open to charges that they were partially responsible for that meagerness. For, as John Kissin of Harvard pointed out, many of their past arguments were applicable to both conflicts: (1) US military intervention required UN sanction. (2) American commitments had to be ratified by the Senate. (3) The US should not get involved in an Asian land war. (4) Foreign adventures led to the neglect of domestic problems. (5) War devastates the country the US tries to help. (6) Foreign intervention harms the US image, especially against "colored" Third World countries.

But, answered the "doves," Israel was a democracy which had never requested or wanted American troops; had the US stood firm, war would have been averted. Still, retorted Kissin, your arguments had encouraged the growth of latent American isolationism and "this new isolationism was at least one of the factors which led the administration to temporize about the Gulf of Aqaba." He then asked: "Suppose that the Israeli army overthrew Prime Minister Eshkol, and installed General Dayan in his place, would it, above all, affect Israel's right to exist?" If not, why should it affect South Vietnam's right to exist?

An irate Theodore Draper conceded that a coup "would certainly not have affected Israel's right to exist," but added that the existence of South Vietnam, unlike the existence of Israel, "was supposed to be temporary." Also, had the Arab armies reached Tel Aviv, the existence of the Israeli people, as much as the existence of the state, would have been at stake. The same was not true in Vietnam. Still, "Vietnam doves" would have to learn to live with what he called "a new scarecrow," the accusation that they fostered "new isolationism." To counter that accusation, he denied that intellectuals impacted public opinion: "If our Vietnam policy were more successful, its critics would be derided or ignored." It was "over indulgence of power in Vietnam" that had made it "in short supply for use elsewhere." In any case, those who called on the President "to act with courage and conviction" on behalf of Israel, "said nothing about unilateral United States intervention."[29] Did Draper mean that it would have been improper for Vietnam doves to urge Johnson to save the Israeli people unilaterally?

The Mideast crisis also raised fundamental questions concerning anti-Communism which underlay much of the liberal opposition to intervention in Vietnam. It was based on the "hope" that it was possible to escape "the Communist/anti-Communist syndrome" by focusing on "the decentralization and dissidence of the Soviet world, in the nationalist and socialist movements in Asia and Africa and in the growth of dissent" in the US. However, remarked *Partisan Review* editor William Phillips:

> The naked power moves of the Soviet bloc in the Near East, together with stale ideology, succeeded in bringing back the old confrontations, so, too, the almost automatic ganging-up on Israel of the Asian and African countries, rationalized by a hodge-podge of racial, national and anti-colonial propaganda, buried another hope – and with it the myth that being dark-skinned and poor and underdeveloped made a nation virtuous and progressive.[30]

Others noted that "If ever there was an expression of Communist solidarity, a unification of forces, a reaffirmation of the Warsaw Pact, it occurred in reaction to Israel's victory. Even Yugoslavia – that prime example of Communist breakaway – returned to the fold, happily and voluntarily." They asked with trepidation: "Or should we consider the Communist International as having transformed itself into an anti-Semitic International now that Eastern Europe, India, the Middle East, and Northern Africa have all joined hands on this issue and are finding new allies – even in the United States?" To continue to adhere to their pre-crisis tenets, concluded some, Jews would have to sacrifice their own people to what others said was best for mankind.[31]

Radicals were just as befuddled. On May 28 Marxist Rabbi Abraham Feinberg started his dinner address with a confession:

> First, I must divulge what has been a very serious conflict during the last few days, namely, the question, how can we continue to criticize the policy of the United States in Vietnam, demanding an end to our intervention in that country, and at the same time hope that the great powers, particularly the United States, will safeguard the beleaguered and desperately imperilled State of Israel?
>
> I have answered that question for myself. I shall continue without compromise to protest against . . . the continued military activities of our government in Vietnam; at the same time that I shall

> hope and pray, along with millions of others, that some measure of firmness and understanding and sense of obligation will be mustered for the protection of Israel.[32]

Morning Freiheit asserted that "Israel must not become a Second Vietnam," and three different "progressive" groups appealed to both American and Soviet UN representatives to do what was "necessary to prevent the illegal closing of the Gulf of Aqaba to Israel, to halt the threats of the destruction of Israel by Arab leaders, as well as threats of reprisal by Israeli leaders."[33] Soon, "progressive" Jews listening to both American and Soviet UN representatives began to doubt the efficacy of such dual appeals. Still, the radical *Jewish Currents* urged its readers to forgo an "appeal to Johnson for unilateral action" because the destructive presence of the US in Vietnam made anyone associated with her suspect in the Second and Third worlds.

The fact that Israel won alone enabled Western "progressive Jewish movements" to declare the Six Day War a "just war," "rejoice" that the planned aggression against her "was smashed," and characterize the Soviet position as "incomprehensible, unjust and disturbing." The Arab "obsession" with the destruction of Israel, they asserted, was not an expression of "anti-imperialism" but of a Pan-Arab nationalism which mandated an accommodation with feudal kings. However, given the Soviet influence in the region, peace could be had only through superpower cooperation which depended on American concessions in Vietnam. Therefore, active opposition to the American presence in Vietnam was needed both to end an unjust war and to help Israel "win a just peace."[34]

Since non-Jewish communist outlets followed the official Soviet pro-Arab line, many communists in the US and elsewhere quit the party. Fidel Castro noted that "true revolutionaries never threaten a whole country with extermination." The fact that the Arabs did, and the Soviet bloc refused to denounce their so doing, undermined their credibility among Western radicals. Listening to live broadcasts of UN debates, Martin Peretz wrote, "a certain naivete about the purity and virtue of the revolutionary world" which had "characterized much Left and anti-war sentiment in America," vanished. It could not survive the "fraternal greetings from Ho Chi Minh to Nasser" or the ganging up of countries considered "victims of American imperialism" on a "little country, and a progressive one at that, threatened to its very foundations." "The willingness to sacrifice small countries for large stakes was supposed to be a Washington specialty," he noted. "Slowly it began to dawn on some elements of the Left that cynicism was amply distributed around the globe, and around the political spectrum." Consequently, reported Milton Himmelfarb, internationalism and "the old idea" that all "our" enemies were "on the Right" became passé.[35]

The term "our" is not accidental. Israel's enemies mistreated their Jewish citizens. Jews in Arab countries were subjected to mob violence and official persecution. Following a series of deadly pogroms, pro-Western Libyan Jews were permitted to emigrate with their personal luggage and $60. In Egypt, police rounded up Jewish males; those of foreign nationality were expelled. Others were first imprisoned, then expelled. A rabbi's plea that "we are Egyptians the same as anyone else," fell on deaf ears. Mahmoud Riad recalls a New York experience:

> Once, as I was returning to my hotel, a young man stepped forward and shook my hand. He spoke Arabic with an Egyptian accent and . . . I discovered he was an Egyptian Jew who had been expelled by the security department. He wished to return to Egypt because he was Egyptian and Gamal Abdel Nasser was his president . . . not Levi Eshkol! . . . I could only tell him that he was one of the many victims of the Arab–Israeli conflict.[36]

In the USSR, the Jewish–Israeli identification was more subtle, but there too "the mobilization of 'Brezhnev's fist' in the direction of the Middle East" meant that three and a half million Soviet Jews began to be regarded by the government, and gradually even by the "broad masses," as "the 'fifth column' of international imperialism." In Poland, Jews were evicted from the Communist Party apparatus; disagreement with Czechoslovak Mideast policy was later a feature of the Prague spring.[37]

In the US, it was black militants who pushed radical Jews into Israeli arms. The June/July 1967 SNCC *Newsletter* horrified the organization's Jewish members, not only by basing its analysis of Arab–Israeli relations on an almost verbatim repetition of a 1966 PLO propaganda booklet, but by accompanying it with anti-Semitic cartoons. One of them showed a hand, marked with a Star of David and a dollar sign, tightening a rope around the necks of Gamal Abdel Nasser and Mohammed Ali. Theodore Bikel and Rabbi Arthur Lelyveld resigned from SNCC.[38]

The ideological-racial line drawn at the 1966 Tricontinental

Conference in Havana took hold. Jewish radicals pointed out that no Arab country had experienced, or was committed to, the kind of social transformation which took place in China or Cuba and that, given communist animosity, Israel had no choice but to take the Western side. They were nevertheless exhorted to sacrifice Israel for the sake of the revolution:

> As the prophetic words were so well expounded by Che Guevara, that we need many Vietnams, the scene of the crisis fluctuates from Southeast Asia to the Middle East. One of the ironies of the situation that has upset the equilibrium of unity in the antiwar forces is the position of support for Israel many members have taken.[39]

Socialist Paul Feldman fretted that disillusioned young Jews would "turn apathetic and conservative." The *National Guardian* worried that a leftist split would damage the peace movement. It would be tragic, wrote *New America* if a desire to gain US support for Israel were to lead to an acceptance of American Vietnam policy. But Peretz explained that "Israel's friends" were not prepared to "agree as to the relative insignificance of a matter that stirred their minds and hearts no less surely and genuinely than the agony of Vietnam." In fact, Peretz added, the time had come for "some vigorous rethinking of attitudes." Leftist blanket opposition to unilateral American intervention had been based "on the confident surety that any decisive response by Washington to a political crisis was likely to be at the service of some landlord class or army junta." But intervention on behalf of an Israeli social democracy would have been as desirable as intervention on behalf of Republican Spain. Indeed, the Munich analogy misapplied to Vietnam applied to Israel except that "this time the Czechs fought back and won, saving the great powers from embarrassment and guilt."

The left, Peretz continued, also needed to curtail its willingness to "swallow an ill-digested, even thoughtless, pacifism" which had started as "reasonable nuclear pacifism" and turned into "a pacifism pure and simple, which still allowed for the violence of revolutionaries." The horrors of Vietnam had made all war seem unjustifiable; "only something like the experience of Israel could have made respectable again in certain circles the notion that some countries fight some wars for good and sufficient reasons."[40] Liberal rabbis found themselves in a similar painful reassessment of their past positions and alliances. Heschel traveled to Philadelphia to enlist his friends from Clergy and Laymen for the Israeli cause. He was rebuffed. A dozen church leaders, including Reinhold Niebuhr, Thurston N. Davis, James O'Gara and John B. Sheerin, did call on "men of conscience" not to remain silent, urged Washington "to honor its commitment to the freedom of international waterways" and asked "Americans of all persuasions" to support Israel's "right to live." But only three of the signatories, John C. Bennett, Martin Luther King Jr., and Robert McAfee Brown were Clergy and Laymen activists. The absence of men like Richard Neuhaus, William Sloane Coffin, and Daniel Berrigan was hard to miss.[41]

Again there was a marked difference between the widespread support given Israel by European Christian clergy and the lack of such support by American clergy. Many clergymen and theologians who were "begged" to issue statements refused and, "in almost every instance," those who did had to be persuaded that it "was a situation in which the strength of interreligious relations was being seriously tested."[42] The following story was typical:

> I held my second meeting . . . with Dr. Carol Shuster, President of the Southern California Council of Churches and Secretary of the Presbyterian Synod of Churches in Southern California. Dr. Shuster had been scheduled to speak this past Sunday at the Hollywood Bowl rally for Israel and at the last minute withdrew. . . . There was an enormous reaction from the Rabbinate and others in the Jewish community and I apprised Dr. Shuster of this fact . . . He withdrew because of substantial pressure which, I understand unofficially, included the National Presbyter. He said that his heart was with the people of Israel but that he was in a terrible position and had to withdraw. Governor Reagan, Senator Murphy, Mayor Yorty and a host of Hollywood stars were present. The absence of our Christian friends was conspicuous. In any event, Dr. Shuster . . . was extremely anxious to have our goodwill and he apologized again and again.[43]

Rabbis found protestations that the "Israeli–Arab relationship constitutes a political issue," and were therefore outside the clergy's domain, particularly goading as they were made by the very same individuals who had solicited Jewish support on no less political or debatable issues as civil rights and Vietnam. Religiously based political activism was the basis of the close ties between liberal churches and reformist Jews and, in any case, as Rabbi Brickner tersely noted, "the survival of the Jewish people is not a political issue."[44]

After the war, many Christian leaders claimed that they had remained silent because they "took Arab threats as propaganda whereas the Jews took these threats seriously." But, during the crisis, the *Christian Century* had warned that it was imperative not to assume that Nasser was "bluffing" and that Israel would surely "not make so naive an assumption" but would resort to arms if not afforded international relief. Yet, it urged the administration to view the conflict in the "larger context," keep in mind US interests in the Arab countries, and consider the possibility that World War III could start in the Middle East just as easily as it could in Vietnam.[45]

Such assertions led Rabbi Brickner of Clergy and Laymen to charge that, by contributing to the world's abandonment of Israel, Christian silence held a measure of responsibility for the outbreak of hostilities which might have led to World War III. Clearly stung, *Christian Century* struck back both at Jewish and Christian "Dawks:"

> We did not . . . urge the United States to intervene unilaterally and militarily on the side of Israel . . . We could not permit our awareness of the perilous state of world peace to be blotted out by strong sympathy for Israel in the present crisis. Nor can we understand those Christian spokesmen who have permitted this to happen. . . . With what amazing speed and dexterity, what involuted rationalizations, these sometime doves flew into a telephone booth and emerged as hawks. . . . They stood aghast – as they should have – before the possibility that the Vietnam war would plunge the whole world into nuclear disaster, but called for military action by the US in an area where the conflicting interests of the great powers can catapult the world into nuclear and global war quicker that it can happen in Southeast Asia. . . . War is the enemy . . . Whether this was true in the past or not is irrelevant.[46]

Emmanuel Gitlin of Drake University protested that it was not accurate to claim "the whole anti-Vietnam war movement for the pacifist camp" and, therefore, it was not "at all accurate to say, "with what amazing speed and dexterity . . . these sometime doves . . . emerged as hawks!" Bennett agreed that, unlike South Vietnam, "Israel was threatened with extermination" but he rationalized Christian silence by noting that support for Israel might have endangered Christians in Arab lands. Jews remembered that such broad concerns were used to vindicate the Church's silence during the Holocaust.

This time Jews had a trump card, liberal Christian fear of renting the peace movement. It led editors of liberal Christian magazines not only to print rabbis' strongly worded indictments of Christian silence, but to urge their readers not to be offended by these indictments because they originated in justifiable Jewish fear that they were "once more threatened by genocide." On the other hand, they asked Jews to remember that "the enthusiasm, affection and admiration of a predominantly Christian nation" were "exceptionally pro-Israel" and constituted a "capital that should be invested, not squandered."[47]

Of course, that capital did not have to be invested with allies that failed. After all, the right had discovered Israel. The John Birch Society contributed $300,000 to the United Jewish Appeal. The Hearst publications were just one of the conservative outlets which celebrated the Israeli victory, and Christian fundamentalists delighted in the Jewish return to the Old City of Jerusalem.[48]

The realization that "Israel had promises and friends, but even if it hadn't wanted to fight on its own, it would have had to," wrote historian Arthur Hertzberg united a "somewhat lonelier and even angrier" Jewry. However, Jews also realized that this time they did not fail each other, nor did history and God fail them. In fact, the spring 1967 emotional roller coaster renewed the belief "that the history of the Jews points to some kind of providential order" in which they have a "special place." So, wrote Milton Himmelfarb, in the manner of old Jewish tradition in which "I" signifies "singular and plural, individual and collective, personal and referring to the Children of Israel." American Jews joined their brethren the world over in reciting the old verse: "I thank Thee, for Thou hast answered me, and art my salvation."[49] Hence, Jews became more Jewish, more religious and, much more dedicated to Israel.

THE COMMITMENT

> We are a people, one people.
> Fathered today in the capital of this nation in which we rejoice as free and equal citizens, we proclaim our oneness with our brethren in Israel. . . .
> With them we vow that the victories won on the battle field shall not be lost at the table of diplomacy.[50]

On June 8, this was part of the commitment made by all 27 national Jewish organizations. Their ultimate goal was to secure American support for "direct peace negotiations" as a condition for Israeli withdrawal. It was a position behind which "doves and non-doves" could unite. Kenen, with his energized AIPAC, organized this newly committed Jewish leadership into a disciplined lobbying army in possession of clear strategic objectives and tactical means of achieving them.[51] Congress, the media and the public would be an easy sale. The administration was a tougher nut to crack. John Roche wrote Johnson:

> Listening to McCloskey yesterday, and reading the State Department's *Staff Summary* today, I was appalled to realize that there is real underground sentiment for kissing some Arab backsides.
>
> This is, in my judgment, worse than unprincipled – it is stupid. . . .
>
> The net consequence of trying to "sweet-talk" the Arabs is that they have contempt for us – and we alienate Jewish support in the United States. . . .
>
> Which brings us back to the question once (perhaps erroneously) attributed to you: "Whose State Department is it?"[52]

Roche argued that State Department handling of Middle Eastern policy was unprincipled, incompetent and damaging politically. Preparing for the June 8 rally, Jewish leaders took a more subtle tack. A Presidential message stressing peace, and avoiding the term "territorial integrity," they argued would "dramatize" Johnson "depth of feeling for the humanity involved" and his "desire to see a lasting and permanent peace in the Middle East." Barry Levinson and Ben Wattenberg even added that, "the Mid-East crisis can turn around a lot of anti-Vietnam anti-Johnson feeling, particularly if you use it as an opportunity to your advantage."[53] Failure to act could have the opposite consequence. Charles Silberman wrote:

> Since I can not believe that my government will willingly disregard its sacred commitments, I can only assume that the critics of our Vietnam policy are right after all: that our effort there is so eroding our resources and, more important, our energies and will, that we are now unable to respond to aggression in other areas, even those where more vital American interests are at stake.[54]

For three days insiders told Johnson that "many people, including Mr. Krim" tried "to reach representatives of the Jewish community . . . but it seemed to have little effect" because "the man in the street" resented Johnson's policy and, unless the President did something, there was "great danger that the Jewish rally" would turn into "an anti-Johnson, rather than a pro Israel, demonstration." That something, insisted Fortas, was permitting "the Israelis and the Arabs to negotiate this out."[55]

Immediate victory was not to be had. Johnson used the Levinson-Wattenberg memo to express his righteous indignation. Spotting Barry Levinson, "Johnson jutted out his right fist and yelled down the hall, 'You Zionist dupe! You and Wattenberg are Zionist dupes in the White House! Why can't you see I'm doing all I can for Israel. That's what you should be telling people when they ask for a message from the President for their rally.'" The message was received and transmitted. It was time to back off. David Ginzberg called Califano to assure him that everything was under control. The main speaker would be Morris Abram, and the theme of the rally would be solidarity with Israel and statements that Johnson was "doing a magnificent job in the Israel crisis."[56] There would be no Presidential statement or appointment, but a Presidents' Conference would have a chance to meet with McGeorge Bundy and Hubert Humphrey.

On the evening of June 7, over 2,000 Jewish leaders from 39 states attended a leadership briefing session, followed by state and regional caucuses. Marvin Bernstein of Princeton told the delegates that, in their meetings with Congressmen and officials, they should advocate "a substantial shift in American policy." Past "prudent ambivalence" should give way to commitment to freedom of Israeli navigation in Aqaba and Suez; bi-lateral peace treaties between Israel and its Arab neighbors, and "readjustment of boundaries to meet Israel's urgent security needs." Such a policy shift was in America's interest, the delegates should explain, because the crisis revealed "illusionary character of Arab unity and the political unreliability of the Arab leadership."[57]

The unification of Jerusalem and the announcement of a ceasefire, turned the rally into a large victory celebration. A student climbed the statue of Lafayette, first to place an Israeli flag on its top and then to set up an American flag. His lobbying elders were thrilled to discover that the victory turned evasive Congressmen into staunch Israeli supporters. Humphrey ignored his promise to Johnson to merely "sit and listen" and engaged in some fence-mending of his own. On May 30, Humphrey had shocked a Shoreham

Hotel gathering by offering to send food packages to Israel instead of promising to keep the Straits open. On June 8, he became the first official to express support for a formal Middle Eastern peace settlement.[58]

But Jewish anti-war activism still proved troublesome. To the standard questions of “Why should we send American boys to fight Israel’s war? After all we fought ‘their war’ in Germany, why should we do it again?” people added “They won’t fight in Vietnam why should we fight in Israel?” A *NYT* editorial questioned “whether opponents of the war in Vietnam would advocate refusal to cooperate if United States forces were dispatched to the defense of Israel instead of South Vietnam.”[59]

In St. Louis, a student volunteer for Israel confirmed that he would go to Israel, but not to Vietnam, because he had “a deep affinity for the Jewish people.” Such comments led St. Louis members of the AJC to urge the national office to mount a campaign clarifying the issue for persons to whom the distinction between the two wars was less clear than to the Jewish community. “To guard against the ugly implications of this situation for American Jews,” wrote John Slawson, was “not to deny the needs of Israel but rather to meet those needs” because “as in all military situations there is a war front and a home front. They are interdependent and the weakness of one caused the debilitation of the other.” Only by maintaining “their position in American life” could American Jews fulfill their role as a home front and effectively seek American “support of Israel and the backing of world opinion.”[60]

The time had come to repair Johnson’s relations with the Jewish leadership. On June 8, Charles Jordan of the American Jewish Joint Distribution Committee convinced Morris Abram that it was “imperative” to establish “a Jewish presence” in South Vietnam. Providing assistance to refugees in the manner already done by the Quakers would appease the President without alienating opponents of the War. The two asked a select group of leaders to attend a June 13 organizational meeting. Invitee William Haber of the University of Michigan questioned the timing of the initiative because “even a quiet involvement in South Viet Nam might be interpreted by many as a diversion from the major concern of the community at this particular time.” But, “It may perhaps be that . . . such an involvement of a Jewish group in South Vietnam would be of aid, particularly with the national administration in regard to Mid-East affairs.” Since the second possibility was the operative one, plans were made on June 13 for a Jewish Service Committee for Civilian Relief in Vietnam chaired by Morris Abram and funded in the main by AID. Jordan's mysterious death delayed the announcement of the project until January 1968.[61] Afterwards, the AJC was able to inform a political scientist who inquired about its position on Vietnam that while it had no official position, its President chaired the Jewish Service Committee. None of this meant that Jews stopped opposing the War. It did mean, that the Jewish leadership had other priorities.

NOTES

1. Murry Baron to Morris Abram, May 22, 1967, AJC Files, CO/Vietnam, JSX 63–8, YIVO.
2. Kenen, *Israel's Defense Line*, 198–9; *Congressional Record – House*, June 6, 1967, 14882; and interview with Roche.
3. Bick, "Ethnic Linkages," 208–9; and Irwin Suall to Arnold Foster, June 27, 1967, ME crisis, box 105, AJCL.
4. "From the office of Senator Jacob Javits," May 29, 1967, AJC files, ME crisis, box 105, AJCL (emphasis in original).
5. These exchanges can be found in NSF, M.E. Crisis, box 18, 16, 16a, 16b, 16c, 16d, 16e, LBJL.
6. American Embassy, Nov. 22, 1967, diplomatic cables, Six Day War, Yad Eshkol.
7. A memo and a letter from S. Mark to Mathilde Krim, May 22, 1967, President's Appointment File, box 67, LBJL.
8. A letter from Lloyd Shefsky, May 20, 1967; "Dear Mr. President," May 23, 1967; and telegram from Barbara Isaacson, June 6, 1967, Gen ExCo126, box 43, LBJL.
9. Neff, *Warriors for Jerusalem*, 113.
10. Quandt, *The Peace Process*, 32 and 511n; interview with Katzenbach; and Harman to Eban, May 22, 1967, diplomatic cables, Six Day War, Yad Eshkol.
11. Rafael, *Destination Peace*, May 30, 1967; diplomatic cables, Six Day War, Yad Eshkol; and Goldberg, LBJ-OH, Tape I, 16.
12. To the President from Ben Wattenberg, May 31, 1967, M.E. Crisis, President's Appointment File, box 67, LBJL (emphasis in original).
13. *Congressional Record – House*, May 24, 1967, 13959.
14. For the President from Walt Rostow, May 31, 1967, NSF, President's Appointment File, May–June 67, box, 66, 1k, LBJL.
15. *NYT*, June 4, 1967; and Merle Miller, *Lyndon* (New York: 1980), 480.
16. *NYT*, June 2, 3 and 7, 1967.
17. *Jewish Exponent*, June 9, 1967; and David Polish, "Why American Jews

are Disillusioned," *The Christian Century* (July 26, 1967), 965.
18. Califano, *The Triumph and Tragedy*, 205; and For the President from Joe Califano, June 5, 1967, NSF, M.E. Crisis, box 18, 112, LBJL.
19. *American Jewish Yearbook*, 1967, 204; and Abraham Heschel, *Israel: An Echo of Eternity* (New York: 1969), 196–7.
20. Alan M. Dershowitz, *Chutzpa* (Boston: 1991), 80, emphasis in original.
21. Between May 15 and June 10 American Jews contributed $100 million to the Israel Emergency Fund, mostly in cash. The sum reached $600 million by the end of the year. The initiative was largely local and spontaneous. *American Jewish Yearbook*, 1968, 206–9; Kenen, 199.
22. Marshall Sklare, "Lakeville and Israel," *Midstream* (Oct. 1968), 2–3 and 19.
23. *NYT*, June 4, 1967; and *American Jewish Yearbook: 1967*, 216–18.
24. *The Village Voice*, June 15, 1967.
25. *The Washington Post*, May 30, 1967.
26. *Le Monde*, May 30, 1967; *NYT*, June 4 and 7, 1967; Walter Laqueur, "Israel, the Arabs & World Opinion," *Commentary* (Aug. 1967), 55–6; Mordecai Nahumi, "The View from Abroad," *New Outlook* (July–Aug., 1967).
27. "Intellectuals & Just Causes," *Encounter*, Sept. 1967, 3–16 and Oct. 1967, 45–50.
28. Arthur Schlesinger Jr. to Gus Tyler, June 13, 1967, papers of Max Kampelman, Misc. 1967, 26E 10 10F, MSA; and *NYT*, June 7 and 12, 1967.
29. *NYT*, June 12 and 15, 1967; "Letters from Readers," *Commentary* (Dec. 1967), 14–20.
30. "Symposium: Liberal anti-Communism Revisited," *Commentary* (Sept. 1967), 58, 64.
31. "To the editor," *Commentary* (Dec. 1967), 6.
32. Feinberg, "Our Mission to Hanoi," 4–5.
33. Morris U. Schappes, "The Middle East Explosion," *Jewish Currents* (Oct. 1967), 3–22.
34. Ibid.
35. Robert Scheer, "The Story of Two Wars" *Ramparts* (Nov. 1967), 85; Martin Peretz, "The American Left and Israel," *Commentary* (Nov. 1967), 28; and Milton Himmelfarb, "In Light of Israel's Victory," *Commentary* (Oct. 1967), 58–4.
36. *American Jewish Yearbook, 1968*, 131–44; and Riad, 59.
37. Alexander Shumilin, "Backstage Events of the 'Six Day War,'" *New Times International* (Oct. 1992), 26; and interview with Brzezinski.
38. *American Jewish Yearbook, 1968*, 228; and Hertzberg, *The Jews in America*, 371.
39. *The Militant*, June 26, 1967.
40. Peretz, "The American Left," 30; and Michael Walzer and Martin Peretz, "Israel is not Vietnam" *Ramparts* (July 1967), 11.
41. *NYT*, May 28, 1967; Winston, "Vietnam and the Jews," 204–5. After the war, William G. Oxtoby noted that "Israel was not so decimated that it had not been able to mobilize an army of men – and women!" "Christians and the Middle East Crisis," 961.

42. Bennett, "A Response to Rabbi Brickner," 204; and Mailing from Irving Jay Fain and Albert Vorspan to UAHC board of Trustees, Rabbis, etc. June 23, 1967, Subject: Middle East, Appendix B, AJC, JSX 5/67–8/67, AJCL.
43. Memorandum from Will Katz and Neil C. Sandberg, June 13, 1967, M.E. Crisis, React-rel., box 105, AJCL.
44. Jacob Neusner, "Communications," *Judaism* (Summer 1967), 363; and *NYT*, June 23, 1967.
45. "American Jewish Committee press release," July 7, 1967, Six Day War, box 105, AJCL; *The Christian Century*, May 31 and June 7, 1967.
46. *The Christian Century*, 12 July 1967, 883.
47. *The Christian Century*, 9 Aug. 1967; and John C. Bennett, "Further Thoughts on the Middle East," *Christianity and Crisis* (26 June 1967), 142.
48. *NYT*, June 13, 1967.
49. *Maariv*, June 2, 1967; Himmelfarb, "In the light of Israel's victory," 57 and 61; and Hertzberg, 373.
50. "A Proclamation," June 7–8, 1967, FAD-67, box 104, AJCL.
51. Kenen, 203 and 207; and Irwin Suall to Arnold Foster, June 27, 1967, M.E. Crisis, box 105, AJCL.
52. For the President from John Roche, June 6, 1967, NSF, M.E. Crisis, box 18, 328, LBJL.
53. Memo to the President from Larry Levinson and Ben Wattenberg, June 7, 1967, President's Appointment file, June–July 1967, box 67, 1m, LBJL.
54. Charles Silberman to Harry McPherson, June 2, 1967, Office files of Harry McPherson, box 42, 25, 25a, 26, LBJL.
55. To the President from Marvin, June 7, 1967, Name file, Mathilde Krim, and To the President from Joe Califano, June 7, 1967, Name File, Abe Fortas, LBJL.
56. Califano, 205.
57. "Days of Crisis: April 1 to September 30, 1967, A President's Conference Interim Report," 1967, 10–12, AJCL.
58. *Washington Post*, May 31, 1967; and Patir, "Miyomano Shel Dover," June 3, 1967, 26.
59. *NYT*, June 10, 1967.
60. To Isaiah Terman from Morton Ryweck, June 8, 1967, AJC files, FA/MID/AR-I, X FCO/VIET, YIVO; and To AJC staff from John Slawson, June 7, 1967, M.E. Crisis, box 105, AJCL.
61. Telegram from Morris Abram to John Slawson, June 8, 1967, AJC, CO/Vietnam, JSX, 63–8, YIVO. Letter from William Haber to Morris Abram, June 8, 1967, Minutes of the American Jewish Service Committee for Civilian Relief in Vietnam, Feb. 1, 1968, AJC, FAD–1 (70), 81, AJCL.

Part IV
The Die is Cast

10 Vietnam and/or the Middle East

THE GLASSBORO DEAL

Glassboro was a summit neither leader wanted; that was the real cause for the protracted haggling over its location. For hovering over them, as Kosygin candidly remarked to Johnson, was the perception that they were about "to sell out someone" in an unseemly package deal.[1] After all, from the moment the Six Day War ended in an unconditional ceasefire, the two Asian conflicts had become inextricably linked. Vast differences notwithstanding, both the US and Israel insisted that troop withdrawal had to follow negotiations leading to peace. Hence, any superpower agreement on the conditions for Israeli troop withdrawal was bound to impact on the American negotiating position on Vietnam, and vice versa. That was the reason that the first CIA estimate ordered by McGeorge Bundy was on the questions: "Can Israel hold what it won? How long? What is the cost to them? To us?"[2]

The Soviets "*too*" were "increasingly aware of the implications" their handling of the Middle East had for "their relationship with Hanoi, Pyongyang and other revolutionaries" and were "very uncomfortable in agreeing . . . to cease fire resolutions which failed to distinguish between 'victim' and 'aggressor'– notwithstanding the scorn Soviets had previously heaped on similar US proposals in Vietnam." The "immediate cease fire," they maintained, was but a *first step* to curbing the aggressor." Subsequent steps, they promised, would include condemnation, withdrawal and compensation.[3]

Not only "revolutionaries," but also "moderates" held the Soviets' feet to the fire. News of Nasser's resignation turned the June 9 European Communists gathering into an acrimonious meeting which lasted 12 hours. Tito led the charge: "Your policy of secret dialogue with the Americans has led to the liquidation of the concept of the uncommitted world. It has led to the overthrow of Third World leaders like Nkrumah, Sukarno and today Nasser. It has strengthened the US grip on India."[4]

Unable to shift the blame to the Chinese, Soviet leaders tried to shift it to the Arabs arguing that they did all they could short of direct military involvement, which was rendered impractical by the Israeli bombing of the Egyptian airports and the swift collapse of the Arab armies. They also held up their generous support for the "people of Vietnam." In the end, Moscow had to sign a joint communique stating that the unity of the Communist bloc could only be maintained by Soviet adoption of a tougher policy towards Washington and an obligation to do "everything necessary to help the people of the Arab countries administer a resolute rebuff to the aggressor." The language was "lifted virtually verbatim from standard Moscow statements on China and Vietnam," noted an American analyst.[5]

Kosygin's journey to New York was part of a larger Soviet salvage effort. It began with the transfer of the UN Middle Eastern debate to the General Assembly in the hope of securing an unconditional Israeli withdrawal resolution. It proceeded with the announcement that Kosygin would head the Soviet delegation and an invitation to other UN members to send their own top officials. De Gaulle said no as he was miffed by Moscow's rejection of his prewar call for a four power summit, and doubted that there was enough give in the Soviet negotiating stance to tempt the US. Wilson, who opposed any prospective "ganging up on Israel," happily followed suit. Moscow's hopes for a Versailles-type Middle Eastern conference were dashed.[6]

The Politburo *ordered* Alexei Kosygin to meet with Lyndon Johnson. Moscow found American media speculations about "Israel's Lesson for American Generals in Vietnam" or "What Moshe Dayan says about Vietnam" disconcerting and hoped Kosygin would take the measure of the man. Summit atmospherics would calm those like De Gaulle who saw a direct superpower clash in the offing. Brezhnev might have also hoped that the expected failure would undermine Chinese accusations of superpower collusion and weaken Kosygin. At issue were not only personalities, but policies. Focusing on the economic needs of his country, Kosygin sought to acquire Western help in meeting them. Focusing on the strategic goals of his country, Brezhnev sought to exploit the American embroilment in Vietnam. The Soviet debacle in the Six Day War had strengthened Kosygin's hand; a failed summit would redress the balance.[7]

Johnson too worried that the lack of advance preparation precluded concrete agreements, and that the summit could be used as a propaganda device by the Soviets. True enough, retorted his press aide, Tom Johnson but the president had to be seen as willing to "take this step *to seek Peace*;" otherwise, "any deterioration in US–Russian relations that may develop, or any increased support by the Soviets to the Arab world or even to Hanoi, would be linked to the fact that no meeting between the President and Kosygin was held." Moreover, his aides mistakenly assured him that Kosygin was in a position to cut a deal.[8]

Johnson came to Glassboro ready for an ambitious superpower agreement which would permit him to redirect his attention to the domestic front. He told Kosygin that they should act like responsible "big brothers" willing to impose reasonable solutions on their impulsive younger siblings and settle between them the outstanding regional and bilateral issues. Kosygin too came ready to deal. But his goal was more modest. He was determined to limit the escalating financial cost of supporting his Arab and Vietnamese allies. The closure of the Suez Canal was particularly burdensome as it left Egypt teetering on the brink of economic disaster and raised considerably the price of supplying North Vietnam.

To strengthen his week hand, he tried to put Johnson on the defensive by accusing the US of bad faith. After failing to restrain Israel as promised, it reversed position by insisting on an unconditional ceasefire just four hours after agreeing to a ceasefire plus withdrawal. This American shift, Kosygin charged, left Moscow exposed to Chinese accusations of Soviet acquiescence to a "sell-out" of the Arabs. Thus undercut, he was no longer in a position to negotiate on behalf of his allies. He did, however, bring along Nasser's personal emissary Mahmoud Fawzi to deal directly with Dean Rusk. Assuming Johnson to be partial to oil interests, Kosygin assured him that Moscow had no designs on Arab oil.[9]

The premier also carried sticks. An American failure to cooperate in forcing an Israeli withdrawal, he repeatedly warned, would result in a lengthy Arab (not Palestinian) national liberation war. Moreover, Kosygin conditioned any progress on bilateral relations, including on the ABM treaty Johnson was anxious to have, on a solution to the Mideast problem. Johnson did not budge though it soon became clear that Vietnam, not the Middle East, was his primary interest. When Kosygin made a sketch of the Suez Canal, Johnson made one of the DMZ.

Kosygin decided to pull a rabbit out of his empty bag. He began the afternoon session with an announcement concerning Vietnam:

He had just received a message from Hanoi which amounted to the following: "Stop the bombing and they would immediately go to the conference table." Moreover, Kosygin offered his good services as an intermediary between Washington and Hanoi and suggested that Johnson meet him again so Kosygin could receive and "transmit any reply the President had to make."

Johnson was far from satisfied. He wanted Soviet help in securing "self determination for the people of South Viet-Nam." Kosygin was not authorized by the politburo to make such a promise. As he told Moscow, he was not even sure Hanoi would agree to negotiate in return for a bombing stoppage. So he asked that American questions be formulated on paper "without reference to Mr. Kosygin or the USSR," addressed to Hanoi and given to him for mere transmission. Of course, when the two men parted, the expectation of a reciprocal American gesture in the Middle East was obvious.[10]

That night, Johnson flew to a Krim-organized fund raising dinner in Los Angeles. He knew that Israel and her friends "felt the usual twinge of . . . apprehension." He also knew that, earlier that day, Nixon had declared in Israel that Jerusalem had a right to hold on to "springboards of aggression" until a settlement ensuring her security was reached. Standing tall, Johnson sent a message to Dawks and Hoves: "I was not elected your President to liquidate our agreements in Southeast Asia. I was not elected your President to run out on our commitments in the Middle East. If that is what you want, you will have to get another President."[11]

Before the summit reconvened, Israel moved to strengthen the President's hand. "Israelis Say Captured Documents Show Egyptians Planned to Strike First," was the headline of a report describing Egyptian operational orders which "indicated that Israel beat the Egyptians to the punch by a narrow margin. Each force had been intent on destroying the other on the ground."[12] In other words, Moscow was not controlling her client very well either. When the two leaders renewed their discussions, Kosygin never dared raise the issue again.

Johnson presented him with a written response to Hanoi's message, which the premier read quickly and commented that "it looked alright to him on the whole." Johnson then handed him a personal note clarifying the American negotiating position: Soviet miscalculation in the Middle East had led American officials to fear other dangerous miscalculations. Then came the expected "quid." Johnson promised to authorize Rusk to be "flexible" in "the search for common language" on a UN Middle Eastern resolution, but warned that Rusk found Fawzi less flexible than Kosygin had indicated.

It was Kosygin's turn to be dissatisfied. Though he wanted a strong anti-Israeli resolution passed, he assumed that he could secure it without American cooperation. His primary objective was the reopening of the Suez Canal. Indeed, if Washington had any doubts as to the importance of the Canal to Moscow, the summit laid them to rest. Kosygin mentioned the Canal by name seven times, in addition to appeals to treat Israel and Egypt like boxers who need to be separated. In contrast, Kosygin did not even mention the need for such separation of forces on the Syrian border.

Neither could Kosygin mistake the President's interest in an agreement on strategic arms limitations, or in an end to Soviet resupply of the Arabs. Thus, when Kosygin reminded Johnson of the Tashkent agreement where Indian withdrawal did not solve the underlying problems, but did prevent the renewal of war, Johnson reminded Kosygin that the removal of weapons to Pakistan preceded the withdrawal of Indian troops. Again, Kosygin was not authorized to make such a bargain. In fact, the very day of the summit, the Soviet president and army chief of staff were in Cairo finalizing the details on rearmament.[13]

As their meeting was coming to an end, Kosygin proclaimed that Moscow wanted peace, but conditioned any improvement in bilateral relations on a solution to regional conflicts. Johnson promised not to send ground troops into North Vietnam, and to withdraw all American troops from Vietnam once a settlement was reached. Kosygin grumbled, "We agreed on next to nothing." Soviet hopes for a swift victory in the General Assembly collapsed, as did the *quid pro quo* agreement; and the US faced once again the agonizing choice of "Vietnam and/or the Middle East."[14]

THE DECISION TO EXIT SOUTH VIETNAM

Henry Kissinger seems to have been caught off guard by the domestic unpopularity of the Nixon administration's linkage policy, but astute Lyndon Johnson kept his linkage policy discussions with Kosygin secret even from his closest advisers. In fact, when Walt Rostow handed Johnson a transcript of the meetings in a sealed envelope, the President "blew a fuse . . . called both Rusk and McNamara and chewed them out" because "he didn't want anyone to see that transcript." Benjamin Read, the State Department executive secretary who helped the translator prepare it, is positive that for years no one did.[15]

Johnson did instruct Goldberg to be flexible on "common language" at the UN. In July, Goldberg and Dobrynin agreed on an "equivocal formula" which was so favorable to the Soviets that Dobrynin assumed that Goldberg had failed to understand its ramifications; and he asked that he be permitted to keep Goldberg's handwritten version. It called for an immediate Israeli withdrawal to the June 4 borders, *and* for an acknowledgment of "the right of each state to maintain an independent national state." As Israel was not mentioned by name and no negotiations implying recognition were needed prior to Israeli withdrawal, Arab countries could have simply claimed that the second clause did not apply to Israel. Eban was about to cry "sell out," but Goldberg told him to trust Arab intransigence. Indeed, unaware of the linkage deal, the Arabs disregarded Soviet advice and held out for an even better resolution.[16]

Throughout July, Jewish leaders urged Johnson to "*make* the Arabs sit down and talk with the Israelis." Nasser too tried to break the stalemate with a personal letter to Johnson. Johnson was more than ready. He asked his staff to find a mediator, and promised to back him: "Look, if you can get a workable plan there, I'll push in all my chips," he said. Expressing concern over Soviet penetration of the Middle East and the renewed regional warfare, Johnson argued "The clock is ticking." All to no avail. Rusk and McNamara insisted that there was nothing to be concerned about, and that it was impossible to find a mediator willing "to set himself up" for an obvious failure. An Arab–Israeli peace held little attraction for them. Finally, Johnson gave up and said that "he saw too many Jewish leaders and from now on they should see Bundy."[17]

Neither were Johnson's men in a mood to pursue a bold idea to use the Israeli victory to settle the Arab–Israeli conflict in a manner which would improve the American position in the region. President Dwight Eisenhower, Admiral Lewis Strauss and Lord Edmond de Rothschild were advocating what the Soviets nervously called "a new Marshall plan" for the Middle East. It called for the allocation of a billion dollars for the building of three large nuclear desalting plants which would provide jobs for Palestinian refugees and water to Israel, Jordan and Egypt. As both Arabs and Israelis were meeting regularly at the International Atomic Energy Agency, they could partake in the planning without formal negotiations.[18]

At first, Eisenhower suggested that Johnson adopt the plan as his own. At Glassboro, Johnson had hinted that Soviet-American cooperation in arms deliveries would lead to similar cooperation in development projects such as desalination. Eisenhower wrote to Johnson. Johnson replied that "we have both felt in our bones" that "desalting would become . . . a basis for movement towards reconciliation in the Middle East." His staff was considering the idea, and Eisenhower should feel free "to continue to pass along" his thoughts on the matter.[19]

As the violence along the Canal accelerated, Republicans began arguing that Johnson was hiding the worsening Middle Eastern situation as he had hid the Vietnamese deterioration in 1964. Senator Howard Baker introduced desalination project legislation, the Foreign Relations Committee held hearings, and the Senate passed unanimously a resolution supportive of the plan. This Congressional activity resulted in an NSC meeting on "Economic Elements of a Middle East Peace Settlement." Rusk set its tone by announcing that "For the moment, 'politics is queen,'" and asking that staff work be done to prepare for Congressional testimony. When Johnson inquired whether there was "merit" in Republican claims that water would "solve the Middle East political problems," Rusk admitted that he thought there was. AID Administrator William Gaud stated that he had no money for it. Vietnam consumed it all.[20]

These were all excuses. At the heart of the reluctance to act forcefully in the Middle East was an intense Atlanticist-Pacificist debate about American foreign policy. Was the US still fighting an anti-Soviet Cold War and, if so, what was the role of regional conflicts in it? A special House subcommittee "Review of the Vietnam Conflict and Its Impact on US Military Commitments Abroad" detailed the manner in which the services "had to institute a heavy drawdown from other areas of personnel skills and certain items of critical equipment especially in aviation (landing teams and helicopters)."[21]

At State, the debate swirled around the final Holmes Report. It stated that Moscow had turned the Middle East into a "field of competition beyond which lie the ultimate targets of Europe and worldwide position of the United States." The question was whether American interests in that region were so threatened as to warrant "a major US effort in the area," or could their protection remain entrusted to local forces? Pacificist Nicholas Katzenbach dismissed the report as "a Cold War document" while Atlanticist Eugene Rostow supported it. Consequently, as Saunders informed Walt

Rostow and McGeorge Bundy, State analysts found it impossible to "ready a short memo for the President" on it.[22] Of course, a decision that the Cold War was not over, the Middle East was important, and regionalism could not block a major Soviet thrust would force a reevaluation of American Vietnamese policy.

Two factors aided Pacificists in the fall of 1967: The Middle East seemed under control, and the Vietnam War was going well. By refurbishing the Egyptian army, the Soviets had kept Nasser in office, increasing their influence on his forces and gaining naval facilities to boot. However, the Arab monarchs had defanged Nasser during the August summit in Khartoum. They agreed to replace the Egyptian and Jordanian revenue lost as a result of the closure of the Canal and Israeli occupation of Arab territories. In return, Nasser promised to withdraw from Yemen, endorsed the renewal of oil sales to the US and Britain, and agreed that all Arab energies be directed towards a future war with Israel. Thus, as long as the Canal remained closed and Nasser was dependent on oil producers' money, America's Arab clients and economic interests seemed safe and the US had no interest in an Arab–Israeli settlement. Indeed, regardless of "European concern," the US "did not encourage" any "action leading towards an early opening" of the Canal at the NATO Council session or anywhere else.[23]

Meanwhile, the Glassboro deal fell apart. Kosygin failed to deliver Hanoi's answer to the American note despite prodding by Rusk and Thompson. In August, worried about upcoming Senate hearings, Johnson temporarily lifted the bombing restrictions he had instituted prior to the Six Day War. Kosygin responded with a "very negative" third person message to Johnson.[24] On October 20, Washington–Hanoi contacts through intermediaries in Paris ended in failure and, the next day, a Soviet radar-controlled missile was used by Egypt to sink an Israeli destroyer. Washington worried about the effect such missiles would have on its carriers in Southeast Asia, but the CIA reported in had "no evidence" that North Vietnam possessed any. Israel retaliated by bombing Egyptian oil installations, and Moscow sent naval units to the Egyptian Mediterranean ports of Port Said and Alexandria. On October 23, the US renewed its bombing within 10 miles of Hanoi. Johnson send a tough letter to Kosygin reiterating that Israel would withdraw only the context of peace, and threatened to renew weapons sales to the area.[25]

When negotiations concerning a Security Council resolution recommenced, it was clear that since Kosygin had failed him on Vietnam, Johnson was about to fail Kosygin on the Middle East. Goldberg insisted that the July formula was an "unfortunate misunderstanding." Dobrynin showed Rusk Goldberg's handwritten note but got nowhere. Kosygin made a last minute appeal to Johnson. Johnson's response is unprintable. The Soviets and the Arabs had no choice but to swallow Security Council Resolution 242 which required withdrawal from "territories," demanded the termination of the state of belligerency, and mentioned Israel by name. As withdrawal from "territories" meant negotiations, a mediator was appointed to help them along.[26]

After all, the US no longer had an incentive to deny Israel the right to her neighbors' acceptance of her legitimacy at a time when it was deploying half a million troops to secure that goal for South Vietnam. The administration had also concluded that since the Vietnam War had "reached a peak," and was "beginning to decelerate slowly," action on the rest of the containment line could be safely delayed.[27] McNamara tried to warn that increased Soviet ability to project conventional force meant that Washington was about to lose its "most important" Cold War "advantage." Brzezinski added that a lengthy Vietnamese war served Soviet interests as its end would "simply free the US to pursue more effectively its policies in Asia and Europe." Rusk retorted that "there will be a hairy period when the Soviets will have to decide whether they will let Hanoi fall without doing more in the way of assistance"; i.e. the Vietnam War was about to be won and therefore it was not the time to ruffle Soviet feathers.[28]

A closed Suez Canal limited the efficacy of the new Soviet military facilities in Egypt and, once the Arabs realized that Moscow could not retrieve their territories, they would turn to the US. The central American task was to prevent Israel from making any "permanent moves in occupied lands" which might dampen Arab hopes of American-induced Israeli concessions.[29] These were the reasons the "wise men" in November reaffirmed their support for Johnson's pacificist policy.

With 1968 came new revelations of American vulnerability. The seizure of the *Pueblo* convinced Johnson that Washington faced "a coordinated plan to smash" its "will and stretch its resources to the breaking point."[30] The battle of Khe Sanh and the Tet offensive demonstrated that, far from being poised for victory, the US was mired in a costly war of attrition.

Serious trouble was also brewing in the Middle East. In August

1967, Nasser agreed to move out of Yemen but, in December, the Soviet Union moved in. In January 1968, the British told the US that they had decided to accelerate their disengagement from "East of Suez." Rusk bemoaned that the US was "facing a difficult period in world affairs and Britain was saying it would not be there." Rostow wrote Johnson: "Don't Mourn, Organize." Battle requested an urgent study "of the naval defense problem in the Arabian Sea." But rather than cooperate, Iran and Saudi Arabia began arguing over the booty one called the Persian Gulf and the other the Arabian Gulf, while the Soviets continued to emphasize the Gulf's proximity to their southern frontier and organized "the first Russian naval presence in the Gulf since 1903."[31]

The meagerness of forces available for non-Vietnamese theaters could no longer be ignored. Even McNamara noted "the shortage of US resources" in the Middle East and recommended that it "be given very high priority." He believed the "needs could be met largely from existing appropriations," but, if not, the US "should not let a few dollars" stand in the way. "The President said he would 'not object to a little more money.'"[32] But money was not easy to come by during a gold crisis fueled by a balance of payments deficit and it did not take the new Secretary of Defense Clark Clifford long to reach the conclusion his predecessor had reached: The Vietnam battlefront was consuming too large a share of the nation's resources.

After all a China raked by a destructive Cultural Revolution no longer constituted much of a threat, and Southeast Asia was hardly the place to confront the Soviet Union. Johnson disagreed. Leaving Vietnam without a Soviet commitment to detente, he confided to Harman, would solve little since it "wouldn't be 24 hours" before the US would face new challenges in other parts of the globe.[33] Clifford asked Johnson to reconvene the "wise men," and revealed his purpose by suggesting that General Matthew Ridgway be added to the group. He wanted to enable the general to express his view that the US lacked "enough strength to meet a new crisis" in areas where it had "alliances and responsibilities." When the "wise men" met in March 1968, Ridgway was there and Paul Nitze told the assembled that "the time had come to wind down the costly sideshow in Vietnam and return to the center stage, facing the Soviets in Europe." Aware that Tet presented Washington with a golden opportunity to place the blame for its precipitous exit on Saigon's failure to meet "their obligations to themselves and to" the US, the "wise men" decided that the time had come to end a regional war which no longer served US Cold War interests.[34]

The President, who knew he had lost the argument, decided not to seek a second term but refused to make the concessions needed for a quick American exit from Vietnam. At Glassboro, Kosygin had conditioned superpower detente on the settlement of the Vietnam and Middle Eastern regional conflicts. In his last year in office, Johnson conditioned regional settlements on superpower détente. His wish to retain leverage over the Jewish state by delaying the sale of Phantom jets, embroiled him in an eight month long battle with Israel, American Jews, Congress and even parts of his own administration who believed that Johnson's Vietnamese and Middle Eastern policies were jeopardizing Humphrey's election prospects. That might not have been Johnson's intention, though he realized that Nixon was more likely to follow in his policy footsteps. Indeed, Nixon later kept the US entrenched in Vietnam and Israel along the Canal-line until he had established detente not only with Moscow but also with Beijing.

NOTES

1. "Memorandum of Conversation between President Johnson and Alexei Kosygin," June 23 and 25, 1967, NSF, U.S.S.R. (Glassboro Memcons), LBJL.
2. Minutes of McGeorge Bundy's committee, June 13, 1967, NSF, M.E. Crisis, box 19, 102, LBJL.
3. Amembassy Moscow to Dept. of State, June 15, 1967, NSF, U.S.S.R., Box 230, 46a, LBJL; *Pravda*, June 12, 1967.
4. K. S. Karol, "Angry Men in the Kremlin," *New Statesman* (18 June 1967), 820.
5. *Pravda*, June 12 and 22, 1967; Amembassy Moscow to the Dept. of State, June 15 and 20, 1967, NSF, U.S.S.R., box 230, 46a and 84, LBJL.
6. Harold Wilson, *The Chariots of Israel* (London: 1981) 358–60.
7. *Pravda*, June 19 and 23, 1967; Dobrynin, *In Confidence*, 167; and Shevchenko, *Breaking with Moscow*, 180.
8. For the President from Tom Johnson, June 20, 1967, NSF, the President's appointment file, Glassboro, box 69, 20, LBJL; and interview with Brzezinski.
9. Shevchenko, 163; and Glassboro Memcons, LBJL.
10. Dobrynin, 164.
11. *JTA*, June 23, 24, 1967.
12. *NYT*, June 25, 1967.

13. Riad, *The Struggle for Peace*, 44–5.
14. Shevchenko, 181 and Glassboro Memcons, LBJL.
15. Benjamin Read, LBJ-OH, Tape I, 25; and interview with Read.
16. Vassilliev, *Soviet Policy in the Middle East*, 73; Eban, *Personal Witness*, 453; and Riad, 47.
17. David A. Korn, *Stalemate* (Boulder: 1992), 49–53; interview with Katzenbach; and "President Johnson's Tuesday Luncheons," July 12, 18, 25, Tom Johnson's meeting notes, 1967, box 1; and Eban, *Personal Witness*, 454.
18. *Izvestia*, June 15, 1967; Max Kampelman to the Vice President, July 28, 1967; and Max Kampelman to Sam Harris, Aug. 2, 1967, Kampelman Papers, HHH VP Correspondence, box 12, MSA.
19. President Johnson to General Dwight D. Eisenhower, July 31, 1967, WHCF, CO 126, box 9, LBJL.
20. *The Baltimore Sun*, Aug. 4, 1967; *Christian Science Monitor*, Aug. 25, 1967; *Congressional Record – Appendix*, 8032; and Memorandum for the Record, Oct. 26, 1967, NSF, NSC Meetings, box 2, 2, LBJL.
21. Special Subcommittee on National Defense Posture of the Committee of the Armed Services, Interim Report, Dec. 13, 1967 (Washington, 1968), 49.
22. "A Recommended American Strategy," Special State-Defense Study Group, July 1967, vol. I, State Department archives; For Mr. Rostow from Hal Saunders, Aug. 17, 1967, NSF, Agency File, box 34, NSC, Vol. 2, 7, LBJL; and *Davar*, March 3, 1968.
23. Kenen, *Israel's Defense Line*, 213; Korn, *Stalemate*, 78–89; and Cable from Ambassador Cleveland, Sept. 13, 1967, NSF, France, box 173, 92, LBJL.
24. Interview with Read.
25. "The threat of the guided-missile patrol boat," CIA Special Report, Nov. 24, 1967, NSF, Israel, box 138; *Congressional Record – House*, Oct. 23, 1967, 29614; and Tom Johnson's Tuesday lunch notes, Oct. 23, 1967, box 1, LBJL.
26. Dobrynin, 161–2; and interview with Rusk.
27. Analysis of Congressman Udall's speech, Nov. 29, 1967, WHCF, Confidential File, ND19/CO1-6, box 194, LBJL.
28. NSC Meeting, Nov. 27, 1967, NSF, box 2, 5, LBJL.
29. NSC Meeting, Nov. 29, 1967, NSF, NSC Meeting, Box 2, 3; "Talking Points for Prime Minister Eshkol," Jan. 5, 1968, NSF, Memos for the President, Box 15, LBJL.
30. Clark Clifford, *Counsel to the President* (New York: 1991), 466.
31. Administrative History, pt. 4, ch. 4, Sec. F, and Memorandum to the President, Jan. 16, 1968, NSF, Name File, Walt Rostow, box 7, 31, LBJL.
32. NSC Meeting on the Near East, Feb. 21, 1968, NSF, box 2, 2, LBJL.
33. Memorandum of Conversation, Feb. 7, 1968, NSF, Israel, box 140, 141, 148, LBJL.
34. Tom Johnson Tuesday lunch notes, March 19, 1968, box 2, LBJL; Walter Isaacson and Evan Thomas, *The Wise Men* (New York: 1986), 689; and Clifford, *Counsel to the President*, 519.

11 The Jewish Sparta

SOLIDIFICATION OF A NEW STATUS QUO

Israel followed Lyndon Johnson's global strategy with trepidation, though not incomprehension. A package deal would deprive her of the war booty she sought most, a negotiated peace settlement with her neighbors. Israeli insistence on withdrawal from "territories" rather than from "the territories" was based less on territorial ambitions than on the fact that such a withdrawal could not be implemented without prior Arab–Israeli negotiations. After all, Nasser's closure of the Straits demonstrated the ease with which Egypt could annul agreements to which it was not publicly committed.

However, the Arabs believed that such legitimizing negotiations meant their collective defeat. In comparison, losses of territory, battles or even wars were only temporary setbacks. That was the reason that at their August summit in Khartoum, Arab leaders resolved to retrieve their territories through diplomatic means "within the framework of the main principles . . . namely, *no truce* with Israel, *no recognition* of Israel, *no negotiations* with it and adherence to the rights of the Palestinian people within their country."[1] Nasser told his Cabinet:

> We will listen to the United States although she wants to make us enter a dark room called "negotiations on Resolution 242." . . . But they know very well that we have not been defeated in the war as long as we have not negotiated with Israel, not signed a peace treaty with her and not accepted the eradication of the Palestinian issue.[2]

As long as Israel believed that the wish to regain territories would be sufficient to induce the Arab states to negotiate with her, she treated them as bargaining chips. Indeed, on June 19, the Cabinet decided to withdraw to the Egyptian and Syrian international borders in return for a peace agreement. Decision on the West Bank was postponed while ideas concerning a Palestinian entity could be developed. Eban asked Washington to relay these proposals to the Arab states.[3]

Once the Khartoum decisions made another round of fighting

probable, the bargaining chips turned into strategic assets. The pre-1967 borders, which exposed 95 percent of the Israeli population to enemy artillery, were not defensible without preemption, which Washington was sure to oppose. The territories would provide Israel with the strategic depth necessary to survive an Arab first strike.[4] Those who had assumed that a single-handed victory would enhance Israel's independence faced a rude awakening. Rabin told a December 1967 Cabinet meeting that "the Soviet Union was interested in continued tension in the area and our dependence on the Americans is increasing." The Soviets rebuilt the Egyptian army with amazing speed, and Israel's air force was down to 55 Mirages. Dayan, who had permitted the army to reach the Canal so that Israel would "have a place from which to withdraw," recommended pulling the sting out of Israeli–Soviet relations by withdrawing from the Suez Canal. Eshkol favored withdrawal from half of the Sinai in return for the right to traverse the Canal and the Straits of Aqaba.[5]

During the war, Eshkol and Dayan began toying with the idea of a Palestinian entity. Israel had always accepted the 1947 two state solution, and its leaders dreaded the role of military occupiers. There were also reports that a strengthened Arafat was planning a general uprising of the Palestinian population. Algeria had trained 200 FATAH members. China provided special leadership instruction for thirty fedayeen and urged all Palestinians "to learn from their Vietnamese comrades and go on fighting 'unflinchingly to final victory.'" FATAH's first "general international communiqué" stated that "the occupation of all Palestine by Israel has made possible one of Fatah's most important long-range objectives – the transference of all its military bases into the occupied homeland."[7]

Israeli security forces were beefed up for their new challenge. Dayan, who quickly appropriated the role of policy maker for the territories, believed that self-rule was the answer. "The Americans in Vietnam," he repeatedly argued, "had the mistaken idea that not only could they run the Vietnamese people's lives for them, but they would also be loved for it." He told the first military governor of the West Bank Chaim Herzog, "Don't make the same mistake as the Americans made it Vietnam. . . . Don't bother to try and make the Arabs love you. Let them manage themselves."[8]

The best way to let Palestinians manage themselves was to create a Palestinian entity. For the first time Israel was in control of the Palestinian territories and, therefore, in a position to solve the Palestinian problem. Only Britain and Pakistan recognized Jordanian sovereignty over the West Bank, and local leaders treated Israelis as liberators and issued a call for a meeting of a provisional Palestinian assembly.[9]

Simultaneously, Arab rejectionism and favorable Cold War configurations began to convince an increasing number of Israelis, including formerly dovish religious ones, that God and history were providing Israel with a unique opportunity. Three weeks after the Khartoum summit, the "Movement for Greater Israel" published its first manifesto. It stated that "Undivided Israel" was "in the hands of the Jewish people" and, just as Israelis "had no right to renounce the State of Israel," so they were "commanded gratefully to receive what this era" had "granted" them: "namely, the entire Land of Israel."[10]

As an Israeli Arab remarked, "the Six Day War split Israel between a land of Israel party made up of poets and a peace party made up of generals." In any case, with peace prospects fast receding, the only effective unilateral Israeli action capable of halting the settlement movement, arresting the integration of the West Bank into Israel proper, and avoiding the abrasions of occupation would have been the creation of a Palestinian entity on the West Bank.[11]

The US totally rejected the idea. On June 22, Rusk told Eban that Hussein "was the key to the Palestinian settlement."[12] George Gruen, the AJC's Middle East specialist, reported:

> Atherton and his colleagues all rejected the concept of an autonomous region under Israel for the West Bank. . . . No one thought Hussein could survive economically and maybe even physically without the West Bank. Atherton pointed out that if he were eliminated, it was quite likely that the Syrians would move down and take over the East Bank, complicating greatly Israel's border security problem.[13]

Did that mean that the American government believed that Hussein would cut a deal with Israel? Not really. It did not consider Hussein to be in a position "to move forward towards a real agreement with the Israelis." In fact, continued Arab monetary support for Jordan to the tune of $40 million a year depended on Hussein's rejection of an agreement with Israel. Arafat had also secured financial support in Khartoum, and established bases of operation in Jordan from which to renew cross-border incursions.[14]

In December 1967, as Eshkol was getting ready to revisit President Johnson, giving the West Bank "a special status" was still the government's preferred solution to the Palestinian problem. However, in return for a peace treaty with Jordan, Israel would return to the green line provided Jordan would agree to an Israeli base on the line of mountains West of the Jordan River, settle the refugees, and permit Jewish access to the Tomb of the Patriarchs in Hebron. In the meantime, Israel would acquiesce to a rearming of Jordan as long as it was again tied to Israel's own rearming.[15]

Eshkol's planned visit to Washington reawakened the question of Israeli-South Vietnamese relations. The breaking of ties with Moscow, and the deterioration of relations with Paris, removed two major obstacles to Israeli acceptance of diplomatic ties with South Vietnam. Israel still needed Third World support at the UN, and had no wish to alienate the liberal-left, but it was also interested in encouraging the right's new interest in Jerusalem. Eshkol confided in William Hearst that he recognized that both Israel and the US were "defending democracy and freedom in different parts of the world" and that "his government was working on ways of showing its sympathy to U.S. position in Vietnam."[16]

The remarks leaked to the press and the anti-war forces. On December 31, Ambassador Barbour told Eshkol that Johnson needed "psychological support" on Vietnam, and an Israeli declaration of intent to establish diplomatic ties with Saigon would suffice. Eshkol intimated that he might countenance some Israeli presence in South Vietnam. Eban, however, reassured the Knesset the very next day that there was "no change in the Israeli government's policy towards Vietnam."[17]

Eshkol departed for the US with the issue still unsettled. His January 1968 meeting with Johnson took place at the Texas ranch. Eshkol wanted Johnson to commit himself to sell Israel Phantoms jets. Johnson wanted Israel to accept more refugees, but "abandon previous effort to set up independent entity on the West Bank." Indeed, she should avoid any "permanent moves in occupied lands." This included the formal unification of Jerusalem as well as a separate solution for the Canal zone. The US even opposed the building of the Eilat-Ashdod oil pipeline as an alternative to the closed Suez Canal.[18]

Washington viewed the territories held by Israel as bargaining chips, and the closure of the Canal as a strategic asset. Not only should Israel "not evacuate one inch of the occupied territories as long as the Arabs refused to conclude peace," but she should increase their value by appearing intransigent.[19] That was the message inherent in Walt Rostow's memo to Johnson on the advisability of Israeli–South Vietnamese ties:

> You will be the best judge of what would help you most. We've had one report . . . that Eshkol may be thinking of an open endorsement of our Vietnam effort and even some active help. We ought to look at that pretty carefully because it would further fix the image of Israel as our stooge – an image we need to blur if we're ever to persuade the Arabs that Israel won't just do what we tell it. It may be that the best help Eshkol could give us would be some strong words to the Conference of Presidents of Major Jewish Organizations in New York and a modest endorsement in his departure statement.[20]

In any case, both Harry McPherson and Walt Rostow told Eshkol that Johnson expected him "to do something about the Jews." Eshkol did as he was told. Such political aid was a small price to pay for a Presidential commitment to deliver Skyhawk aircraft promptly and sign a deal for the Phantom sale before the end of the year.[21]

Eshkol's statement to the Conference was phoned in by Evron and given to Johnson the following morning. The prime minister told the Jewish leadership that while conflicts "in Southeast Asia, in the Middle East and the less publicized conflicts in Africa and Latin America" were not "entirely identical," they all involved aggression and needed to be "solved by direct negotiations." He ended with a personal endorsement of the American policy: "I am absolutely convinced that the US is genuinely seeking a peaceful solution of all the conflicts in the world, including all those I have mentioned above."[22] The uproar that followed revealed just how explosive American Middle Eastern policy had become.

It all began with a *Newsweek* revelation that, following some "sharp trading down at the ranch," Johnson promised Israel Phantoms in return for Eshkol telling Jewish anti-war leaders that what Johnson did in Vietnam was "right." Columnist Paul Scott "reconstructed" the entire Eshkol–Johnson dialogue.[23] Here was a concrete manifestation of the much denied implication of the Tarlov affair, a clear *quid pro quo*. It was not the blackmail aspect which concerned Republicans but, as Nixon told Eshkol, Johnson's failure to appreciate the Soviet danger in the Middle East. "By holding the supply of aircraft "in ransom for the votes of Americans of Jewish faith," a Republican Congressmen complained, Johnson was "playing politics with free world security."[24]

Republicans regarded victorious Israel as America's "best and only reliable friend," an anti-Soviet bastion in the Middle East. Failure to supply her with means to defend herself only intensified the danger of an unwanted regional war. After all, while Eshkol visited Johnson, Brezhnev visited Nasser. Precisely, retorted State's Arabists, Moscow had succeeded in turning the Israeli victory to its advantage. The US must, therefore, improve her relationship with the Arab states, and Israel must help by not pushing for Phantoms; by getting Congress to renew arm sales to pro-Western Arabs; and by permitting the US to negotiate on her behalf. In any case, the Phantoms were needed for Vietnam.[25]

Afterwards, reporters asked Dayan the question Bundy had asked the CIA: "Can Israel in your opinion remain in this situation for an indefinite period of time?" Dayan replied that "the key is in the hands of the US That is to say, if the US is prepared that we should stick to this policy of ours, i.e., as long as there is no peace we will maintain the status quo – we can do it."[26]

Dayan knew that the Sinai passes afforded far superior defensible positions, while continued Israeli presence on the Canal meant "struggle, and, perhaps, another round in the war." He expected Moscow to permit Egypt to restart hostilities for the limited goal of retaking the Canal, knowing full well that the US would not interfere with such an undertaking.[27] Four major Israeli cities were added as Soviet nuclear targets at the end of 1967. Ben Gurion's disciple was not going to repeat Eshkol's 1966 mistake. Dayan convinced the Cabinet to go nuclear, which it did in 1968. Israel's dovish treasury minister Pinchas Sapir remarked, "There will be no more Auschwitzes."[28]

With their "Samson Option" in place, Israelis reconciled themselves not only to another long siege, but also to becoming occupiers. Dayan decided to increase the economic integration of the West Bank and Gaza with Israel proper. The two nations might as well learn to live with each other. Peace would be a long time coming. Given their history, Jews were bound to be a different kind of occupier. To prevent, or at least delay, another round of fighting Israel had to secure a visible American commitment to the *status quo* in the form of Phantom sales.[29]

GLASSBORO DEAL REDUX?

American–Israeli relations in the winter of 1968 seemed oddly reminiscent of those of the winter of 1965. In his February meeting with outgoing ambassador Harman, Johnson emphasized America's isolationist mood and threatened to leave the Middle East. Israel might be able to hold her own with her neighbors, Johnson said, but "it might not be superior to the Soviets." The scare tactics worked again. It was in Israel's interest, Dayan candidly explained, "to reach, as far as possible, an understanding with the US, to strengthen their hand and make them stay in the Middle East." Therefore, Israel agreed to cooperate with UN negotiator Gunnar Jarring; assured her supporters that there was "no problem on the Phantom planes," and dropped her objections to arms shipments to Jordan. Abba Eban even confided in Jewish Congressmen that "he would be very upset if President Johnson were not reelected."[30]

Johnson announced his withdrawal from the Presidential race in March and, in May, Israel received reports that Harriman and Thompson wanted Israeli concessions to assist the Paris negotiations. American officials, including Johnson, emphasized that the Arabs had "a unique opportunity" to deal with a president who was "beyond the domestic pressure of the Jewish vote" and who delayed action on the promised Phantom sale irrespective of the JCS analysts' conclusion that Israel was "in an inferior military position." The media was filled with speculations of an imminent package deal.[31]

In fact, refusal to supply Israel with Phantoms became equated with a willingness to sacrifice Israel for a better deal in Vietnam, an unpalatable position for presidential candidates. Not surprisingly, on May 9, both Eugene McCarthy and Robert Kennedy called for Phantom sales. McCarthy even declared that the US had "a much clearer commitment" to Israel than to "anything" in "Southeast Asia," and it should do whatever necessary to honor that commitment. Republican presidential contenders Richards Nixon, Nelson Rockefeller, and Ronald Reagan followed suit.[32]

Just as Washington and Moscow had not cut such a deal in Glassboro, Luke Battle indignantly asserted, so they would avoid doing so in the future. Moscow had "historic ambitions in the Middle East" which were "unlikely to be altered by events in Asia," nor did the US "trade on the interests" of its "friends" for her own "benefit."[33] Battle hoped his remarks would help Hubert Humphrey, who was stuck carrying the unwanted baggage of the administration's policy in Vietnam and the Middle East. Instead of worrying about an American sellout, Walt Rostow told Israel's new ambassador Yitzhak Rabin, Israel should do what the US was doing in Paris and get "Nasser engaged in the process of making peace." In Paris, Rabin retorted, Americans and North Vietnamese were doing the "probing in *direct negotiations*." Rostow ignored the comment.[34]

The assassination of Robert Kennedy on the first anniversary of the Six Day War reinforced the Vietnamese–Israeli connection as Sirhan Sirhan was carrying a newspaper article which described Kennedy as a Vietnam dove and a Middle East hawk. Johnson insisted that he did not "know the reasons for the attack on Senator Kennedy." "We cannot permit a wave of anti-Arab sentiment among the American public at a time when we are trying to restore good relations with our friends in the Arab world," explained a "top official."[35]

In fact, the preparations for another superpower summit were accompanied by a determined administration assault on Israeli popularity in the US. Officials brought to media attention Soviet assertions that American "hopes for a reduction of world tensions and results in the Paris peace talks" depended on Israeli withdrawal. Johnson no longer argued that he was withholding the Phantom sale to limit Soviet weapon supplies to the Arabs; He simply said that he did not want the sale to jeopardize his pursuit of détente with Moscow. Congressman Halpern remarked that this was "a cynical way of conducting world diplomacy."[36] Rabin tried to counterattack. He encouraged Congress to pass an amendment to the foreign aid appropriations bill requiring Johnson to sell Israel no fewer than 50 Phantom jets. But Humphrey's friend Kenen, who apparently resented being sidelined by Rabin's diplomacy, rushed to the White House and cut a deal to replace the House resolution mandating the sale with a joint Congressional resolution recommending it.[37]

It did not take Rabin long to find himself at odds with the organized Jewish leadership. Rabin complained that Israel cooperated with large Jewish Democratic contributors in exaggerating Democratic administrations' benevolence towards Israel. The Six Day War demonstrated the pitfalls of basing Israel's security on presidential good will. Nixon and the Republicans supported a strong Israel as a matter of American self interest. This was a much more solid basis for mutually advantageous relations. In any case, Israel should use the upcoming elections to secure the Phantoms and scuttle another Glassboro deal.[38]

When the 1968 Republican convention opened, Rabin was there. The Republican platform criticized Johnson's Middle Eastern policy, advocated the sale of Phantom jets to Israel, and condemned the "continuing anti-Semitic actions by the Soviet Union." The previous day, Humphrey had broken ranks and came out in support of Phantom jet sales to Israel.[39]

"At the moment the Soviets moved into Czechoslovakia, we were about to announce talks with them on strategic missiles, Mideast and Vietnam," Johnson mournfully remarked. In fact, the appearance of Soviet tanks in Prague did not convince Johnson to cancel his trip to Moscow. Instead, he informed the Soviets that they could take the heat off Czechoslovakia by agreeing to a Glassboro redux. "This time," Johnson told Dobrynin, "he 'had more freedom of action.'"[40] He signaled the meaning of that freedom via another pointed delay of the Phantoms sale.

The Soviets responded by promising to supply Egypt with hundreds of additional tanks, jets and 100–150 pilot instructors. They also unveiled a peace plan which called for an Israeli withdrawal within a specified time in return for Arab declarations of the cessation of a state of war, to be deposited at the UN, and including guarantees of Arab–Israeli borders by the Security Council by the Four Powers. The settlement of issues related to refugees, Israeli passage through the Suez Canal, and Jerusalem would be delayed.[41]

Eshkol wrote Johnson that Israel saw the plan as a way to return her to the old vulnerable borders without solving the basic Israeli–Palestinian conflict. Nor did he trust Soviet guarantees, as Moscow had "helped unleash the June 1967 war," invaded Czechoslovakia, fermented "hatred of the Jews in Eastern Europe," poured weapons and propaganda into the Middle East, and undermined Western interests in it. Eban rushed to New York, met with Rusk, and declared: "The Middle East is not an international protectorate." A Gallup poll revealed that one out of three Jews supported Nixon.[42]

Atlanticists in Congress were up in arms and, after less than four months on the job as the US ambassador at the UN, George Ball resigned. Congressional leaders claimed that Ball did not like the outline of a planned summit deal involving Israeli/Western concessions in the Middle East in exchange for Soviet concessions in Vietnam and refused to become associated with it.[43] In any case, enmeshed as she was in Vietnam, Washington was in no mood to give anyone security guarantees. This is evident from the following June 13, 1967 exchange:

> McNamara: 1. Belligerency: state of mind will continue. 60m [miles] vs. 2.5m [miles]. 2. Territorial question without US guarantees!
> Bundy: I don't see President asking Senate for guarantees.
> McNamara: I don't think we ought to get him into this.
> Bundy: A deep policy question: *How firm is the US Commitment to Israel?*[44]

Israel very much wanted an answer to that question because, in September 1968, General Fawzi declared that Egypt had entered a new phase of "active defense." The Canal became a battle line and 25 Israeli soldiers died within a month. With 2,000 Soviet military advisers dispersed in the Egyptian army, an American commitment "to neutralize the battlefield" seemed so crucial that Dayan, of all people, claimed that Israel had one. But both State and the President quickly denied it.[45]

During the yearly General Assembly debate, Rusk met with Gromyko, but they failed to reach an agreement. There would be no summit and no package deal. On October 8, Eban was again being helpful on Vietnam. He told the General Assembly that there was an urgent need "for the establishment of peace on the basis of the Geneva Agreement, in conditions which would let the peoples of Viet-Nam, South and North, determine their future, free from intimidation or constraint."[46]

On October 9, in response to Eban's "constructive" address and to the joint Congressional resolution, Johnson authorized Rusk to begin talks on Phantom sales with Israeli officials. On October 10, a Soviet commentator explained that the US army had used Phantoms for "mass killings of civilians in Vietnam" and Israelis were "particularly attracted by its ability to destroy an average sized village in a few minutes."[47] However, Israel was too relieved to pay much attention to the Soviet insinuations. The danger of a second Glassboro package deal seemed over. Of course, within months, Richard Nixon would take Lyndon Johnson's place. Accompanying him would be a linkage advocate named Henry Kissinger.

NOTES

1. Korn, *Stalemate*, 281.
2. Riad, *The Struggle for Peace*, 75.
3. Brown, *Chotam Ishi*, 113; and Eban, *Personal Witness*, 438–9.
4. Ofira Seliktar, *New Zionism and the Foreign Policy System of Israel* (London: 1986), 157–9.
5. Brown, 110–11; and Haber, *Hayom Tifroz Milchana*, 250, 295–7; and *Davar*, June 2, 1987.
6. Haber, 240 and 294; Brown, 113; Mon'im Nasser-Eddine, *Arab–Chinese Relations* (Beirut: 1981), 285–6; and Yezid Sayigh, "Turning Defeat into Opportunity," *Middle East Journal* (Spring 1992), 243.
7. "Press release No. 1," Jan. 1968, *International Documents on Palestine*, 1968.
8. Shabtai Tevet, *The Cursed Blessing* (London: 1969), 32; and Haber, 323.
9. Jon Kimche, *There Could have Been Peace* (London: 1973), 259–60.
10. Eban, *Personal Witness*, 460.
11. *Haaretz*, June 3, 1988.
12. Eban, *Personal Witness*, 438.
13. George Gruen to Simon Segal, July 28, 1967, AJC, Middle East Crisis '67, FAD/67, box 105, AJCL.
14. For the President from McG. B., June 27, 1967, WHCF, ExCo 1–6, box 9, LBJL, Sayigh, 250.
15. Haber, 303; Korn, 128–35; and *Davar*, June 2, 1987.
16. *Los Angles Herald-Examiner*, Dec. 10, 1967.
17. Interview with a source close to Eshkol; and *Haaretz*, Jan. 2, 1968.
18. "Talking Points for Prime Minister Eshkol," Jan. 5, 1968, Israel, box 138, 95; Department of State to Amembassy Tehran, Dec. 28, 1967; and from Amembassy Tehran to Secstate, Dec. 30, 1967, NSF, Iran, box 136, 188, 200, LBJL.
19. Rafael, *Destination Peace*, 181.
20. "Issues for Eshkol," Jan. 5, 1968, NSF, Israel, box 138, LBJL.
21. Interview with a source close to Eshkol; and Haber, 321.
22. "Part of the statement which Prime Minister Eshkol made in New York Jan. 9 to the Conference of Presidents of Major Jewish Organizations in America," Jan. 10, 1968, NSF, Israel, box 138, LBJL.
23. *Newsweek*, Jan. 16, 1968; and *Wichita Falls Record News*, Jan. 23, 1968.
24. *JTA*, Jan. 22 and 24, 1968; *Congressional Record – House*, Jan. 23, 1968, 717–18; and *Haaretz*, Jan. 11, 1968.
25. *The Los Angeles Herald Examiner* and *The Baltimore Sun*, Jan. 7, 1968.
26. *Maariv*, April 30, 1966; and Korn, 105.
27. *Haaretz*, Jan. 19, 1968; and *Davar*, June 2, 1987.
28. Hersh, *The Samson Option*, 177–9.
29. Korn, 134–5 and 129.
30. Memorandum of Conversation, Feb. 1 and 7, 1968, NSF, Israel, box 140/141, 143 and 149, LBJL; and *Haaretz*, Jan. 19, 1968.
31. *Haaretz*, May 3 and 5, 1968; *NYT*, May 15, 1968; *The Baltimore Sun*, May 17, 1968; *Chicago Sun Times*, May 22, 1968.

32. Kenen, *Israel's Defense Line*, 218; and *JTA*, May 10 and 16, 1968.
33. An address to the American Jewish Congress, May 16, 1968, NSF, Israel, box 140, 141, 139a, LBJL.
34. Memorandum of Conversation, May 17, 1968, NSF, Israel, box 140/141, 231a, LBJL.
35. *JTA*, June 7, 1968.
36. *JTA*, July 17 and 27, 1968.
37. Kenen, 219; and *JTA*, Aug. 5, 1968.
38. Zevet Itonaim Bachir, *Hayoresh* (Tel Aviv: 1974), 37.
39. *JTA*, Aug. 5 and 6, 1968.
40. Tom Johnson's Tuesday lunch notes, Nov. 26 and Oct 14, 1968, box 3, LBJL; and Dobrynin, 180–1.
41. *NYT*, Sept. 26, 1968; "Soviet initiative for an Arab–Israeli Settlement," Oct. 2, 1968, NSF, Iran, box 136, 286, LBJL.
42. Levi Eshkol to the President Johnson, Sept. 29, 1968, NSF, Israel, box 140, 141, LBJL; *NYT*, Oct. 1 and 2, 1968.
43. *JTA*, Sept. 27. 1968.
44. Bundy committee, NSF, M.E. Crisis, box 19, App. I, 102, LBJL.
45. Korn, 93–5; and *NYT*, Oct. 27, 1968.
46. Tom Johnson's notes, Nov. 26, 1968, box 4; and General Assembly debate, *U.N. Chronicle*, July–Dec., 1968, 5.
47. *NYT*, Oct. 10, 1968; and B.B.C, Oct. 12, 1968 (SU/2897/A4/1).

12 Organizing the Homefront

IDEOLOGICAL READJUSTMENT

"American Intellectuals and Foreign Policy" was the title of an article Irving Kristol published in the July 1967 issue of *Foreign Affairs*. It did not include a word about Israel or the Middle East. It only pointed out that the US was an imperial power "because what it does *not* do is just as significant, and just as consequential, as what it does." It is the responsibility of intellectuals, Kristol wrote, to provide the imperial power with intellectual and moral guidance. Unfortunately, an alienated American intellectual class was undermining the country's domestic social equilibrium and limiting its policy makers' ability to exercise their imperial power responsibly or effectively. Without a major change in that class' demeanor, the US would end up relinquishing her imperial role, leaving the world in the hands of the imperial powers of "Soviet Russia and Maoist China." Kristol doubted it would be possible to modify intellectual community behavior "in the immediate or even near future." Still, he and some other Jewish "brains" were determined to try.[1] As a less circumspect Jewish radical explained, Jewish survival hung in the balance:

> As Marxists and international bankers, millions of Jews were murdered by Hitler and Fascists. As imperialists, reactionaries, and capitalists, Jews are being murdered by Soviet Russians and their Arab puppets. Yesterday we stood in the way of Hitler and had to be removed. Today we stand in the way of the Soviets.[2]

Since the US was the only power which was willing and able to back Israel, Jews had to do their utmost to insure that the US was as powerful as possible and as effective in projecting her power as possible. Since intellectual fermented ideological dissent undermined American effectiveness as an imperial power, it was important to convince intellectuals to alter their behavior. By placing the new-leftist critique of American foreign relations within the three century old isolationist tradition, Kristol undercut the critique's moral and intellectual force. And by labeling intellectuals a new "alienated" class in search of power and recognition, he undermined their claim to apolitical objectivity. Nor would he permit this new "priestly" class to shirk responsibility for the consequences of their teachings by underestimating "the esteem in which the public" held them or the degree to which political leaders depended on their guidance.

Did that mean that intellectuals or Jews had to support the Vietnam war? Not necessarily. Kristol deduced that the war not only could not be won, but its influence on the country mandated its end. They only had to smooth the leadership's road out of that quagmire so as to prevent a "patriotic working class" anti-liberal backlash or an isolationist victory. This could be achieved by evacuating the Vietnamese front and gutting the Cold War of its moral and ideological content. After all, the behavior of the superpowers during the Mideast crisis was as devoid of such overtones as any nineteenth-century great power contest.

For the planet to survive in the nuclear age, Kristol insisted, great powers must eschew attempts to revise the status quo by the use of force. China, the only great power which had yet to shed its ideological mooring, challenged this essentially "conservative" doctrine with her support for "wars of national liberation." US forces went to Vietnam not to fight communism, but "because wars of national liberation are a dangerous anachronism in the nuclear age." There was nothing arrogant, immoral or genocidal inherent in this failed effort. If they did not wish to bring about a new era of American isolationism, intellectuals had better stop hunting for "guilty men" and start explaining these realities to the public.[3]

Kristol demanded that the educated classes curtail their support for violent change abroad. Nathan Glazer demanded that "the Jewish intelligentsia" cease its tolerance for student radicals and black nationalists at home.[4] Charges levied by UN representatives of Jordan, Saudi Arabia and Syria that American Jews engaged in "unAmerican activities" and constituted a "fifth column" which subverted American national interests rekindled fear of anti-Semitism.[5]

Young blacks also failed to distinguish between Israel and the diaspora. A 1967 Black Panther journal included this poem:

> We're gonna burn their towns and ain't all
> We're gonna piss upon the Wailing Wall
> And then we'll get Kosygin and de Gaulle
> That will be ecstasy, killing every Jew in Jewland.[6]

Paul Jacobs, who organized an encounter between Evron and blacks at Watts, wrote that besides ignorance of the realities of Israel, "two major themes emerged from the heated discussion, the alleged exploitative role of some American Jews inside the ghettos and Negroes' identification of Arabs as supporters of the colored peoples of the world."[7]

The striving of blacks for a sense of power naturally drew strength from the belief that they were part of a global colored people's movement destined to overturn the existing power structure which had shortchanged them. Should Jews continue to dismiss the significance of the anti-Semitic ranting of black radicals? No, argued Meir Kahane and Joseph Churba, who in a book entitled *The Jewish Stake in Vietnam* highlighted the influence of the January 1966 Tricontinental Conference in Havana on the black power movement, as well as the anti-Israeli partnership between China, North Vietnam, the NLF, the USSR, the Arab states and the PLO. Since the war in Vietnam had emerged "as a symbol in the great struggle for civilization," Jews had an abiding interest in preventing the victory of the anti-Semitic–anti-Zionist side. After all, free to divert their resources from Vietnam, they might redirect them against Israel.[8] Nathaniel Weyl, author of *The Jew in American Politics*, concurred. Jews had to recognize that their welfare was no longer threatened by conservatism but by "the global threat to Israel and Western civilization posed by Soviet and Chinese Communism and by the strident, racist nationalism of the new, impoverished states of the Asian and African world."[9]

The problem was less black militancy, contended Jay Kaufman of B'nai B'rith, than Jewish support for that militancy. Thus, delegates "obsequiously forsook their voting rights" at the National Conference of New Politics (NCNP) and agreed to black militants' demands that they pass resolutions condemning "the imperialist Zionist war," establishing "white-civilizing committees" and supporting the Vietcong. "The irony of the black corruption of the NCNP," noted one reporter, was "that the militants kept deriding white liberals and Jewish money, yet the conference organizers had raised some $6,000 to feed, house and transport scores of black people to the convention." Even more ironic, added Milton Himmelfarb, was Jewish radicals' willingness to back black nationalism while opposing Jewish nationalism.[10]

In fact, it was the Jewish intelligentsia which taught black students to glorify the violence of revolutionaries, rebels and even criminals, contended Nathan Glazer. Its members were the ones who paid for an ad on behalf of Eldridge Cleaver in the same *Black Panther* magazine which headlined a story about "Palestinian Guerrillas versus Israeli Pigs." Glazer even named names. He was writing after the 1968 New York City teachers' strike in which Jewish teachers were told that they were "Middle East murderers of colored people" unfit to teach black children.[11]

Thus, by insisting that the Six Day War be viewed within the global context, the left had forced everyone to take sides. The fact that black nationalists and many new-leftists not only took the anti-Israeli side, but did so in an overtly anti-Semitic fashion, helped a group of intellectuals (who came to be known as Neoconservatives) to combat the anti-Israeli forces which damaged US ability to provide Israel with the backing she needed in the post-1967 era.

Radicals could no longer count on unconditional Jewish largesse. Martin Peretz responded to *Ramparts*' backing of Arab and black militancy by curtailing his financial support for the magazine. Some young radicals organized themselves into a new "Jewish left." They demanded Jewish studies programs, defended Zionism on campus, published underground newspapers, and experimented with novel forms of communal prayer. Meir Kahane's Jewish Defense League attracted those who wished to prove that they were just as tough as the Black Panthers. They all backed the emerging Soviet Jewry.[12]

Caring less about alienating Moscow, and more about the increase in Soviet anti-Semitism, Jewish organizations mobilized the community on behalf of Soviet Jewish human rights. Systematic efforts were also made to bring the weight of the American academic community to bear on the subject: 2,000 professors from 115 universities signed a *NYT* ad on behalf of Soviet Jewry.[13]

None of this is intended to imply that Jewish intellectuals, especially liberal rabbis, easily accepted the new global alignment. They did not. For example, in his presidential address to a convention of Reform rabbis, Jacob Weinstein maintained that the PLO–NLF connection was unfortunate, as was the Soviet attempt to use intransigence in the Middle East "as a leverage for concessions in the settling of the Vietnam War." However, Jews had to "beware of package deals" and resolve to continue their opposition to the Vietnam War while, at the same time, "be strong as lions, swift as eagles, cunning as serpents" and "not permit that which Israel" had "gained by so much precious blood and sweat to be nibbled away through the devious diplomacy of big-power plays."

Weinstein acknowledged that the administration might have to make "some concessions to Russia's pro-Arabic alignment in the Middle East in order to assure cooperation in bringing the Viet Cong and Ho Chi Minh to the negotiating table." Indeed, "it would be naive" of Israel to expect to "be able to isolate the dialogue." But these problems belonged to politicians who had "to strip themselves perforce of the handicap of idealism." Rabbis could afford to pretend that those choices did not have to be made and continue their anti-war activism in disregard of rank and file complaints that they were using their pulpits in a manner harmful to Jewish interests. Moreover, their central organizations should provide rabbis who had been dismissed by their congregations as a consequence of that activism with psychological and financial aid.[14] After all, while Jewish peace activism had no impact on American policy towards Israel, explained rabbi David Polish, it prevented the domestic spread of leftist anti-Semitism.[15] These were no idle matters in an election year in which Vietnam, the Middle East and their interrelations took central stage.

SHOULD JEWS REMAIN DEMOCRATS?

On the whole, Jewish peace activism revived after the Mideast crisis. When General Lewis Hershey called on local draft boards to reclassify and induct those engaged in anti-draft activities, Jewish organizations issued a joint press release reaffirming their support for the right of dissent. The perception that US failure to stand by Israel had been attributable to the Vietnam War further undermined Jewish support for both Johnson and his Vietnam policy. Speeches criticizing "the myth of national interest" and "commitment to South Vietnam" were heard even on the JWV's convention floor.[16] Eshkol's address backing Johnson's Vietnam policy had little impact. His audience understood that he and other Israelis were doing what they had to do. Joachim Prinz said: "I would have thought very little of them if they didn't ask. They had responsibilities too."[17] During the annual AIPAC policy conference, both Republican and Democratic Congressmen criticized the lack of adequate administration support for Israel and blamed it on events in Vietnam.[18]

On March 28, Abe Feinberg placed a full page ad in the *NYT* entitled "A Personal Statement about President Lyndon B. Johnson."

The text contrasted the 1957 Republican policy towards the Middle East with the 1968 Democratic one, and asserted:

> Now, as before, President Johnson believes that Israel and her neighbors must themselves work out the terms of a peace for the Middle East. Now, as before, in the Middle East as elsewhere, he opposes one-sided recommendations that would ask one party to grant concessions without reciprocal moves by the other.[19]

So desperate were "Johnson's Jewish friends" to keep Johnson president that, after he withdrew from the Presidential race, they tried to convince Israel to agree to far reaching concessions for the sole purpose of handing Johnson a major diplomatic victory. Johnson was the best president Israel could ever expect, they insisted, and such a victory would persuade him to run again. Behind their unusual request was the conviction that, without Johnson, Nixon was bound to win.[20]

Their reasoning was reflected in Kristol's article, "Why I am for Humphrey." McCarthy and Kennedy, Kristol maintained, were minority candidates. Their charm to liberals consisted of their ability to communicate with radicals. However, most voters were "non-black, non-young and non-poor" and, to win, it was with them that a candidate had to communicate; only Nixon and Humphrey had a chance to do so effectively. Kristol supported Humphrey because Nixon appealed to "*the wrong majority*," one that was "sullenly resentful of the social changes" that swept the country and bound to be "impulsively reactionary" towards future ones.[21]

To the chagrin of Kristol and the Democrats, Nixon refused to cede the Jewish vote. On September 9, in a speech before the triennial convention of B'nai B'rith, Nixon threw down the gauntlet: An American policy which merely maintained the balance between Israel and her neighbors ran the risk of Arab miscalculation. It was safer to provide Israel with a technological edge which more than offset Arab numerical superiority. American interest in the Middle East exceeded that in Vietnam, and the US had to make that "crystal clear" to Moscow. Americans had a "firm and unwavering commitment to the national existence of Israel" because Israel was "threatened by Soviet imperialism" and because she had "displayed guts, patriotism, idealism and a passion for freedom." Nixon also promised to initiate regional peace talks, and strongly denounced Soviet anti-Semitism.[22]

Johnson and Humphrey also addressed the conference, but they only made vague promises to maintain the balance of armaments and even failed to mention the Phantom sale. Jewish Democrats were incensed. They worried that Nixon's greater support for Israel would translate into Republican votes. A *NYT* editorial asserted that the American commitment to Israel was "clear and outside the political debate" and chided Nixon's willingness "to go well beyond that basic pledge to project a new, dangerous, open ended and ultimately self-defeating commitment." Klutznick complained that it was "abnormal" for Israeli military needs "to be aired in a national campaign." Klutznick suggested that a Democratic advocacy of "a security pact with Israel"; and a discount prices for military hardware would demonstrate the party's recognition that Israel was America's "partner in the defense of the Middle East against Soviet expansion."[23]

A week later, Hubert Humphrey made an unscheduled appearance before the Zionist Organization of America. First, he made "very clear" that he was "speaking for himself." Then, he called for the prompt sale of Phantoms to Israel once she signed the non-proliferation pact. Later, his spokesperson explained that no *quid pro quo* was intended. Humphrey also drew a parallel between prospective Middle Eastern peace talks and the Paris peace talks on Vietnam, and revived his 1966 comparison between Palestinian insurgency and "Communist wars of national liberty." A few weeks later, Humphrey found it just as difficult, but just as necessary to distance himself from Johnson's Vietnamese policy.[24]

The reason for Humphrey's change of heart can be found in the polls. In 1964, his addition to the ticket had raised the prospective Jewish vote for the Democratic ticket from 94 percent to 97 percent. Gallup polls taken between May 25 to June 3, 1968 showed Nixon with only 4 percent of the Jewish vote, Humphrey with 79 percent and Wallace with 4 percent. But the September polls gave Nixon 31 percent of the vote, Humphrey 51 percent and Wallace 4 percent. Nixon's Jewish advisor Max Fisher credited the shift to the promise to tip the balance of power in Israel's favor.[25]

The liberal Jewish leadership mobilized. Arthur Goldberg became the co-chairman of the Humphrey–Muskie campaign. Jacob Kanter organized a group of "opinion makers" into the National Coordinating Committee for Humphrey–Muskie. Meetings were held in major cities. Over 60,000 personalized letters were sent soliciting support and funds. An ad endorsing the ticket was placed in the Jewish press which reached 90 percent of the Jewish voters and in the *NYT*. It emphasized Humphrey's commitment to law and order, human rights, social reform, Israel ("We know his commitment is heart-felt and not an election year posture"), world peace and peace in Vietnam. Among the signatories were Vietnam hawks and doves: Jacob Blaustein, Irving Fein, Abe Feinberg, Abraham Heschel, Philip Klutznick, Joachim Prinz, Abraham Ribicoff, Dore Schary, Abraham Sachar and Lewis Weinstein. There was also a "young, American Jewish leaders" group which raised money, wrote letters and made phone calls.[26]

Their strategy was to cast doubt on Nixon's sincerity by holding him responsible for the Eisenhower administration's handling of the 1956 Suez War, while wrapping Humphrey in the Kennedy mantle. Neither Johnson, nor the Six Day War, were mentioned. In the end, 81 percent of the Jews voted for Humphrey as compared to the over 90 percent who had voted for Johnson; 17 percent voted for Nixon and 2 percent for Wallace. Most election analysts celebrated the tenacity of liberal Jewish voting patterns.[27]

But the battle for keeping Jews Democrats was not yet over. Paul Warnke wanted to use the Phantom sale to gain full access to any Israeli facility the US deemed to be connected to nuclear development. Rabin said no. So Clifford delayed the completion of the agreement until after the elections, and then renewed that demand. Rabin was furious. He would have to renegotiate the sale with a new administration. He called Feinberg. Feinberg called Rostow, who was dining with Clifford and asked him to tell Clifford that Johnson had promised that there would be no conditions attached to the sale. Clifford called Johnson, who concurred.[28]

Johnson asked Eban to tell Eshkol that "Lyndon B. Johnson had kept his word." The Phantoms agreement was concluded before the end of 1968. He also insured that Jewish Democratic middlemen, like Abe Feinberg, retained their credibility. Five days before leaving office, Johnson even added a little bonus in the form of a letter from Rusk to the Soviet charge asserting that a Middle East settlement could only be secured by a signed agreement concluded in negotiations between the parties involved; Israel was not obligated to withdraw from all the territories. "Perhaps," writes Rabin, "Johnson wanted to be remembered, at least by Jews, as a president who benefitted Israel." Feinberg told an interviewer, "When the Phantoms were delivered to Israel, I was the only American present at the airfield."[29] His victory helped keep most Jews (including Neoconservative intellectuals) in the Democratic party for another decade.

NOTES

1. Irving Kristol, "American Intellectuals and Foreign Policy," *Foreign Affairs* (July 1967), 395–9; and Isaacs, *Jews and American Politics*, 166.
2. Melvin I. Urofsky, *We Are One!* (New York: 1978), 376.
3. Irving Kristol, "We Can't Resign as 'Policeman of the World,'" *NYT Magazine* (May 12, 1968), 26–7 and 105–12; and "Why I Am for Humphrey," *The New Republic* (June 8, 1968), 21.
4. Nathan Glazer, "Black, Jews & the Intellectuals," *Commentary* (July 1969), 35.
5. *Security Council Official Records*, 1358th Meeting, 7–9 and 1359th Meeting, 4–6, June 13, 1967.
6. Charles Silberman, *A Certain People* (New York: 1985), 204.
7. *JTA,* Feb. 27, 1968.
8. Meir Kahane, Joseph Churba, and Michael King, *The Jewish Stake in Vietnam* (New York: 1967), 23, 97 and 140.
9. Weil, *The Jew in American Politics*, 9 and 171.
10. Jay Kaufman, *Black Anti-Semitism and Jewish Racism* (New York: 1969), 67; and Jeffrey L. Hodes, "New Left in Disarray," *The New Leader* (Sep. 11, 1967), 7.
11. Glazer, "Black, Jew & Intellectuals," 81.
12. Jack Nusan Porter and Peter Drier, eds., *Jewish Radicalism* (New York: 1973).
13. *American Jewish Yearbook, 1968,* 117.
14. *CCAR Yearbook*, 1967, 8–11.
15. David Polish, "Vietnam and Jewish Responsibility," *Congress Bi-Weekly* (Jan. 22, 1968), 13–15.
16. Joint News release, Dec. 6, 1967, AJC, CO/ Vietnam, AJCL; and *Jewish Currents* (Oct. 1967), 3.
17. Bick, "Ethnic Linkages," 208.
18. *NYT*, March 5, 1968; *JTA*, Jan 25, March 12 and 22, 1968.
19. *NYT*, March 28, 1968. Underline in original.
20. Rabin, *Pinkas Sherut*, 220; and interview with Kampelman.
21. Kristol, "Why I am for Humphrey," 21.
22. *JTA*, Sept. 10, 1968.
23. *JTA*, Sept. 11, 1968; and *NYT*, Sept. 10, 1968.
24. *JTA*, Sept. 17, 1968.
25. "Humphrey Polls," Max Kampelman Papers, HHH 1968 Campaign, 26E 10 7B, MSA; and *JTA*, Oct. 21, 1968.
26. A letter from J. H. Kanter to Dwayne Andreas, Nov. 14, 1968 and Attachments, Max Kampelman Papers, HHH 1968 Campaign Corresp. Misc. 26E 10 7B, MSA.
27. *American Jewish Yearbook 1969*, 100.
28. Hersh, *The Samson Option*, 191–2.
29. Eban, *Personal Witness*, 474; Rabin, 234; and Bick, 167.

Linkages

In his memoirs, Henry Kissinger distinguishes between two types of linkages, those by virtue of reality and those used as a negotiating tactic. In fact, the first often leads to the second. Thus, the American decision to keep the Vietnam War a one front war meant that increased involvement in Southeast Asia inevitably decreased commitment elsewhere. With little fanfare and much misplaced confidence, the new frontier was replaced by the Johnson doctrine of regionalism.

For her Cold War rival, the Soviet Union, the American withdrawal was an opportunity to realize historic ambitions and improve her strategic Cold War position. The growth of Soviet influence in the Mediterranean seriously damaged American efforts to sell the Vietnam War at home and abroad as countries, such as Israel, turned down repeated American requests to place their flag alongside the American in Vietnam for fear of offending the USSR.

But this, Washington surmised, was an acceptable price for Soviet acquiescence to the War in Vietnam and her cooperation in thwarting Chinese attempts to open a second front in Kashmir. In the summer of 1966 however, after China began imploding, a Soviet Union increasingly hurt by its manifest inability or unwillingness to protect fellow communist North Vietnam served notice that further American bombing escalation would lead to a Soviet response in the Middle East. Not sufficiently impressed, or too desperate to care, Johnson ignored the warning. Hence, the 1967 bombing of Hanoi and Haiphong led to the Middle East crisis and focused world attention on the reality of the linkage between the two Asian Cold War fronts.

Covert linkage diplomacy began with Johnson's May 19th letter to Kosygin, flourished during and after the Glassboro summit, and ended when Johnson left office. Security Council resolution 242 is its remaining legacy. Nixon merely replaced a covert linkage diplomacy with an overt one. In the meantime, the great strides made by Moscow in the Middle East contributed to the March 1968 Johnsonian decision to accept Clark Clifford's advice and talk to the American people about "the prospects for peace in Vietnam" and not about the "grave challenge" to America in Vietnam.[1] Ultimately, as De Gaulle had predicted, the Vietnam War had to be settled before any progress could be made in the Middle East.

Regional conflicts may have deep historic roots. However, in an interdependent world, their ebbs and flows are linked to their global context if for no other reason than because regional leaders are forever scanning the international landscape in search of new windows of opportunity. It did not take long for Arab leaders from Nasser to Ben Bella to perceive that the Vietnam War was such a window and sponsor the creation of Palestinian Liberation Organizations. In the Vietnam era, transforming the interstate Arab–Israeli conflict into a Palestinian war of national liberation had distinct strategic as well as ideological advantages. Israel could retaliate but not go to war on a country which supported cross-border infiltrators as she did in 1956 because, not wishing to be distracted from Vietnam, the US forbade it.

Israel fashioned "a new neutralist" foreign policy in the hope of securing a superpower agreement on the Middle East in the "spirit of Tashkent." She set aside the nuclear option, continued to improve her relations with the Second and Third worlds, and avoided diplomatic ties with Saigon. Inspired by Vietnam, Syria began in 1965 to advocate and support an active people's war against Israel. The more manifest American inability to win the unconventional war in Vietnam became, the more adherents of a Chinese style people's war gained influence in the Arab world and elsewhere and the more difficult it was for the leader of the Communist world to oppose it. Moscow, therefore, told Israel that she had to put up with increasingly effective Palestinian sabotage or be treated as if she were acting on behalf of the "aggressive forces" responsible for the Vietnam War.

At the same time, regionalism undermined the nonaligned movement by reducing American economic aid to regional powers, such as Egypt, and contributing to the overthrow of charismatic leaders like Ben Bella, Sukarno and Nkrumah. When the Soviets expressed their wish for an Egyptian squeeze on Israel, a vulnerable Nasser fearful of being overthrown, concluded that a window of opportunity had just opened to humiliate Israel, reestablish himself as the leader of the Arab world, and get American economic aid renewed.

Within days, obvious American fear of a second front and Soviet self confidence convinced him that it was actually a door which had blown wide open. The world retreated, the Arabs united, and the direct showdown Nasser had always wanted was his for the taking. How could Nasser, or the Soviets for that matter, know that a totally isolated Jewish state would effectively reorganize her leadership and gamble its entire existence on one throw of the dice, the ability of her air force to destroy those of her enemies on the ground, and win?

Ironically, it did not take Nasser or Dayan long to realize that all the war did was to increase their dependence on their respective superpowers. Egypt had to overcome its objections to foreign bases, and Israel had to prove her value as a knight in the global chess game. Of course, socialist, secular, conciliatory ideologies were poorly suited for good knights. Capitalistic, religious, chauvinistic ideologies fit the bill much better. It took a full decade, and another round of fighting, before the Israeli political culture transformed itself sufficiently to meet the new need. But the writing on the Israeli wall was clear by the end of 1968, and so was the writing on much of the diaspora's wall.

For diaspora Jews, survival has always depended on an accurate reading of the larger society in which they lived. In the early sixties, American Jewish religious and secular leaders took advantage of Jewish electoral and financial clout to forge alliances, including one with the Democratic Party, which sought to make America a more hospitable, liberal and just place. When success and the Vietnam War threatened to undermine these achievements by alienating their young, redirecting the nation's resources from domestic reform to military adventures, and threatening world peace, Jewish leaders quickly organized in opposition to it. Their response helped prove the relevancy of their age old tradition.

But the good times did not last. By the fall of 1966, Johnson reminded the Jews that they were a vulnerable minority. While the American Jewish leaders were still debating the appropriate tactics to deal with Johnson's warning, the roof caved in on Israel. Suddenly, the dangers of a second Jewish Holocaust seemed much more imminent than the dangers of a nuclear one. When three weeks of fear and trembling were followed by a joyous return to Jerusalem, a large number of Jews decided that the eclipse of God was over and traditional Judaism remained viable in the modern world.

There are linkages between history and ideology, as well as between history and theology. The Six Day War united Jews the world over. It also presented them with a new powerful enemy: the USSR, her allies and sympathizers. Jews reorganized themselves to meet the challenge. Israel became the battlefront, Western Jewry the homefront, and Soviet Jewry the POWs. To have a chance, Jews needed to have America as an ally. A group of American intellectuals, already concerned about the threat to liberalism posed by the radicalism of the New Left, took it upon themselves to help create a domestic political culture conducive to an America willing and able to fulfill her imperial role, and perhaps even win the Cold War. This group of intellectuals would later be known as Neoconservatives.

NOTES

1. Clifford, *Counsel to the President*, 520.

Index